Problems of New Power
MOROCCO

Published simultaneously
in Great Britain
by Prentice-Hall International
London

Problems of New Power

MOROCCO

By I. William Zartman

Atherton Press
70 Fifth Avenue, New York
A Division of Prentice-Hall, Inc.
1964

MOROCCO: PROBLEMS OF NEW POWER
I. William Zartman

THE AMERICAN ASSOCIATION
FOR MIDDLE EAST STUDIES SERIES

The Modern Middle East
Richard H. Nolte, Editor

Morocco: Problems of New Power
I. William Zartman

Leadership in a New Nation:
Political Development in Israel
Lester G. Seligman

ACKNOWLEDGMENTS

The author is grateful to the United States Navy, which brought him to Morocco in February, 1958, for a two-year stay, and to the Social Science Research Council, whose research grant enabled him to stay there during much of 1960 to complete this study. Gratitude is also expressed to the American Association for Middle East Studies for advice and support in the preparation and publication of this book. The progress of the study owed much to the kindness and openness of many people—Moroccans, Frenchmen, and Americans —more numerous than can be fully acknowledged in this brief mention. Furthermore, the political position of many of these people prevents my giving them public credit; their help and information have made this study possible, however, and any inaccuracies are certainly not their fault. Where attributed, the phrase "in an interview" will be used to designate the author's meetings with the person named. Two names deserve first mention. The late Si Mbarek Bekkai, Morocco's first premier, was not only the source of information and encouragement, but also a valuable friend. Louis Fougère, his technical counselor, is also an esteemed friend and spent much of his very valuable time reading the entire manuscript. Benjamin Rivlin has given much kind assistance as AAMES's reader of the manuscript. Remy Leveau, Warren Clark, Mohammed Bennis, and Douglas E. Ashford have also been helpful, and the first two have read parts of the manuscript. Kamili Mahfoud, Mohammed Bouzouba', and my many other friends in the Moroccan Army also taught me much about their country. My colleagues Richard Walker and Gordon Tullock also gave helpful comments. I especially thank David Hilling and Charles Amarquaye of the Geography Department of the University of Ghana and F. F. Baughman for timely and skillful assistance in cartography. In lieu of specific attribution of source, the following figures, among others, must be thanked for their time in interviews: Mahjoubi Ahardan, Mohammed Awad, Hajj Ahmed Balafrej, Hajj 'Omar ben 'Abdeljalil, Mohammed Benjelloun and his division heads, Mohammed Boucetta, Mohammed al-Fassi, Ahmed Reda Guedira and the cabinet of the prince, Hussein Hajbi, Ahmed Lyazidi, 'Abderrahman Yusufi, Mohammed Zeghari, Hassan Zemmouri and the Election Bureau, Maurice Duverger, Jean Lacouture, Charles W. Yost and the American Embassy staff, and Capt. John Counihan and the Naval Facilities at Port Lyautey. Obviously, the responsibility of none of these people is engaged in this study. Many secretaries have worked on the manuscript, but I am especially grateful to Mrs. Cloris Grogan. Finally, it is possible that the study could have been completed without the assistance of my wife, but it would have been difficult and certainly much less enjoyable.

Reference in the text is made to a number of newspapers by their short titles:

Times	*The New York Times,* New York edition, independent daily
Tribune	*New York Herald Tribune,* Paris edition, independent daily
Monde	*Le Monde,* Paris edition, French daily
Echo	*L'Echo du Maroc,* Casablanca edition, French daily
Vie	*La Vie économique,* Casablanca edition, French weekly
Vigie	*La Vigie marocaine,* Casablanca edition, French daily
PM	*Le Petit Marocain,* Rabat edition, French daily
AG	*L'Avant-Garde,* Casablanca edition, UMT weekly
at-Tahrir	*at-Tahrir,* Casablanca edition, UNFP daily
ar-Rai	*ar-Rai al-'Amm,* Casablanca edition, UNFP daily
al-'Ahd	*al-'Ahd al-Jadid,* Casablanca edition, UNFP daily

Phares	*Les Phares,* Rabat edition, Liberal Independent weekly
an-Nidal	*an-Nidal,* Rabat edition, Liberal Independent weekly
al-Hayat	*al-Hayat ash-Sha'ab,* Casablanca edition, Communist weekly
La Nation	*La Nation,* Casablanca edition, Communist weekly
al-'Alam	*al-'Alam,* Rabat edition, Istiqlal daily
al-Istiqlal	*al-Istiqlal,* Rabat edition, Istiqlal weekly
al-Fellah	*al-Fellah,* Rabat edition, UMA biweekly
Démocratie	*Démocratie,* Casablanca edition, PDI weekly
al-Maghreb	*al-Maghreb al-'Arab,* Rabat edition, Popular Movement weekly

A number of periodicals and official publications have also been used frequently. They appeared infrequently, so their issues are listed:

Revue des communes rurales et des municipalités, Ministry of Interior, four numbers irregularly spaced in 1959 and 1960

Maroc-Documents, Ministry of Foreign Affairs, twelve numbers irregularly spaced in 1958 and 1959

Notes et Documents, Ministry of National Education, appearing monthly until May, 1959

Education Nationale, Ministry of Education, monthly after October, 1959

Bilan et Perspectives de l'action du Ministère de l'Agriculture, Ministry of Agriculture, October, 1959

CONTENTS

LIST OF TABLES AND MAPS

A Danièle

Problems of New Power
MOROCCO

ONE

INTRODUCTION

The importance of Africa and the rest of the developing world has far outrun our scholarship. This is partially because of the difficulty of extracting information from the disorganized, evolving, and often suspicious regimes of newly independent countries. This is also the partial result of the lack of analytical tools to deal with the problems of new power. This study, the product of nearly three years of living and doing research in Morocco, attempts to fill gaps in our knowledge of methodology, of Morocco, and of the under-developed world in general. The essential problem faced here is the problem of new power in the hands of a young political leadership trying to find its path through the ways of government.

I

The broad purpose of this study is to present information and to use a methodology which can be useful in understanding Arab and African countries. Methodology in this area is in a develop-mental stage, as is the subject matter. In new areas of study, much of the success in understanding and analysis depends on asking the proper questions and recognizing the salient phenomena. The sub-stance of this study is therefore presented in the hope that it might act as a model—to be refined where necessary—for the study of similar societies, as well as deepen understanding of Morocco itself. The conclusion brings into focus the forces and questions which are basic to the understanding of any developing government.

3

Since the early 1950's, when the idea of looking at government in terms of its decision-making functions was formulated, decision-making has been recognized as a helpful approach to both domestic and international problems of political science. The original works on this approach are still being reprinted, but their applications are scarce. Although the approach was developed for general application and first used in connection with France, in the developing world it is of even greater usefulness. Comparative government, dealing with older, developed government systems, usually takes either a functional or an institutional approach. Where political life is highly sophisticated, a study of the legislative, executive, and judicial branches of government—often strengthened by complementary analyses of the role of public opinion and public participation in government—can easily cover the functions of government and even follow the natural divisions into which that government falls. In fact, this approach, now very descriptive, is actually following the normative pattern which three or more centuries of political theorists have declared that governments should have in order to be modern, democratic, and efficient. But developing countries have not reached this level. Where governmental life has settled into comfortable patterns, a study of its organization can tell how it works as an institution. Yet developing countries are only looking for institutions, and the institutions they do have perform varying jobs at various moments. Thus, functional and institutional approaches are not only unhelpful; they are misleading, inappropriate, and suggestive of normative judgments about institutions not yet established.

In a situation in which institutions are evolving and in which functions are *ad hoc,* the decision-making approach is more helpful. Here the unit of investigation is the problem. In early decision-making studies, the problem area suggested was international relations or foreign affairs, but the approach is equally applicable to domestic issues. By following the issue along its course as it is shaped by circumstance, propelled by political and social forces, and dealt with by the government, understanding of the process of governing can be acquired. By choosing a number of significant problems and subjecting them to this type of analysis, judgments can be made about the relation of situational, external, and governmental forces in the political process. Analysis of the role and power of individual decision-makers can also be made, as can an evaluation of their general power, not from an examination of what their position should be, but from a study of what is. This book is the first study to use the tools of decision-making analysis to examine an underdeveloped country's government.

As used in this study, decision-making refers to a complex process of dealing with a problem. On one hand, when the phrase, "the prime minister decided . . ." or "the king appointed . . . ," is used, it means that the action was actually committed by the designated agent, not that a symbolic seal or a formal approval was involved. But the study of a problem through decision-making must also include non-decisions, avoiding decision, and the conscious or unconscious postponement of decision. For, on the other hand, decision-making also includes the evolution of a problem under the influence of external forces and the course of an issue through day-to-day operations. Most importantly, it includes the limitation of possibilities in preparation for the ultimate choice of one possibility. This aspect will be emphasized, as much as the making of individual, personal decisions.

II

The specific task of this study is to elucidate the nature of Moroccan government and politics between 1956 and 1961, the independent reign of King Mohammed V. If the decision-making approach is to be used, the choice of problems to be studied is crucial. They must be important and representative. The five problems treated here have been chosen with these two criteria in mind, and an attempt has been made to cover all major aspects of governmental activity. Problems have been chosen from diplomatic, military, economic, social, and politico-administrative policy. The narrowing of these problem areas to a specific problem is more delicate. The problem must be researchable; material must be available. It must be controversial; there must be pressures for conflicting policies. It must be of sufficient duration to cover the five-year independent reign of King Mohammed V. These additional criteria helped select the specific problems. Although the problems were consciously chosen, an element of random sampling was present, for the differing patterns of decision-making appeared only after the initial research was done.

Many diplomatic problems were available; few of them are researchable. Unfortunately, the problem of relations with the new states of Africa or the orientation of Moroccan policy vis-à-vis the Arab world was abandoned for lack of material. Problems of relations with the former colonial powers, France and Spain were also discarded for lack of precision; any aspect of this problem would be

too broad to handle in depth. The problem of American base negotiations fits well into the five-year period, from the first mention of
the topic at the time of independence to the agreement at the end
of 1959 and the evacuation over subsequent years.

The military problem was perhaps the easiest to choose, for it
is the broadest. The organization of the army encompasses both the
formation of the military units—organization in the strictest sense
—and the operations in which the army was engaged. The third
section under this topic involves the political battle for control of
army organization, the important complementary facet of the problem that is inseparable from the first two aspects.

Nothing poses so many intriguing problems as the new nation's
economic policy. In Moroccan economic life, no sector has the importance of agriculture. Although the policy of industrialization
would for this reason be instructive, it is vague. The unresolved con-
troversy over agrarian reform—from the meaning of the phrase
down to its actual implementation—offers a case study in negative
decision-making, for agrarian reform has never taken place. It has
been strongly advocated, however, and it is a continuing problem,
the importance of which is emphasized by the recurrent crises in
Moroccan agriculture.

The area of social problems also offers many specific cases. Education was chosen as one of the dominant problems, if not the
dominant problem, in this field, and the policy of Arabization in
primary and secondary education is a researchable and controversial unit that was of interest during Mohammed V's reign and continues to be so.

The choice of a representative problem in the political field
was more obvious and provides a fitting final case for this study.
The biggest problem of Moroccan government is its evolution, and
the most significant event in this area has been the organization of
elections. First mapped out with imprecision in 1955, the road to
the timid beginnings of democracy led to an abortive law in 1957
before it ended in the holding of elections on May 29, 1960. In the
process, basic problems of civil liberties, an instructive sociological
sidelight in the rural organization, and much political activity
come to light.

There is a final reason for the choice of these five cases, refer-
ring to the broad purpose of the study. Each of these problems has
substantive relevance to the problem of new power in the new countries of the Arab-African area. The crucial role that the military
has played in Egypt, Sudan, Ethiopia, Iraq, Jordan, Syria, the

Congo (where Moroccan Army units were sent by the United Nations to organize a new national army), and others makes the study of military organization with its political aspects a pioneer analysis of broad relevance. The coexistence of a guerrilla force (the Army of Liberation) and a regular army (Moroccan units in the French and Spanish armies) poses a problem common to Algeria as well, and the tacit admission that the army is a force for internal security rather than for external defense will make the Moroccan experience relevant to other developing countries for some time to come. The problem of American bases exists in Libya, Ethiopia, and Saudi Arabia and, if extended to bases of other Western nations, in Algeria, Tunisia, Egypt, Kenya, and many other areas of west Africa, to name a few. Even more important is the general problem of finding a foreign policy; Morocco's search for a framework and its discovery of "non-dependence"—at first a slogan in search of a meaning—are developments which parallel strikingly similar—and often overlooked—evolutions in other countries of Africa and the Middle East. Similarly, the agricultural and educational policies of new nations are without exaggeration the cornerstones of their development. The difficulties in finding a policy and implementing it are endemic to the developing world. More precisely, the specific aspects of agrarian reform and recasting education in a national language have broad relevance, and the narrow problem posed by Arabization has pertinence to all former colonial lands of the Arab world. Finally, the pressure for the forms of democracy posed above all by the slogans of popular nationalism is similar throughout the newly independent world despite cultural and political differences. The Moroccan way of dealing with this problem can throw some light on the rough and smooth spots in other nations' paths to democracy.

III

One important question must be answered, however: To what extent is Morocco typical of the other new states which can be studied as developing societies? Certainly there are many unique points in the Moroccan experience; to rise above these, must we attain a level of abstraction that makes any comparison meaningless? One suggestion of typicality comes from the confusion over whether Morocco and the rest of north Africa belong in Africa or in the Arab world. The very confusion suggests—quite rightly— that there are elements of similarity to both regions. If this is true, Morocco and its neighbors can serve as helpful models for comparative study of countries from Algeria to Angola and from Pakistan to Portuguese Guinea.

As the last African country to fall to the great African hunt which began in the mid-nineteenth century, Morocco had a forty-four–year colonial experience that was in many respects similar to that of other African and Arab countries. Although Morocco had known European interference and sporadic occupation since the Moors were driven from Spain at the end of the fifteenth century, European power rivalries prevented its final occupation by any one power until 1912, after France, supported by England, had been given a free hand by Germany in exchange for territory in the Congo basin. An attack by mountain tribes against the sultan in his capital at Fez provided the occasion for his rescue by French troops, already stationed in coastal regions of the country to protect French interests and citizens. Following Sultan Moulay Hafid's invitation of military intervention, he signed the Treaty of Fez, establishing a formal protectorate on March 30, 1912, and abdicated. On May 1, Marshal Louis Lyautey was named the first and most famous resident general.

The residency was the head of the French government that was parallel to the *makhzen* (Moroccan government). The Treaty of Fez committed France to "institute in Morocco a new regime including . . . the organization of a reformed Sherifian *makhzen*," and to maintain "order and security" through the pacification of the country. The latter task took until 1936, but work on the first obligation did not await pacification. Colonial rule was direct and indirect, thus combining features of other systems used in the Middle East and Africa. Since the *makhzen* with its vizirates (ministries) and its grand vizir (premier) was neither replaced nor reorganized by the protectorate, but was duplicated by the residency and the delegations (ministries), the two systems worked more-or-less hand in hand, the *makhzen* frequently dealing with the Moroccans and the residence with the European colony. In local matters, military commanders, civil controllers, and officials in the Office of Indigenous Affairs headed effective government at various levels, but administration was usually done in cooperation with tribal and city authorities. These prominent Moroccans must not all be thought of as collaborators; a number of leading nationalists were in the *makhzen*, and many of them had had local administrative posts. After the rise of the independence idea, during World War II, and the mounting tension which followed between the protectorate and the sultan, the *makhzen* was placed in a position of increasing subservience by the residency. After the deposition and exile of the sultan in 1953, most of the remaining nationalists left government service. Yet many of those in lower civil service positions remained after independence to provide the experience and skills necessary for running a government.

In the north and the extreme south of the country, two protectorate zones were subleased from France by Spain and, for all practical purposes, were governed autonomously. Although the sultan was recognized as ruler of all Morocco, his representative (*khalifa*) in Tetuan was head of the Moroccan government in the northern zone. A delegate general occupied a position similar to that of the residency. Although the Spanish were in the northern zone before 1912, the limits and legal status of the Spanish protectorate were fixed the same year as those in the French zone. Disputes over Tangier delayed its international status until 1923. The extreme south, Tarfaya, below the Dra River, was under superficial Spanish control until 1958.

The effects of the protectorate—slightly longer than in most of the Middle East and slightly shorter than in black Africa—were typical of any colonial regime, even though Morocco was not a full colony. Public works and welfare were advanced, order and central government restored, urbanization and industrialization accelerated, national consciousness sharpened, and European notions of politics, mores, and progress introduced. The protectorate was of more direct benefit to Morocco than to the Moroccans; although the people generally bettered their condition, they also were less favored, proportionally, than the Europeans, whom they outnumbered. But the biggest contribution to political unrest was not the size of the gap that the protectorate permitted between the two communities, but the increased awareness of this gap.

Although Morocco has existed as a political entity, with numerous interruptions, since Roman times and as a national and geographic unit since the eleventh-century Almoravid dynasty, it is still struggling to attain national consciousness and unity. The violent wave of xenophobia which swept over it at the turn of the nineteenth century was a traditionalist manifestation typical of Arab areas at that time but different from modern nationalism. Paradoxically, as in Sudan, Egypt, and Nigeria, this political current was to end in the establishment of colonial rule. In 1930 came the first awakening of modern national consciousness and the beginning of the nationalist movement. Through the Berber *dahir* (edict) of that year, the protectorate attempted to divide and conquer by making a legal distinction between Arab and Berber. By 1934 the basic elements of the nationalist movement were in place; the young sultan was called "king" in a popular demonstration in Fez, and the Moroccan Action Committee was formed to formulate grievances and demand reforms. The king was the rallying point of Moroccan national consciousness. The protectorate recognized this and deposed and exiled him in 1953, but, in so doing, it enhanced his symbolic value. Mohammed V remained the symbol of Moroccan nationalism during his lifetime. Beyond this point, however, national consciousness is only developing. The biggest obstacles are geography, tribal organization, and the social structure.

Morocco is not a natural or homogeneous geographic unit. It is shaped like a giant *khaima*, the dark bisymmetrical camel's-hair tent used by the Moroccan nomad. Its ridgepole, running northeast-southwest, is the Atlas Mountains, lying in three parallel and overlapping ranges—the Middle Atlas southeast of Fez and Meknes, the High Atlas southeast of Beni Mellal and Marrakesh, and the Anti-Atlas southeast of Taroudannt and Agadir. Due south of Marrakesh is Tubkal Peak (13,665 feet), the highest African mountain west of Lake Tanganyika and the Nile. East of the Atlas lies a region of high plateaus stretching into Algeria. North of Fez and Meknes, the Rif Mountains rise as a barrier along the Mediterranean coast from the African pillar of Hercules at Ceuta to the other Spanish *presidio* of Melilla; the Rif meets the Middle Atlas at the narrow Taza Gap. West of the Middle Atlas and south of Rabat and Casablanca lies a hilly upland amenable to cultivation. The rest of Morocco is plain, but the lowlands south of the Atlas are pre-Saharan desert spotted by oases and lightly populated, whereas the northern plains are the agricultural areas of the country, heavily populated and dotted with the coastal and inland cities which attract Morocco's growing population.

Horizontally and vertically, the geography divides the population. The pastoral Berber populations of the mountains, the nomads of the desert, and the sedentary farmers of the irrigated oases and the coastal plain are all distinct from one another and the urban populations in their ways of life and means of livelihood. The crucial ties in such a diverse society are those of transportation and communication, but in Morocco these are only developing. There are about 30,000 miles of roads, a third of them surfaced. Only four surfaced roads (plus countless trails) cross the backbone of the Atlas; the four roads run along the coast, southeast and southwest of Marrakesh, and south of Fez. There are still no passable roads running across the Rif to the coast. Railroads are largely for freight and cover only 1,200 miles of roadbed in the coastal plain, through the Taza Gap, and along the Algerian frontier; no railroad crosses the Atlas. The country is crossed by bus, truck, and bicycle traffic, but snow in the mountains cuts communications in winter, raises prices south of the Atlas, and makes goods scarce and commerce sporadic.

Newspapers are printed in Rabat and Casablanca and distributed in inland cities; they cover the urban areas but are kept from the rural regions by a barrier of illiteracy. Morocco has one thick telephone book and over 130,000 telephones (in 1960). Throughout the realm, the Moroccan National Radio can be heard in Arabic, Berber, English, French, and Spanish. There were 550,000 radio sets in 1961. Rumors are rife, and news is rare; the most widespread means of communication outside the cities still remain the crier and the exchange of gossip in the weekly market.

Like most of the Arab and African countries, Morocco has a dominant tribal structure. Three hundred, the figure usually given for the number of tribes, compares favorably with statistics of some other African countries. A firm count is difficult, however, for fractions, tribes, subconfederations, and confederations all play varying roles in the allegiance and social life of the Moroccan. More relevant than statistics is the fact that tribes (in any of the above forms) were the dominant form of social and political organization in the past and that this predominance, still important in the *bled* (countryside), is being eroded by contemporary political events. Next to residual state ownership, tribal ownership was—and still is—the predominant system of land ownership. The tribe was also the socioeconomic unit, often autarkic in its production and consumption and closed in its social organization. Although the tribe did not have a separate religion, as is often the case in black Africa, tribal versions of the Muslim religion are frequently characterized by purely local borrowings from the pre-Islamic past. Social customs are also tribally determined and oriented.

Tribal relations were theoretically secondary to the power of the sultan. The multistate systems or semi-anarchic group relations which existed from time to time in Africa were not characteristic of tribal government in Morocco. Thus the problem of the chefferies of Guinea, paramount chiefs of Ghana, or emirs of Nigeria differs from the Moroccan problem, but the difference is only one of degree. The protectorate ruled the tribes as units and ruled the country through important tribal leaders, such as Hajj Thami of the Glawa, pasha of Marrakesh and lord of the Atlas. The protectorate aided in breaking the power of the tribes, on the other hand, by accelerating the process of urbanization; in the process, it created the conditions for a successful independence movement. The nationalist revolt was slower to appear and less important among the rural tribes, where the Army of Liberation was its major arm, than in the cities, where urban resistance was highly developed.

When independence was realized, the social preponderance of the tribal structure made the problem of the tribes not one of breaking down their political dominance, but one of breaking up their social isolation. In the winter of 1958, Riffi and Middle Atlas tribes became dissident when they found themselves neither left alone nor helped by the new Moroccan government. Two winters before, the governor of Tafilalt united local tribes under his control in a revolt against centralized government. The Popular Movement, a rural and largely Berber political party that was connected with the 1958 events, glorified the leader of the 1956 revolt after his death. A chance to mobilize national sentiment and effectively replace tribal patterns in many areas was found in the rural communes, created in 1959, and in their communal councils, elected in 1960. Yet the government was slow to use the communes as a basis for the social and economic mobilization and education as originally conceived, and the councils were allowed to take little part in local government. The tribes thus continue to act as social units, even though their powers of military resistance and their position as administrative institutions have been removed. Since there is a gap between political and social reality, the tribes in Morocco continue to resist change. They are frequently bypassed, but not totally overcome.

There is a well-defined, if changing, social structure in Morocco as a whole. In the traditional society, up to eighty per cent of the population was tied to the land, either as a small landowner, a farmer-grazer in the tribal system, or a sharecropper. Although incentive may be expected to have been higher among the first group mentioned, the three segments were generally equal in standard of living and way of life. An urban artisan and merchant class, including some very prosperous families, comprised much of the rest of the society. There was very few laborers, except for domestic workers or children who were assistants and apprentices. A heterogeneous elite capped the social structure; it included the *makhzen* and palace cliques, a small group of large rural landowners usually living in the cities, the *'ulema* (religious doctors) and other mem-

bers of the religious intelligentsia connected with Quranic learning, and the sheikhs, *muqaddem,* caids and other members of the
rural or tribal judicial-administrative hierarchy. Often these four
groups overlapped. An important subsegment too powerful to be
included simply within the *makhzen* was the army, whether tribal,
mercenary, or professional. Thus, the society resembled the traditional world of the Middle East, its percentages strictly Moroccan
but its composition typically Arab. It should be noted that, with
the possible exception of the *gish* (army) tribes who received their
land from the king in return for their military support, there is
nothing in this social system which can properly be called feudal.
Modern doctrinaire attacks on the Moroccan "feudals" is a neo-
Marxist distortion of the term.

These social groups still exist, although their relative share in
contemporary society has diminished to make room for new groups.
Even these new groups cannot be called classes in the Marxian sense.
Their class consciousness is scarcely developed, and their ties with
their group of origin remain strong. Soussi merchants in Casablanca
build houses and store nest eggs in Tafraout in the Anti-Atlas, Berber mountaineers from the Rif and the Middle Atlas spend half a
year on Algerian farms or in Casablanca factories earning enough to
"retire" for the rest of the year with the families they left behind,
and modern farmers work together with traditional *fellahin* (peasants) in the Moroccan Agricultural Union (UMA).

Nearly one-third of Morocco's 11,600,000 people are urban
dwellers, and nearly one-third of these 3,400,000 people live in
Casablanca (965,227, of which 114,471 were foreigners in 1960).
Here, in the newer industrial towns along the coast—Rabat, (227,-
445), Tangier (141,714), Kenitra (Port Lyautey; 86,775), Safi (81,-
072), al-Jadida (Mazagan; 40,302), and Mohammedia (Fedala; 35,-
010)—and the mining centers—Oujda (128,645), Khouribga (40,838),
and Youssouffia (Louis Gentil; 8,302) in the interior—a growing
proletariat is appearing. It carries the hopes and efforts of industrialization on its back, but it has not developed its skills, education,
and economic strength enough to take a responsible role in government or to avoid being caught between prices and wages. The total
700,000-membership claimed by the Moroccan Labor Union (UMT)
and the smaller General Union of Moroccan Workers (UGTM)
gives an idea of the size of this proletarian group although the
actual membership is only about one-third of these claims.

Another new urban group is the businessmen, ranging from
wealthy individuals, many of whom have had Horatio Alger careers,

to small Soussi grocers who represent the epitome of the adaptable trading spirit of the Arab world (although in this case they are Berbers). According to registration figures for Chamber of Commerce and Industry elections in May, 1960, this group numbers about 100,000, a figure which should be tripled or quadrupled to include families. In the larger traditionalist cities of the interior— Marrakesh (243,134), Fez (216,133), Meknes (175,943), Tetuan (101,352), and Ouezzan (26,203)—and the smaller ones of the coast —Salé (75,799), al-'Airash (30,763), and as-Sawira (Mogador; 26,-392)—the traditionalist complement to the businessman—the artisan—is strong, numbering close to 500,000 with his family.

Another segment of the urban population is composed of the educated Moroccans, those who have received some schooling; in 1956, of the 1,200,000 school-age children out of schools, fewer than 200,000 came from the towns and cities and more than 1,000,-000 from the *bled*. Of the Moroccans aged twenty-seven to thirty-four in 1958, about 42,000 had primary educations, and only about 1,500 had secondary educations. The number of citizens with the basic training necessary to fill the demands of professional, administrative, and other types of modern service is thus limited, as it is in other developing nations.

Changes in the structure of rural society have been much less marked than those in the urban regions. Of the seventy per cent of the population who lives in the countryside, 3,300,000 people make up the rural labor force. About 1,000,000 families are engaged in subsistence farming; fewer than 2,000 families use mechanized equipment and modern methods. An additional 120,000 work as sharecroppers, meagerly supporting their families, and 70,000 work as salaried agricultural laborers, often with only seasonal employment. Under the traditional system of agriculture, half of the farm labor force is underemployed, working fewer than four months a year.

The general social structure of the country, then, is characteristic of the developing areas of Africa and Arab Asia, with a large rural mass living in largely primitive conditions on autarkic subsistence agriculture; a small educated elite that is active in politics, government, and a limited market economy; and between them a serious gap, occupied rather than bridged by such small restive groups as the proletariat and the transitional commercial class. Extremes of wealth and poverty, rather than a vigorous middle class, are not doctrinaire myths but reality. The per-capita income of $147 is therefore only a rough index of the country's development.

⌠ The most important dynamic element in the social picture is the growth rate, which Moroccan leaders were surprised to see was 3.2 per cent according to the census of 1960. Nearly three-quarters of the Moroccan population was younger than Moulay Hassan when, at the age of thirty-one, he ascended the throne at the end of February, 1961. This age distribution means that Morocco's manpower potential is great, but that the problems of feeding, training, employing, and utilizing this growing young mass are greater. Unprepared to take part in the national life, it can become a growing element of dissatisfaction and disorder, a dead weight about the neck of the nation. This population increase compounds the problems of urbanization and modernity typical of the developing world, for it is most remarkable in the cities of Casablanca, Rabat, Kenitra, Khouribga, Safi, and Salé, all but the last the growing modern centers of Morocco. On the other hand traditional cities in the former Spanish zone, such as Asila, Xauen, al-'Airash, and Nador have lost population, and other traditional centers like Azzemour, as-Sawira, Marrakesh, Ouezzan, Sefrou, Settat, and Tetuan have registered only small gains. When compared with the results of the previous census, taken in 1952, the growth in urban concentration is clearly shown; 71 instead of 73 per cent of the country lives in rural areas (including villages of fewer than 2,000 people), and 19 instead of 16 per cent lives in cities of over 500,000.

In this situation the prime movers of national consciousness have been the political organizations, although their effect is limited. Partisan evolution in Morocco is similar to that of parties in any new country which has attained its independence by violence and in many ways resembles even those who have gradually attained self-government through elections.

As the king symbolized the unity and independence of the country, an active political elite backed by a number of semi-clandestine groups organized and cooperated to attain independence by direct action. By 1937 the reform group of 1934 had split into geographic and personality factions, all with similar but competing programs. The hardening line of resistance and particularly the programmatic unity brought by the substitution of the single goal of independence for a number of reforms led to the formation of the Independence (Istiqlal) Movement in 1944. This was followed in 1951 by a Moroccan national front, which loosely united the four major nationalist factions under the leadership of the 1934 elite.

⌊ Three groups became evident in the nationalist movement.

The original leaders, especially after 1952, were deported ('Allal al-Fassi) or went into exile (Hajj Ahmed Balafrej, Mohammed Laghzaoui) to direct the international aspect of the nationalist movement and to provide guidance for the home front from the security of foreign shores. A second generation of younger leaders sprang up to lead the active resistance on Moroccan soil (Mehdi ben Barka, 'Abderrahim Bou'abid). Many of these were also later jailed or deported, but they remained in closer contact with resistance activity, and some of them were connected with terrorist groups (Mahjoub ben Seddiq, Mohammed al-Basri) or with the Army of Liberation (Mahjoubi Ahardan, 'Abdelkrim Khatib). The third group was an active fraction of the popular masses who listened to the old leaders and worked under the younger generation in guerrilla, terrorist, and propaganda activity, sometimes even taking decisions as well as actions into their own impatient hands. From this group came the popular martyrs ('Allal ben 'Abdullah, Mohammed Zerqtouni). On the symbolic level, the resistance became synonymous with the independence movement; the goal, the movement, the party, and even the clandestine newspaper became welded together in the unifying confusion of a powerful name—Istiqlal.

On the attainment of the goal, the old-guard leaders returned to resume political leadership, supported by the actions of the younger leaders, who again took second place, and of the enthusiastic, impatient masses. The Istiqlal party took advantage of independence to assert its dominant position, but it agreed to join with the smaller resistance groups in the first government of National Unity presided over by an independent nationalist, Hajj Mbarek Lahbil Bekkai. The parties provided the cadres for the new governments, urban resistance members were largely absorbed into the police, and the Army of Liberation—the last die-hard group to recognize the monarchy's independence—were integrated into the Royal Moroccan Army and its nominal reserve or given minor posts in the local administration. Other civil servants were recruited from among former employees of the ministries under the protectorate or from the newly trained cadres of Moroccan youth.

The Moroccan political scene continued to be dominated by the Istiqlal during the first three years of independence, but the monolithic appearance of the party was deceptive. During 1956 and 1957, the Istiqlal campaigned vigorously to turn sympathizers of the nationalist movement into members of the political party and accompanied this campaign with a drive to infiltrate government services and with pressure to form a homogeneous (i.e., all-Istiqlal)

TABLE 1

THE FIRST SIX GOVERNMENTS—PART A

Government	I Dec. 7, 1955— Oct. 25, 1956	II Oct. 26, 1956— Apr. 16, 1958
Premier	Mbarek Bekkai (ind.)	
Vice-premier	Mohammed Zeghari (ind.) │	
Foreign Affairs	*Ahmed Balafrej (Ist.) ▶ *	
Ministers of state	Ahmed Guedira (LI) † Driss Mhammedi (Ist.) † Mohammed Cherkawi (PDI) † 'Abderrahim Bou'abid (Ist.) †	
Interior [Undersec'y]	Lahcen Lyoussi (ind.) ‖	Driss Mhammedi (Ist.)
Economy		'Abderrahim Bou'abid (Ist.) ▶
Finance	'Abdelkader Benjelloun (PDI)	['Abdullah Chefchaouni (ind.)] ‡ ▶
Commerce	Ahmed Lyazidi (Ist.)	[Ahmed Lyazidi (Ist.)] ‡
Industry	Thami Ouezzani (PDI)	
Agriculture	Ahmed Nejjai (Ist.)	'Omar b. 'Abdeljalil (Ist.)
Education [Undersec'y]	Mohammed al-Fassi (Ist.)	
Youth	Ahmed Bensouda (PDI) │	
Justice	'Abdelkrim Benjelloun (Ist.) ▶	
Civil Service	│ Rashid Mouline (LI)	
Telecommunication	Leon Benzaquen (ind.)	
Defense	Ahmed Guedira (LI) ‡	Mohammed Zeghari (ind.) ‖
Information	['Abdullah Ibrahim (Ist.)] §	Ahmed Guedira (LI)
Labor	'Abdelhadi Boutaleb (PDI)	'Abdullah Ibrahim (Ist.)
Public Works	Mohammed Douiri (Ist.) ▶	
Housing	Mohammed b. Bouchaib (PDI) │	
Health	'Abdelmalek Farraj (ind.) ▶	
Habous	Mokhtar Soussi (ind.)	Mekki Baddou (ind.) ▶
Undersecretaries of state in brackets	* April 27, 1956 † Charged with French negotiations ‡ March 22, 1956 § Undersec'y of state, Premier's Office ‖ Replaced by Mhammedi, May 4, 1956	* Arrows (▶) following names indicate continuance to next government. ‡ Undersec'y of state, Economy ‖ Replaced by Lyazidi, Sept. 12, 1957

TABLE 1

THE FIRST SIX GOVERNMENTS—PART B

Government	III May 12–Nov..22, 1958	IV Dec. 24, 1958—May 20, 1960
Premier	Ahmed Balafrej (Ist.)	'Abdullah Ibrahim (UNFP)
Vice-premier	'Abderrahim Bou'abid (UNFP)	
Foreign Affairs	▶ Ahmed Balafrej * (Ist.)	'Abdullah Ibrahim (UNFP)
Ministers of state	[Mohammed Boucetta (Ist.)] †	
Interior	Messa'oud Chiguer (ex-Ist.)	Driss Mhammedi (ex-Ist.)
[Undersec'y]	[Driss Slawi (Ist.)]	[Hassan Zemmouri (ind.)]
Economy	▶'Abderrahim Bou'abid (UNFP)	
Finance	▶['Abdullah Chefchaouni (ind.)] ‡	
Commerce	[Ahmed b. Kiran (Ist.)] ‡	[Driss Slawi (Ist.)] * ▶
Industry	[Mehdi 'Abdeljalil (Ist.)] ‡	
Agriculture	['Abdelhafid Kadiri (Ist.)] ‡	Thami 'Ammar (UNFP)
Education	'Omar b. 'Abdeljalil (Ist.)	'Abdelkrim Benjelloun (ex-Ist.) ▶
[Undersec'y]	[Mohammed Tahiri (Ist.)]	
Youth		
Justice	▶'Abdelkrim Benjelloun (Ist.)	Mohammed Bahnini (ind.)
Civil Service		
Telecommunication	Mohammed Awad (ex-Ist.)	Mohammed Medboh (ind.) †
Defense	Ahmed Lyazidi (Ist.)	Mohammed Awad (ind.)
Information	[Ahmed Senussi (Ist.)] §	['Issa Benchekroun (ind.)]
Labor	Bashir b. 'Abbas (Ist.)	Ma'ati Bou'abid (UNFP)
Public Works	▶Mohammed Douiri (Ist.)	'Abderrahman b. 'Abdelalli (ind.) ▶
Housing		
Health	▶'Abdelmalek Farraj (ind.)	Yussef b. 'Abbas (Ist.) ▶
Habous	▶ Mekki Baddou (ind.) ‡	
Undersecretaries of state in brackets	* Arrows (▶) in front of names indicate continuance from preceding government. † Undersec'y of state, Foreign Affairs ‡ Undersec'y of state, Economy § Undersec'y of state, Premier's Office	* Undersec'y of state, Economy † Replaced by Awad, Aug. 29, 1959 ‡ Until Aug. 30, 1960

TABLE 1

THE FIRST SIX GOVERNMENTS—PART C

Government	V May 26, 1960— June 1, 1961	VI June 2, 1961— Jan. 5, 1963
Premier	Mohammed V *	Hassan II
Vice-premier	Moulay Hassan	
Foreign Affairs	Driss Mhammedi (ex-Ist.) †	Ahmed Balafrej (Ist.)
Ministers of state		Mohammed Fall Ould 'Omeir (Maur.) * 'Allal al-Fassi (Ist.) † 'Abdelkrim Khatib (Pop. Mvt.) ‡ Hassan Ouezzani (PDC) §
Interior	Mbarek Bekkai (ind.) ‡	Ahmed Guedira (LI)
[Undersec'y]		[Mfeddel Cherkawi] ‖
Economy	Mohammed Douiri (Ist.) #	
Commerce		
Industry	▶ Driss Slawi (ex-Ist.)	Ahmed Joundi (ind.) **
Agriculture		[Ahmed 'Osman] ‖
Education	Hassan Zemmouri (ind.) §	Ahmed Guedira (LI)
	▶'Abdelkrim Benjelloun (ex-Ist.)	Rashid Mouline (LI) ††
Justice	▶ Mohammed Bahnini (ind.) #	Mohammed Boucetta (Ist.) #
Civil Service	Mohammed Boucetta (Ist.)	
Telecommunication	Mohammed Cherkawi (PDC)	Mohammed b. 'Abdeslam al-Fassi (Ist.)
Defense	Moulay Hassan	Mahjoubi Ahardan (Pop. Mvt.)
Information	Moulay Ahmed al-'Alawi (ind.)	
Labor	'Abdelkrim Khatib (Pop. Mvt.)	'Abdelkader Benjelloun (PDC)
Public Works	▶'Abderrahman b. 'Abdelalli (ind.)	Mohammed Benhima (ind.) ‡‡
Health	▶Yussef b. 'Abbas (Ist.)	
Habous	Ahmed Bargash (ind.)	
Undersecretaries of state in brackets	* Succeeded by Moulay Hassan, Feb. 26, 1961 † Replaced by Benjelloun, Oct., 1960, then by Boucetta, Jan., 1961 ‡ Succeeded by Guedira, April 14, 1961 § Replaced by Guedira, March 21, 1961 # Replaced by 'Abdelkhalek Torres (Ist.), Oct., 1960	* For Mauritanian affairs † For Islamic affairs, resigned Jan. 5, 1963 ‡ For African affairs § Without portfolio ‖ July 18, 1962 # Resigned Jan. 5, 1963 ** Replaced by Benhima, July 18, 1962 †† Replaced by 'Abbas, Oct. 1962 ‡‡ Replaced by Slawi, July 18, 1962

government. The latter effort partially succeeded in October, 1956, when one minor party was eliminated in the formation of the second government, a new National Unity coalition, again under Bekkai. In May, 1958, with the formation of the third government, homogeneity appeared to be attained, for only two ministers were non-Istiqlal and independent and the premier was party Secretary General Ahmed Balafrej. However, the pre-independence division between old-guard leaders and second-generation activists, supported by labor, led to increasing factionalism and the fall of the government before the year was out. On Christmas Eve, 1958, the fourth government was formed of activists and independents under a leading activist sympathizer, Moulay 'Abdullah Ibrahim, and on January 25, 1959, the party split. The scissionists formed a short-lived Confederated Istiqlal and then, on September 6, 1959, freed themselves from the magic name and united with activist elements ,from other parties in the National Union of Popular Forces (UNFP). On the eve of the May, 1960, elections which Ibrahim's government had organized, the king revoked its mandate and created the fifth government, with himself as premier, the crown prince as vice-premier, and the ministries held by representatives of groups and parties, excluding only members of the UNFP. This coalition governed Morocco until after the king's death on February 26, 1961.

The other parties ran like hidden currents through this stream of events, sometimes rising to play a momentarily crucial role but usually submerged. At the time of independence four minor organizations existed, the most important being the Democratic Istiqlal party (PDI) and the Liberal Independents. The PDI was a small opportunist group which had split for personal reasons from the prewar nationalist movement. In accordance with the king's desire to balance the Istiqlal, it was granted disproportionate participation in the government. The party was eliminated from the second government, and its problems of influence were compounded by its position of irresponsibility. During 1959, it, too, split into two, the activist wing joining in the UNFP and the original leaders consolidating under the name of the Democratic Constitutional party (PDC). The PDC was present in the fifth government.

The Liberal Independents were also a personal group centered about two influential friends of the Palace, Rashid Mouline and Ahmed Reda Guedira. They resisted the demands for homogeneity and retained participation in the cabinet until the formation of the third government. Liberal Independents returned to favor and influence in the formation of the fifth government. In the northern zone the National Reform party (PRN) joined the Istiqlal after independence, and the even smaller Moroccan Unity party (PUM) continued its separate existence.

The urban concentration of partisan activity by both the original Istiqlal and the minor parties was both the cause and the result of rural resentment. Just as nationalism was slower in finding an active manifestation in the countryside than in the cities, so a political organization representing specifically rural interests did not appear in the open until over a year after independence, although the intervening period was bridged by a secret organization which kept up the contacts of the Army of Liberation. In early October, 1957, the Popular Movement was suddenly announced and just as suddenly, on October 24, was outlawed; the Istiqlal was in no mood for competition at that time, and the king acquiesced. Only after the publication of the civil liberties laws at the end of the following year did the party reappear, this time to stay. It lost only a few of its leaders to the newly formed UNFP the next year and for the first time participated in the government (the fifth), although Bekkai, the first premier, had been an active sympathizer of the movement.

Results of the 1960 municipal and communal elections indicate the strength and followings of the parties. The Istiqlal, with about half the seats, still remained the strongest party, with a large mass following in every province, but particularly in the traditional cities and villages of the interior. The UNFP, winning between one-third and one-quarter of the seats (according to conflicting interpretations of the results), drew the bulk of its strength from the new industrial cities of the coast and the rural villages in the Souss valley between the High Atlas and the Anti-Atlas. Popular Movement strength lay in the Atlas Mountains and the desert and plateau east of the Atlas, where the UNFP fell short; less than one-tenth of the national total of seats were won by the movement. The PDC, Liberal Independents, and PUM showed their lack of a popular base by winning less than three per cent of the seats, most of this number going to the PDC. The few supporters of these parties were scattered through the country. More significant were the seats won by candidates without any party affiliation; at least one-quarter of the winning candidates were independents, evenly spread through most of Morocco. Political organization in Morocco is still largely an urban phenomenon and has far to go before it can claim effective mobilization of the entire population.

TWO

The important thing is to find a
program; we can always find a man
to apply it.

—Mohammed V

DIPLOMATIC PROBLEM
Evacuation of American Bases

When Morocco awoke an independent nation in March, 1956, it found that it faced a diplomatic anomaly within its borders. Although sovereign, it had on its territory five major bases of a power with which it had never signed a military agreement. Barely independent, it was already committed in foreign policy by the presence of foreign, non-protectorate troops as a consequence of the military cooperation between the United States and France. Four principal bases of the United States Air Force and the one United States naval air station, with their subsidiary units, posed a foreign-policy problem which had to be solved.

The bases in question were two active installations of the Strategic Air Command (SAC) at Sidi Sliman and Ben Guerir, near Meknes and Marrakesh respectively, and an inactive SAC base at Bensliman, near the Moroccan Army camp between Rabat and Casablanca; an air force matériel depot with SAC and fighter units at Nouasseur, by Casablanca; a naval air station at Port Lyautey; an air force radar warning system that ran along the ridge of the Atlas ranges from Marrakesh to the eastern frontier; and a navy communications system based on Sidi Yahya and Sidi Bouknadel on either side of Port Lyautey. The air force bases contained about 7,500 military personnel until mid-1956, when the ceiling was increased by 2,000, and the naval installations had about 2,000. These figures can be doubled to show the number of Americans—military, civilian and dependents—who were part of the base system. The naval installations were under a commander of naval activities who was directly subordinate to the commander, Naval Air Forces, Eastern Atlantic and Mediterranean, in Naples; the air force complex was headed by the commander of the Seventeenth Air Force in Rabat. In 1956, without changing the status of the bases, the air force administrative headquarters moved to Wheelus Field, Libya and then to Torrejon de Ardos, Spain, for political and geographical reasons.

Although American forces had been in Morocco in small numbers since the World War II debarkment along Morocco's Atlantic shore, the base network was established as a result of secret agreements signed between French Foreign Minister Georges Bidault and the American ambassador to Paris, Jefferson Caffrey, on December 22, 1950, within the general framework of NATO defense arrangements. At the time of the negotiations and after, the United States requested that the negotiations be communicated to Morocco or that Morocco be consulted, but Paris consistently refused. France's sensitivity to the political situation in Morocco at that time was also reflected in the agreements, for the American position was subordinate to the French and isolated from the Moroccans in important respects. France was empowered to fix the ceiling on personnel figures and for three years had refused the increase finally granted in April, 1956. Contact between Americans and Moroccans at all levels was reduced as much as possible by the protectorate. Because of urban terrorism during the Resistance and even after independence, all *medinas* (native quarters or cities) were declared off limits, although individual friendships between two naturally curious peoples often circumvented this rule. More important, all upper-level contact with Moroccans was channeled through the French, whose Quartermaster Corps handled hiring, firing, and wage scales for the 6,800 air force and 1,000 navy employees.

The French position, as stated by Foreign Minister Christian Pineau, was that disposition of the bases must be settled by tripartite negotiations. There were four points of French interest. One, the legal status of the land was unclear. The land had been expropriated, but paid for, by France and was then leased to the United States for nothing. Two, the French were responsible, according to the Bidault-Caffrey agreements, for the security of the bases. This could be taken to mean the internal security, which the French ensured through small military detachments who watched the gates and fences—doubled by more security-conscious American units—or it could mean the military security and defense of the bases, which remained dependent on the French Army throughout Morocco. Three, the French were interested in keeping predominant influence in independent Morocco when economic or military influence was to be exercised. In 1956 France was becoming vividly aware of the law of power vacuums and was particularly smarting over the flow of American influence into its troublesome former colony of South Vietnam. Four, in addition to the security guards, the naval base of Port Lyautey was in reality a twin French and American base, and some of the minor installations also were.

Decision-making in the base question was frequently and subtly influenced by sporadic incidents involving the bases. The two special incidents of 1956, however, before the actual negotiation began, are more illustrative of the inherent tripartite problems of the question, even if two of the sides were interested in keeping negotiations in their company and out of the crowd. When the king and the prince hastily returned to Morocco after the French kidnaping of five Algerian leaders in October, 1956, they pointedly refused to land anywhere other than the American base of Port Lyautey, snubbing the French with an implicit fear for their personal security in their own country.

It was the complex nature of the same base which led to another incident a month later. When relations between France and Morocco suddenly deteriorated following the October kidnaping, Morocco began the first of its waves of pressure on the French for a troop withdrawal. Supply ships normally unloading at Casablanca were met by a strike from the UMT longshoremen, and in late November and early December four ships were rerouted to Mehdia, the small French navy port just outside the fence of the American base at Port Lyautey, where they were unloaded by French sailors. Local civilians isolated the base with roadblocks for twelve hours, and on November 26–27 the same UMT union in Casablanca refused to unload supplies for Nouasseur from the "Norfolk Victory," in retaliation for "American complicity" in the Mehdia bypass. The strike was solved by negotiations, but the Moroccan Foreign Ministry protested to the American Embassy without receiving "satisfaction." The principle of public pressure on the question of American bases was thus early established.

The American position recognized that renegotiations would be necessary, although there consistently seems to have been more good will than speed in settling the matter. In fact, there was a certain amount of diplomatic spadework to be done before any talking could begin.[1] The legation at Tangier was replaced by a chargé d'affaires at Rabat in June, three months after independence, but American statements maintained merely that negotiations would have to await the appointment of a full ambassador. In October, 1956, Cavendish Cannon, former ambassador to Greece, presented his letter of accreditation to the king.

To the United States, a base had two aspects. It was a strategic element of the concept of mutual defense of the free world, established through joint recognition by the United States and another country of their common interests in being prepared for war and strong for peace. Its importance was first as a deterrent, strengthening the free world and thereby discouraging attack by totalitarian forces, and second as a military establishment from which to resist attack. The base question was, therefore, diplomatic before it was military. By the same token, it was not a commercial proposition; American bases are not rented, although frequently they are accompanied by an aid program designed to strengthen the economy of the free world partner, thus further strengthening free world defense. A base was also a group of American citizens living abroad under defined conditions, established through a status-of-forces agreement (SOFA), such as had recently been signed with Libya. In American thinking, the recognition of the former element would lead to a detailed agreement on the latter element.

From the very beginning of the Moroccan problem, there was also a double escape clause in Pentagon estimates. Across the Straits of Gibraltar an even greater complex of air and naval bases was under construction in 1956, with an uncertain ready date but with the future capability of either augmenting or replacing the Moroccan complex. In the United States, equally uncertain in time of perfection, an intercontinental and intermediate range ballistic missile program, which would probably render obsolete all foreign air bases, possibly SAC itself, was being developed. Both the Americans and the Moroccans were aware of these elements in United States thinking, although neither knew when they would reduce the value of the Moroccan bases.

In the face of the French post-colonial outlook and America's Cold War point of view, the Moroccan position was unclear. In

---

[1] Negotiations first awaited French ratification of the Franco-Moroccan diplomatic convention of May, 1956, which restored Moroccan control of foreign affairs. In an interview Balafrej suggested that the Americans were held back by an initial desire to include the French, but then embarked on negotiations alone. The Pentagon's delays in preparing the initial brief may have also accounted for the late start in negotiations.

1956 the question of American bases was so far behind the problem of French troops stationed in Morocco that little public fervor and only intermittent official notice were aroused. To Morocco, the question was one of turning the *de facto* situation into a *de jure* one. The bases were noticeably there, but legally non-existent, Morocco maintained, since it had not been consulted on the Bidault-Caffrey agreements. This stand was proclaimed by the king before his return to Morocco in 1955 and formed the basis of the Moroccan position ever since. "As soon as a freely elected Government is installed, it will take cognizance of the terms of the Agreement and will make its own decisions," the sultan said.[2] Ahmed Balafrej, secretary general of the Istiqlal party, had been appointed foreign minister on April 27, 1956. When he joined Bekkai's government to set up the new Foreign Ministry, he kept his party post and thus became the highest partisan figure in a position of responsibility. Balafrej's first action on the bases was simply to formulate the same reservations on their legality. In May, he officially told France: "I have the honor to inform you that the Moroccan Government reserves its position entirely concerning the Franco-American Agreement of 22 December 1950." At the same time and again in July, Balafrej asked to see the Bidault-Caffrey agreements, a request that America and France discussed between themselves without reaching any positive conclusion.

In fact, to Morocco the bases were above all a matter to be reconciled with Moroccan sovereignty. The king was sympathetic toward the continuation of the bases provided that they were subject to the authority of his government, and he left his ministers to work out the details, as he had announced. Balafrej was wary of American involvement in his problems with the French Army, refused trilateral talks, and did not "recognize" joint bases, but was not antipathetic to the bases per se; he said, at least, that they constituted a guarantee of Moroccan liberty and security as long as there was no American interference in Moroccan affairs.[3] But he also saw the habitual coincidence of United States bases and an American aid program and was actively interested in the latter to increase Morocco's economic independence from France. Negotiations in the immediate future were expected to be devoted principally to revising the financial clauses of the tenure agreement and putting it on a Moroccan instead of a French basis. Party leaders and an unidentified member of the government not connected with foreign affairs

---

[2] *Daily Express* (London), November 15, 1955.
[3] *Times*, December 24, 1956; *Tribune*, November, 1955. This, of course, was the attitude hoped for by the United States in mutual security arrangements.

went even further and in the summer of 1956 were heard talking of demanding rent, the most frequently quoted annual figure being close to the $500,000,000 which went into the construction of the bases. In a *New York Times* interview Balafrej himself attempted, without too much success, to disavow this inflated figure but he did not totally exclude the idea of rent in preference to other forms of aid.

One of the earliest public discussions of the bases in an organized fashion from a nongovernment source came from the Istiqlal's daily Arabic newspaper, *al-'Alam,* usually more outspoken than the party's French-language weekly, *al-Istiqlal.*[4] In a collection of ideas of mixed parentage, the paper demanded an immediate government proclamation "that we do not accept the establishment of war bases on Moroccan soil," in order to avoid ideological involvement; at the same time, it could accept as much as a ten-year delay in evacuation if a sufficient rent were to be paid, at the end of which time the bases and all equipment would be turned over to Morocco. It was the first time evacuation was mentioned publicly.[5] The *al-Istiqlal* article also mentioned one of the key ideas of Balafrej, however, in stating that "in case of World War, the Government should impose special conditions compatible with the interests of Morocco alone." The absence of a rental figure and the presence of the idea of some joint control of the bases suggest that the article, written when Balafrej's supremacy in foreign affairs was undisputed in his party, had his approval.

It was in this context, then, that the opening base negotiations were set. Morocco, searching for a foreign policy, was in direct opposition to the colonial point of view of France and sought to find out from America how highly it valued its Cold War defense installations and how their existence could be reconciled with Moroccan sovereignty. A high enough value would incidentally strengthen Morocco's bargaining position with France on questions of economic and military aid or might even provide the desired measure of economic and military independence from the former protector. The problem in defining the new *de jure* situation was at the same time one of deciding the type of agreement to be negotiated. Was the question to be "settled" or "regularized," would the conditions

---

[4] See *Tribune,* August 15, 1956; *al-'Alam,* August 10, 1956. The Istiqlal National Council called for the opening of direct negotiations (*al-Istiqlal,* August 24, 1956).

[5] The first mention, that is, outside of Moroccan Communist party (PCM) demands. As early as December 5, 1955, the PCM had sent a delegation to the king asking for evacuation.

be those of "tenure" or of "withdrawal," would agreement be one for "staying" or "leaving"; in brief, were the talks to be positive or negative?

THE FIRST STAGE

External events and the first stage of relevant negotiations worked in a backhanded way to clear up some of these problems. The kidnaping of the Algerian leaders in October, 1956, led to the rupture of diplomatic contacts and military and economic talks with France. Following the establishment of the United States Embassy, Balafrej made arrangements to visit Washington, and Prince Moulay Hassan and the eldest Princess, Lalla 'Aisha, planned a good-will trip to the United States. Balafrej met several times with the State Department and Defense Department in late November to discuss aid and bases. The two nations' positions were explained, with no attempt at a final conclusion, and on his return the foreign minister was only able to say vaguely that "a solution will certainly meet the comprehension of His Majesty the King."

The request for aid was separated from the question of the bases, and the United States acted with unaccustomed speed. The day of his return to Rabat Balafrej met four experts from the International Cooperation Administration (ICA) on a preparatory study tour, and, on their departure two weeks later, the king told them Morocco "counts on American aid." In April, following a request for $37,000,000 necessary for its planned development-budget projects, Morocco signed an agreement with the United States providing for $20,000,000 ICA aid.

By this act, however, the aid question was divorced from the bases, and any "mutual assistance" between the two issues was lost. On May 11, 1957, the first negotiations on a base agreement were opened between the American Embassy and the Foreign Ministry. The State Department, in cooperation with the Defense Department, had been working on a draft treaty along the normal SOFA lines, similar to the Libyan treaty. During the meetings the Moroccan delegation was led by Balafrej or his immediate assistant, Mohammed Boucetta, who fully reflected the minister's thinking. Other members of the ministry also attended, as well as purely technical advisors when the discussion turned to specialized subjects. Negotiations on secondary matters were carried on by commissions, with infrequent talks between the ambassador and Balafrej. The meetings were sporadic and reached few conclusions on either the question of tenure or such secondary questions as military postal facilities, radio transmissions, legal jurisdiction, hiring of local labor, exchange facilities, and customs. Scheduled meetings were canceled by the Moroccans because they were too busy on other business.

The structure of authority in the Foreign Ministry, typical of most Moroccan ministries, contributed to the difficulties. Outside of Balafrej and Boucetta, there was no one in the foreign-policy field who could make decisions. Both the prince and the premier were uninterested in the matter; the prince was present at the first meeting to show the king's interest, but did not return. No collegial body other than the cabinet had any authority in the field, and the cabinet would act on foreign policy only on the initiative of the foreign minister, whereas the king's role was only to set general guidelines or to take ultimate action in a crisis.[6] The negotiators at the lower level were, therefore, only emissaries between the conference table and their ministers. They received proposals, collected questions and explanations, and carried them back to the ministry to be judged by the deciding elite. When Balafrej went to Spain in July and then to southeast Asia in August, the talks stopped, for there could be no answers.

If the procedure was hobbled, the approach to the subject matter was also somewhat lame in 1957. Early meetings were devoted to an exposition of the American position. The Moroccan negotiators were friendly but unhelpful; the American stand was rejected, either outright or by such extreme counterproposals as a demand to abolish exchange and fleet/army post office facilities or a demand to establish joint control over the operations. There was no attempt to engage in negotiations, and conversation ran out as the summer ran on. There was also no unified approach; postal arrangements were considered from the point of view of sovereignty, customs arrangements from a financial standpoint, and so on.

The Moroccans wanted to approach the problem as a general ensemble and to regularize it within the framework of an over-all definition of Moroccan-American relations, with the details falling into place later. They sought some formula—or even institution— that would reflect the realities of Morocco's position in world politics and define its relations with the United States. Yet the nature of this framework was unclear to them, and it appeared to

[6] An interministerial commission, composed of Balafrej, Defense Minister Zeghari, Interior Minister Mhammedi, Public Works Minister Douiri, and Economics Minister Bou'abid, had a vague role in preparing the general lines of the Moroccan position (al-Istiqlal, April 20, 1957).

their American opposites that they vaguely hoped for imaginative suggestions from the Americans. The same attitude is expressed from the other side in similar terms in *al-Istiqlal* on September 28, 1957.

> The Moroccan delegation seeks above all to place the problem of the bases within the general framework of Morocco-American relations and, of course, refuses simply to renew the Franco-American Agreement of 1952 [*sic*]. While awaiting a definition of this framework, the experts are presently studying technical and practical problems which stem from the installation of these bases; jurisdictional competence, circulation of individuals, privileges and immunities, etc.

Any chance of coming to grips with the problem was further lessened by the American ambassador's estimate of the situation. Cannon appeared to look on the bases as sleeping dogs which he preferred to let lie. Whatever may be the long-range judgment of this estimate, in contemporary fact he was right. Throughout Moroccan press and party programs, the emotional phrase, *jela'* (evacuation) of the foreign bases, was indeed beginning to be prominent, but not until the end of 1957 were the American bases associated with this demand for the withdrawal of ex-colonial military forces.[7] Whereas the French and Spanish *troops* were considered an affront to Moroccan sovereignty, it was simply the lack of a legal *agreement* that was the anomaly of the United States bases. When the bases were spoken of in the press, they were the subject of separate attention largely devoted to a reputation of Morocco's nonrecognition of the 1950 agreement and an indication of the smoothness and friendliness of Morocco-American contacts on the matter.

In fact, the bases continued to operate in a *de facto* SOFA condition, even in the absence of a status-of-forces agreement. Until the public appeal for *jela'* was broadened to include the United States bases, the negotiators were free of public pressure to hasten an agreement. Unfortunately, when external events and the evolution of Moroccan foreign policy finally brought the bases to the front page, the pressure was not to be toward the acceleration of negotiations, but toward withdrawal. Unhurried, the decision-makers did not decide; harried, they were to lose their power of decision.

[7] An exception, which also illustrates the uncertainty of current thinking, was the strange formula used by Balafrej when he visited India: America, Spain, and France were "either to get their troops out of Morocco or arrange conditions for temporary stay" (*The Washington Post*, August 24, 1957).

If the talks of 1957 allowed the Americans to see that their offers were far from the Moroccans' views, they also gave the Moroccans time to discover that, instead of looking for a framework into which to fit the bases, they were actually looking for a foreign policy. In the euphoria of interdependence before Balafrej's appointment in 1956, a Mediterranean pact had been mentioned as the keynote of Moroccan foreign relations, and Moroccan negotiators in Paris had spoken of a "total military alliance" with France.[8] A bilateral alliance with France was too narrow for the views of Balafrej, but a Mediterranean pact was suggested to the American negotiators in the hope that they would give the idea some shape and dimension. NATO was also possible, although, if the Moroccans ever awaited an invitation to join, they only vaguely proclaimed their availability, and their wish went unrequited. The Baghdad Pact had also been suggested as a possible framework, particularly during the visit of Feisal II of Iraq in May, 1956, although by the following year the idea had been dropped if only for geographical reasons. A likely framework was made available in May, 1957, when Rep. James P. Richards came to consult Morocco on the Eisenhower Doctrine. Although the king agreed with the "very principles" of the doctrine, "the Eisenhower Doctrine was conceived for the countries of the Mideast" and "could not be applied to Morocco without adaptations implied by the political, geographic and diplomatic situation of this country which is engaged in negotiations with France and Spain."[9] If this was a framework, Morocco did not make the most of it. Yet the word continued to be used in base negotiations, and, as late as a speech of August, 1957, Information Minister Ahmed Reda Guedira announced, "Bilateral agreements or the inclusion of Morocco within a broad system of defense in existence or to be created—the choice that His Majesty the Sultan will make will certainly be the best adapted to the situation of the country."

It was the king who formulated one guideline. Seizing on the grammatical notion of a hyphen to express the geographical and cultural crossroads position of Morocco, the king began as early as 1956 to talk of his country as a "hyphen" (*trait d'union* or *wusla*) between east and west, north and south. To the new French ambassador, to the International Summer Conference at Toumliline, to

---

[8] *Monde,* February 14, 1956; Mohammed V: "The position of Spain between Morocco and France will facilitate relations among the three countries, and in this trinity, the two states will always help the third" (*ibid.,* April 6, 1956).

[9] *Ibid.,* March 9, 1957.

the French and Algerians in a conciliatory speech at Oujda in 1956, and to the newly invested crown prince in 1957, the king spoke of Morocco as a "hyphen" or "link" in international affairs.[10] In drawing the guidelines of policy, the king followed one of his principal concepts of his political role and left implementation to the organ of the government competent in the particular field. Unfortunately for the base negotiations, this guideline gave a more precise picture of Morocco's role in the Algerian problem, for example, than it did of a frame in which to place American bases. It is hard to frame anything in a hyphen, and the base negotiations dissolved in the summer of 1957.

THE SECOND STAGE

The second stage of negotiations took the base question from the Foreign Ministry and put it into other hands. Cannon saw Balafrej in September, 1957, between the latter's visit to Asia and his trip to the United Nations and spoke of the American desire for a settlement. (In Washington, D.C., Balafrej had seen John Foster Dulles, who also emphasized the need for an agreement.) There was no longer any question of resuming talks in Rabat, however, for the long-expressed desire of the king to return Pres. Franklin D. Roosevelt's visit of 1943 had led to the preparation of a state visit to Washington in November, 1957. Although the king was not making the trip as a formal negotiator, he wished to enlarge his field of consultations prior to the visit and so convened the year-old National Consultative Assembly to hold a great debate on foreign policy. Instead of being strengthened by a popular mandate for the forthcoming talks, at the outcome of the debates the king found himself with a foreign policy changed and committed and a Foreign Ministry weakened by its association with a new organ in the decision-making process.

Morocco's first great debate lasted four sessions in an atmosphere of growing Istiqlal criticism of the coalition government (of which it was the major member), of a slowly forming split in the same party between its activist and old-guard wings, and of a highly vocal opposition demagogically critical of the government. Balafrej made a succinct statement of the government's position on the bases, reprinted in *al-Istiqlal* on November 17, 1957:

[10] The basis for this idea was laid as early as the king's Tangier speech on April 7, 1947; see also *Monde*, July 30, August 31, September 28, 1956; *al-Istiqlal*, July 13, December 28, 1957; *Times*, November 26, 1957; Mohammed V, *Le Maroc à l'heure de l'indépendance* (Rabat: Ministry of Information and Tourism, n.d. [1958]), pp. 134, 218.

We have entered into negotiations with the USA on this
question in the hope of arriving at a provisional solution to
this illegal status while awaiting a Government position on
the basic problem: the existence of the bases themselves.

This statement was doubly significant. It raised the possibility
that the government might take a negative stand on "the basic
problem." It also recognized the absence of defined policy both on
the present status of the bases and on Morocco's desires for their
final disposition. There is no indication that at this time indecision
stemmed from a division in the government; it was, rather, the
result of the deciding elite's attention's having been diverted to
other more pressing problems, such as relations with the French
and Spanish, and also of the lack of any attempt to formulate a
definite stand on the future status of the bases.

In his speech and in his answers to the sharp questioning that
followed it, Balafrej specifically rejected several frameworks—
such as the Baghdad Pact, NATO, or a common defense agreement
with the former protectors—for Moroccan foreign policy and, avoiding the hyphen suggested by the king, spoke of Morocco's foreign
position only in terms of "friendships," "freedom of choice," and
"ties of solidarity." [11] It was the discussion that provided the long-
sought framework—not the positive hyphen of the king, but the
more negative notion of "non-dependence" coined by Mehdi ben
Barka, president of the assembly and leader of the activist wing
of the Istiqlal.[12] Sensitive to anything which might disrupt party
unity at a time when the Istiqlal was pressing for a homogeneous
(all-Istiqlal) government, Balafrej was quick to pick up non-dependence as a guideline for foreign policy. The final resolution of the
assembly incorporated the slogan, although it made no mention of
the United States bases and appeared to continue to use *jela'* in
reference only to the French and Spanish troops. Yet adoption of
non-dependence by an official organ of government made the assembly debate a turning point in the base negotiations, and the
search for a framework for the bases led to the formation of a principle for excluding them.

[11] Nonalignment vis à vis NATO and the Cold War was formulated as early
as January, 1950, by 'Allal al-Fassi in a speech in Tangier and by the Istiqlal
in a statement in September, 1950. A succinct expression of all the grievances
along these lines is found in *al-'Alam,* April 15, 1959. During the great debate,
the only member who had kind words for a pro-American foreign policy was
'Abdellatif Sbihi, an independent.

[12] *Al-Istiqlal,* November 16, 1957.

Outside of the assembly, this decision was sharpened in political statements. An activist-dominated affiliate of the Istiqlal, the National Union of Moroccan Students (UNEM), which frequently served as a sounding board for the party, ended its second annual congress with a demand for base negotiations "with the view of fixing the date on which the air bases would be handed over to the Moroccan authorities." [13] Changing opinion was also reflected in the position of the Liberal Independent party, fighting to retain its place in the government. Before the assembly debate, Minister of State Rashid Mouline issued a party communiqué praising the American role in Moroccan independence, calling the bases "an element of equilibrium," and asking their evacuation only after the French and Spanish had gone. The Istiqlal party press flew into a patriotic rage; *al-Istiqlal* said Mouline "did not even know how to chew chewing gum correctly," and *at-Tali'a,* organ of the UMT, spoke confusedly of anti–anti-Communism and emotionally of atom bombs in the Middle East.[14] In their next statement, in early 1958, the Liberal Independents looked to a mutually acceptable evacuation agreement. Whatever earlier ambiguities there might have been, no one was publicly for the bases after the National Assembly debate. It was in this atmosphere that the king prepared for his trip to Washington.

The neutrality implied in non-dependence and the nonisolation insisted on when the phrase was discussed in ben Barka's *al-Istiqlal* editorial posed conceptual problems about the bases. To demand immediate evacuation would be an act as inimical to the policy as the conclusion of a military alliance. Balafrej therefore conceived of a two- or three-year negotiated solution which would permit Morocco to retain both the bases and its future freedom of choice and in any case would avoid the necessity of making an immediate decision.

The king's agenda for his talks with President Eisenhower and Secretary of State Dulles included the three topics of aid, Algeria, and the bases. The discussions were on a high enough level to be polite and inconclusive; whenever the talks touched a concrete point, the same broad and basic differences appeared in Washing-

[13] *Monde,* September 11, 1957.
[14] See *al-Istiqlal,* October 19, 1957; *al-'Alam,* October 20, 1957; *at-Tali'a,* (Casablanca), October 18, 1957. At the same time and for the same partisan reasons, Information Minister Ahmed Reda Guedira was under bitter attack by the Istiqlal for incompetence. On the 1958 statement, see *Vigie,* April 11, 1958; Guedira, *La deuxième crise ministérielle marocaine* (Rabat: n.d. [1958]).

ton as in Rabat. Since it was realized that the king could not return empty-handed, a vague declaration was formulated. According to the final communiqué, the two governments were to

> . . . pursue the negotiations now in progress with full respect for the sovereignty of Morocco. Pending the conclusion of an agreement, the two Governments expressed their desire to proceed, by means of a provisional solution, to the appropriate adjustments of present conditions. . . .

Commentary by ben Barka in *al-Istiqlal* made it plain that the temporary solution meant a short-term tenure pending evacuation.

Morocco heard the last official mention of the hyphen in the Speech from the Throne in November, 1957. (In early 1959, the Foreign Ministry's publication *Maroc-Documents* was to carry an article entitled "Le Maroc, trait d'union entre l'Orient et l'Occident"; on the indicated pages of the review, however, appears an article on "Operation Plow.") [15] At the end of December, 1957, the Democratic Independence party (PDI) exercised its frequent role as the vanguard of radicalism by making an explicit demand for immediate evacuation and thereby broadening *jela'* to include Americans as well as French and Spanish.[16] At the Afro-Asian Solidarity Conference in Cairo, the PDI presented the Political Commission's Subcommittee on Imperialism with a demand for support in the suppression of American bases in Morocco. The terms of reference for the base negotiations were therefore completely changed by the beginning of 1958. One may search for specific decisions which might have been made and find none, for the limitation of choice imposed by a chain of events had as much effect in deciding the bases question as any action of the decision-making elite.

INTERVENING INCIDENTS

The twenty months (1958 and the first half of 1959) between early and late negotiations gave time for the impact of the events of late 1957 to sink in. Throughout this time, scattered incidents

---

[15] *Maroc-Documents*, IX (1959), 661–663. The term was used once again by *al-'Ahd*, November 2, 1959, in another context, approving Premier Ibrahim's trip to the Middle East. The role of the assembly debate was explicitly acknowledged by ben Barka in opening the next session of the assembly on November 9, 1958: "This [foreign policy] study was at the origin of the adoption of the orientation of non-dependence which characterizes Moroccan foreign policy."

[16] The PDI showed early interest in the American bases. A conference of the party at Itzer on October 16, 1956, called for "the settlement . . . of the American base problem."

and sporadic negotiations kept the topic alive, and, because it remained alive, it continued to undergo changes in its terms of reference similar to those begun in 1957. The effect of these changes was to limit choice, to negotiate, and to decide more effectively than any of the formal agents of choice, negotiators, or decision-makers could do.

Following the king's return, formal negotiations were resumed. A quick stop by Secretary of State Dulles in Marrakesh on January 23, 1958, to see Balafrej was also the occasion to express the American desire that the talks begin moving. Discussion between the American Embassy and the Foreign Ministry was for the most part limited to the question of tenure rather than to the side talks in the specialized commissions, but the difference of opinion remained unbridged. There was, in fact, even less consensus on the terms of reference: were the bases or the agreements under discussion? was evacuation or continuation at stake? The Moroccan point of view as formulated in a counterproposal of March, 1958, continued to adhere to a two- or three-year agreement, with evacuation after that time vaguely understood. The original American proposal for continuation seems to have provided for a temporary agreement to run until a permanent solution was negotiated, the full term running about twenty years. Obviously, either of the proposals would have been consistent with the letter of Balafrej's views as expressed in Washington, as well as with the White House communiqué; it was rather in the meaning of the terms that the final "wide divergences of views" showed up. American negotiators saw the Moroccans change their terms of reference without the Moroccans' actually being aware of this development in their thinking or the evolution of their foreign policy. One embassy member spoke of the Moroccans' "evolving" under negotiations. Another said, "At some point in the negotiations it was clear to both of us that they were talking of evacuation." A third put it, "Balafrej sensed a change in the wind and by mid-1958 the evacuation handwriting was evident on the wall." This type of action is certainly not an example of clear decision or the result of conciliation attempts, but rather a case of decision-making of the most informal sort.

Probably Balafrej's most original contribution to the negotiations was his insistence on a Moroccan role in determining the mission of the bases. Although this topic was little mentioned in press reports,[17] it might have provided a meeting ground between evac-

---

[17] See, however, *al-Istiqlal,* December 19, 1959. Details of this point come from an interview with Balafrej.

uation and the continuation. As with the framework and other possible points of agreement, however, Balafrej appears not to have had a clear idea or proposal on his stand, and certainly he never conveyed one to the American negotiators. The idea was sometimes expressed as nonutilization and sometimes as inactivation of the bases; it was later explained to mean not so much converting all bases to the stand-by status of Bensliman as to mean a Moroccan role in determining the operations of the bases. American troops would wear civilian clothes, and the bases would be utilized as technical training camps for Moroccans. Balafrej was interested in ensuring that the airfields would never be used as a "base of aggression"; he also appears to have sought a distinction in appearance and in function between the American bases and the French and Spanish installations. None of these ideas, however, was sufficiently tempting to entice the Americans to develop details. The Moroccans waited in vain for an answer to their counterproposal, and meetings petered out sooner than they had in 1957.

I

During this time a series of incidents kept the negotiations alive in the public mind. In each case the incident was of the type that could be used by the activist faction as a club with which to beat the government. Although these events had no direct effect on the actual negotiations, they had a discernible effect on the Moroccan negotiators and makers of foreign policy. In some cases, the susceptibility of the king and foreign minister to popular pressure was manifested in an attempt to outspeak the critics; the policy-makers forced themselves into being committed because they could not face criticism over lack of attention to independence and national welfare. The result was to limit further the choice of decisions. In other cases, incidents led to greater procrastination, with the Moroccans putting off difficult decisions because it was becoming increasingly evident that the decisions were becoming more difficult. The circle was, of course, vicious; as decisions were put off, the popular pressure rose, and incidents had a cumulative effect, making decisions even more difficult and procrastination even more provocative.

The first of the five incidents was the pressure on the French to evacuate. Besides intermittent attention to American bases, the Moroccan Foreign Ministry, goaded by more serious incidents and more impassioned popular pressure, was also devoting sporadic efforts to the problem of the French troops. It is not germane to

outline the history of this action, but it is relevant to the American
problem to show the relation between the two troop questions and
the changes in this relation since 1956. When the American negotiations began on a bilateral basis in May, 1957, the French lost out
in their bid to participate in the Morocco-American solution. They
continued, however, to claim an interest in the American bases,
which continued to contain French units of varying sizes. To the
French—who were probably right legally—such matters as French
responsibility for security and French ownership of the land remained unchanged pending the negotiation of a superseding agreement; some of such agreements would also appear to require
French acceptance. Yet France was not simply seeking new diplomatic experiences. To the extent that French demands slowed
down the settlement of the American question, Moroccan pressure
for settlement of the French problem was also mitigated. The
French, therefore, were believed to have suggested to Rabat that
it come to agreement with the Americans, after which the French
role could be defined. It was an argument that was to backfire in
1960, but by then two years of time had been won.

The Moroccans, on the other hand, were reluctant to make
concessions to the Americans that could be used as a precedent in
negotiations by the French. Instead of benefiting from the early
distinction, the American problem was sucked into the Moroccans'
thinking on all foreign troops as time passed. In a speech before the
Istiqlal in Casablanca in April, Balafrej warned that the American
and Spanish bases were next in line for serious attention after the
French base question was settled.[18] Ironically, the question of precedent worked to the detriment of the Americans in a narrower way.
The SOFA condition evolved through the protectorate left the
United States bases with customs, postal, and commissary privileges
that were more extensive than those of the French. After the protectorate, the Moroccans used this inequality to rebuff SOFA proposals that attempted to maintain the favored American position.[19]

Probably the most striking incident in the history of the negotiations was the Sidi Sliman bomber accident, an event which was

[18] *Times*, April 12, 1958. On the extension of *jela'*, compare *at-Tahrir*, May 16
and June 27, 1958, with July 4, 1958, when the United States was specifically
included. *Monde*, April 24, 1958, considered Balafrej's speech at the Conference
of Independent African States in Accra to include American troops in the demand for evacuation.

[19] Many Americans lived in military housing on the bases. Morocco wished
them to live and buy in town, as did the French, whose PX's were very limited.
For two good accounts of life on the bases, see *Times*, March 22 and December
30, 1957.

kept completely out of the public press, but which made a greater
impression on Moroccan leaders than any other base-connected
incident. In April, an air force bomber reportedly carrying an
atomic weapon burned on the Sidi Sliman runway. The base was
evacuated in some disorder, the supercaid was called in from
Kenitra, Premier Bekkai was awakened in Rabat, and the ambassador called on the king. There was no explosion, but the fearful
tremors of "what if" shook the government leaders. Direct effects of
the incident were limited and ironic; the local branch of the Base
Workers' Labor Union (USBA), affiliate of the activist UMT, approached the American labor attaché for a 100 per-cent pay raise
in the face of such occupational hazards. In a country rife with
scurrying rumors of politics, magic, and other signs and wonders,
an atomic bomber accident was only in the natural course of
things.[20] The effect the incident had on Balafrej's demand for nonutilization, however, was important; in the absence of such an
agreement, the incident brought home the need for evacuation.

In June it was the base at Nouasseur that came into the news.
On June 28, the Air Matériels Command (AMC) stationed at
Nouasseur completed its phase-out, and SAC units in Morocco were
henceforth to be supplied directly from the United States. Command
of Nouasseur passed from the commanding officer of the AMC, formerly the largest unit on the base, to the commanding officer of the
SAC unit, the next largest command stationed at Nouasseur. At the
same time, the SAC commander in Morocco moved his area headquarters from Sidi Sliman to Nouasseur. No Moroccan official was
invited to the ceremony, and the government was not informed of
the change of command.[21] On June 29–30, the *Petit Marocain* announced that Nouasseur

> . . . has become since yesterday, by decision of the high com-
> mand of Washington, an operational airfield, Strategic Air
> Command, depending henceforth on the airbase of Madrid
> itself integrated into the NATO system of defense.

The immediate reaction came from Vice-Premier and Economics
Minister 'Abderrahim Bou'abid, the leading representative of the

[20] It also made other dangers credible. On rare occasions, military planes jet-
tisoned gas tanks near a lone village in the countryside, leading to articles such
as that of *al-Hayat* (Communist), April 14, 1958, entitled "The Bombing of al-
Borouj." After this article, all *al-Hayat* could say of the Sidi Sliman incident
was "American Base Workers Disapprove Atomic Dangers in the Country"
(May 30, 1958), an obvious example of what happens when one cries wolf.
[21] The pasha of Berreshid, a nearby official, was invited in a personal capacity,
much to his subsequent embarrassment (*PM*, July 1, 1958).

activist faction in the government, who, without any attempt to
check the facts of the story or to clear it with the Foreign Ministry,
criticized the action as a provocative attempt to commit Morocco
in the Cold War. A member of the Foreign Ministry spoke with the
American chargé d'affaires and was given the facts of the ceremony.[22] But the public action of Bou'abid and the pressure of the
political faction he represented committed the king and Balafrej
to taking official action in order to avoid being outflanked by the
activists.[23] A crowd of several hundred marched on the embassy on
June 29, although nobody was home; the next day the High Committee for National Defense met, bringing together the king, the
prince, Balafrej, and Bou'abid, as well as the ministers of defense,
interior and public works, its other regular members. Nouasseur
was integrated into the question of the other foreign bases, a
question already on the agenda. On the same morning, Boucetta
delivered an official protest to the chargé, charging an "inimical
act" and "provocation." Ben Barka carried the message to its most
effective target a week later, when he spoke to a nationwide meeting
of the Istiqlal party inspectors and told them of the gravity of the
Nouasseur affair and of the importance of an energetic reaction
from the people and the government. Equally illustrative of the
situation was Bou'abid's reply when told his information was false;
his statement, he said, should stand because of the damage already
done in the eyes of Moroccan public opinion. Because of such incidents, public pressure became an integral part of the decision-making process, even if no outright decisions were made.

The port incidents in June and July illustrate the effect of this
popular element. In June a navy ship of the Military Sea Transport
Service became involved in a maritime courtesy dispute in Casablanca. Not equipped with a Moroccan flag, it claimed it was a military ship instead of a commercial vessel and was excluded from the
necessity of flying the host country's colors while in port. The UMT
longshoremen refused to unload, the ship finally was redirected to

[22] See the embassy communiqué, July 29, 1958, emphasizing (1) no SAC unit
is tied to NATO, (2) the Moroccan bases were not tied to the Spanish defense
system, (3) SAC is under operational control of headquarters in Omaha, (4) the
change in command was routine, and (5) there was no change in the functions
and character of the bases in Morocco. Rumored changes of command had already posed problems in rumor-rich Morocco; the grapevine had it that Ceuta
was to be turned over to the United States for use as a base (*al-'Alam* and *al-
Hayat,* May 30, 1958).
[23] An example of another course of action was the public demonstration on
January 31, 1960, against the French atomic explosion at Reggan. On instructions
from the king, this demonstration was kept down by government order, policy,
and fire hoses.

the supply base at Livorno, Italy, and the port of Casablanca was shut to American cargo to the bases. On July 22, the Dutch ship "Lijnbaan" appeared unannounced off Safi from Livorno with cargo for the base at Ben Guerir; a communications failure had prevented its pre-filing with the port authorities. The UMT at Safi refused to unload. Boucetta promised that the matter would be arranged and the cargo discharged, but, when he spoke with the union, he saw that only army intervention could ensure the unloading, although it would probably bring bloodshed as well. Caught by public action he had helped encourage a month before, Boucetta reported to the embassy that, if pressed, he could keep the promise, but that it would be "preferable" if the ship went away. The "Lijnbaan" sailed on, still loaded. On August 11, the "African Patriot" tried to land and met the same fate, the UMT again showing the force of its initiative and pressure over government actions. The port boycotts never reached the lengthy or total dimensions used against the French, nor did they ever touch the flow of American military personnel, but they put the government at the mercy of popular pressure and kept the question of the bases in the public eye.

Last in the series of early 1958 incidents was the question of the bases' use in the Lebanese intervention which began on July 15. A newspaper account said, incorrectly, that Nouasseur was being used as a staging base for the sudden flow of American units to the eastern Mediterranean. On the same day that the first marines landed at Beirut, the National Consultative Assembly met to discuss the two-year plan submitted by Bou'abid. In a heated outburst, the assembly turned to the Middle East at the end of its debate and on July 18 passed a resolution denouncing the intervention, asking the king to protest against the "colonialist aggression" and "the use of our territory as a base of attack against people who are fighting for liberty and independence," and demanding the withdrawal of troops from the Middle East and the use of "effective measures" to ensure the withdrawal of all foreign troops in Morocco. Few issues could so unite Arab spokesmen as the invasion of an Arab country by Western troops, and both currents of opinion in the assembly— old-guard Istiqlal and opposition—rose in the impromptu foreign affairs debate to condemn the intervention and Morocco's supposed role. Balafrej, in an interview with *Action,* a Tunisian magazine, decried the intervention but did not mention the role of the bases. In the United Nations, the Moroccan representative joined other Arab countries in denouncing the American intervention. It was probably only a coincidence and the inaction of the king that kept the matter from going further. At the same time as the Lebanese intervention, King Feisal II was overthrown and killed in Iraq, and the British intervened in Jordan to hold the throne of King Hussein. Mohammed V could not be expected to sympathize with regicide; he looked with serious apprehension at the cries of approval in the assembly, and the actions of the army and the mobs in Baghdad are said to have had one of the strongest impacts that he had ever experienced. The incident was quickly quieted in Morocco, and the United Nations representative was called on to modify his stand. Public pressure did not force an immediate decision, but it did serve to reinforce the currents of non-dependence and nonutilization and limit policy-makers' freedom of action.

II

This chain of events in 1958 was interrupted by changes in the leading personalities. On April 16, the government of Bekkai had fallen for a second time, victim of bitter party rivalries, and on May 12 Balafrej assumed the Prime Ministry while retaining direction of foreign affairs. Mohammed Boucetta was made undersecretary of state for foreign affairs, consolidating his already strong position as Balafrej's lieutenant, but the foreign minister had to give attention and time to the whole spectrum of governmental activities, making the problem of obtaining foreign-policy decisions more difficult than ever. Perhaps more than any other department, the conduct of foreign affairs needs strong direction. Yet throughout his administration Balafrej's position was additionally weakened, at times to the point of impotence, by bitter and growing party strife. As premier he was even more sensitive to external pressures than he had been as foreign minister, and Boucetta, although an able lawyer, was young and only gaining experience.

On June 23 and 31, Cannon went to see Balafrej and the king, respectively, and heard of the urgency of the problem. The following month he retired from the diplomatic service. With the withdrawal of Cannon, the question of American bases slipped into its second summer quietus, broken only by the incidents of June and July. Charles W. Yost arrived in late June and presented his credentials in August, bringing a new approach to the problem. Yost felt that damage was being done to United States interests by letting the negotiations drag. Even before Yost was accredited, Balafrej was reached to obtain clarifications of an interview in which the foreign minister had openly spoken of evacuation and had appeared to ex-

clude any temporary agreement. He refused to enter into discussions
before Yost's accreditation, however.

In fact the Moroccan position had hardened. On August 5
Boucetta said in a radio interview that evacuation was the Moroccan demand for all foreign troops, no matter of what nationality.
In mid-1958 government and popular pressure on French troops
had grown to the point at which the king decided on a general
consultation on the question, and in early August he invited all
political parties to give their views and to examine a dossier prepared by the Foreign Ministry. After the Algerian events of May,
1958, a real fear of invasion by French troops raised Moroccan
concern over foreign troops to a fever pitch. Consultations ended on
August 7 and completed the year-long process of incorporating the
American bases under *jela'*. Under the title, "The American Bases,"
al-Istiqlal wrote on September 20, 1958:

> Their existence, even de facto, is contrary to one of the domi-
> nant [principles] of our foreign policy, non-dependence and
> non-adherence to foreign military alliances. . . . Our major
> concern is therefore to realize the evacuation of all foreign
> troops installed on our territory, an evacuation which is the
> logical and natural consequence of our independence. . . .
> Negotiation can only be carried on on the basis of evacuation.

At the same time a new element appeared in the party consultations. In the face of the firm French position, the organs of popular
pressure left the Foreign Ministry room for a minimum demand:
the recognition of the principle of evacuation. On September 10,
1958, *al-'Alam* wrote, "The best act that the occupying countries
could accomplish before going to the coming session of the UN is to
satisfy the desire of Morocco and proclaim the principle of evacuation. . . ."

Yost moved rapidly to capitalize on the new situation created
by his arrival and to salvage as much of the slowly deteriorating
situation as possible. One of his first actions was to present Balafrej
and the king with a reply to the Moroccan counterproposal of the
previous March. Washington would accept the principle of evacuation with a seven-year delay before actual withdrawal. The message was discussed in the Council of Ministers, and the foreign
minister was instructed to prepare a reply. The same day, the Moroccan National Radio announced the American agreement in
principle and, reiterating the Moroccan demand for evacuation,

looked forward to an agreement on a timetable.[24] Unfortunately, the effect was lost in the manner and the moment of the ambassador's *démarche*.

Instead of publicly announcing the message and using it to counter the consistently negative discussion of the bases in the press, the ambassador was authorized only to make a statement to the king. Concern over the effect of a public pronouncement on the question of the French bases seems to have been the principal reason. Beyond the control of the negotiators, the message was further stripped of its effect by being made during the dying days of the government. In November, Balafrej vacated both the Foreign Ministry and the presidency of the council, and on Christmas Day the same two offices were taken over by 'Abdullah Ibrahim, a leader of the activists. To Ibrahim, the principle of evacuation had never been admitted, and the impetus gained in renewing the negotiations fell off because of the pressure of other problems on the new government.

Ibrahim's arrival in the Foreign Ministry brought significant changes to the conduct of Moroccan foreign affairs. Ibrahim believed in personal diplomacy; together with his desire to bring substantive changes in the orientation of Moroccan policy, this belief led him to numerous voyages outside the country. Although his contacts were often popular and personable, his training for the direction of a foreign ministry was inadequate compared with that of Balafrej, who had spent the resistance in diplomatic posts. Ibrahim's relations with his ministry were frequently tense, increasing the difficulty of coordinated decisions in the foreign field. Ahmed Benhima, the secretary general of the ministry throughout much of 1959, was frequently at odds with Ibrahim, and, when the foreign minister made his trip to Washington, he was accompanied

[24] This is a controversial incident because of the paucity of public information. It can, however, he adequately reconstructed from a combination of sources; see *PM*, September 11, 14, 16, and 18, 1958; *al-'Alam*, September 15, 1958; Moroccan National Radio announcement, 8:15 P.M., September 15, 1958; *al-Istiqlal*, October 18 and November 22, 1958, November 19, 1959; *Monde*, September 17, 1958; Speech from the Throne, November 18, 1958. An excited article, "Without Commentary," in the outspoken column, "Main in the Street" (*al-Istiqlal*, September 27, 1958) illustrates the dangers of the secrecy approach with its subsequent rumors, worries, and suspicions. *Times*, May 8, 1958, quoted Balafrej as saying that the United States had recognized the principle of evacuation at that date, whereas in an interview Boucetta said it was recognized when the king was in Washington the year before. *La Nation* (Communist) charged that the principle was being admitted only to evacuate the troops but keep the bases (September 12, 1958).

by his cabinet director from the presidency of the council, Nasser ben Larbi, not by 'Abdullah Lamrani, his cabinet director from the Foreign Ministry. As his administration continued, even Ibrahim's relations with the king cooled in foreign affairs as they did in domestic matters. Finally, the premier was, if anything, more vulnerable to external pressure than Balafrej had ever been and needed to bring home a tangible success from time to time. Arrayed against him on one side was the majority party, the old-guard Istiqlal, moved to bitter criticism by the activists' secession from the party in January, 1959.[25] But Ibrahim was selected "as an individual and not as party representative" and was blocked or tempered in his wishes by the king; through Ibrahim, the activist group, unhampered by desires to maintain party unity by placating the old guard, kept one foot in the government, but its other foot was the self-appointed opposition, ready to kick the government whenever and wherever necessary. The licensing of new newspapers during 1959 increased the facilities of the various oppositions.

III

The second half of the 1958–1959 transition period was filled with a series of incidents that differed from those of 1958. Part of the revised American approach was the attempt to obtain agreement on side issues outside the framework of a general agreement if an over-all detailed accord could not be immediately negotiated. However, because of the tension in the atmosphere, even the most well-intentioned attempts—some initiated by the Moroccan government itself—to normalize aspects of the bases question usually resulted in a less favorable situation for the bases. These 1959 incidents and their role in whittling away at the bases question are instructive because they show the role of people other than the foreign minister in dealing with the bases.

In an attempt to disengage the bases from their tripartite aspect, the United States negotiated the withdrawal of the nominal

[25] See al-'Alam, April 15, 1959 (to summarize the story: bases incompatible with independence, sovereignty, and non-dependence, according to Istiqlal Action Committees); ibid., February 26, 1959 (government silence on bases is reprehensible, according to 'Allal al-Fassi); ibid., June 27, 1959 (no independence without American evacuation, according to 'Allal al-Fassi). Ibrahim, in Cairo for the 'Id al-Kebir, said the bases problem was being solved: Spanish negotiations were on the verge of a conclusion, the French on the verge of withdrawal, and the Americans on the verge of a solution; al-Istiqlal answered, "Actually, it is known that no steps towards evacuation have been taken for six months" (June 20, 1959).

French security units on the air bases. In April the 300-man force was removed, and the Moroccan government was duly notified. In the Council of Ministers meeting a week later, a report presented by Bou'abid was adopted, providing for the replacement of the security guards by troops of the Moroccan Army in order to assert Moroccan sovereignty over the bases. At the same time the French declared that their rights in the question were in no way altered by their ceasing to provide for base security. The Moroccan Army never arrived, and the Americans henceforth took care of their own security, as, in fact, they always had, and the psychological impact of the move was totally lost. In the course of this exchange, Morocco was given another opportunity, however, to assert that evacuation remained its only acceptable objective.

Three months later, a similar incident occurred over the hiring of the nearly 8,000 local workers on the bases. The labor office for the bases was maintained by the French Army; one of the subjects discussed from the beginning of talks in 1957 was the regularizing of this situation to conform with American base agreements in other countries so that, through an indirect-hire system, Morocco would be the legal employer and the bases the legal utilizer of local labor. It was not until the French security forces were withdrawn that successful discussions could begin. In July the annual service contract ran out; the French hiring office was allowed to lapse and was replaced by an agreement negotiated by the embassy and the Labor Ministry. A Moroccan Office of Administration of Civilian Personnel Employed at United States Bases was created, with the approval of the UMT, as an adjunct of the Labor Ministry but paid by the United States. The office was given monthly slices of the $11,500,000 annual payroll, which it distributed in wages to base workers. Unfortunately, announcements of the move in *The New York Times* and *Le Monde* of Paris intimated that the arrangement was a step "nearer a solution of the base problem"; al-'Alam and al-Istiqlal picked up the notice with criticism,[26] and the Foreign Ministry felt obliged to point out that, although it now handled American money to pay the base workers, it had not changed its stand on the "illegal" bases themselves. Again, any positive element in this minor settlement was lost, and the incident became the occasion for renewed talk of evacuation.

Several other aspects of the base question were brought to light

[26] *Times,* June 2, 1959; *Monde,* August 5, 1959; *al-'Alam,* September 6, 1959; "The Moroccan government has . . . by this act tacitly recognized the legitimacy of the bases" (*al-Istiqlal,* August 8, 1959). The agreement was signed on August 4.

in the Casablanca customs case. One of the major criticisms against
the bases, second only to the principal line of attack in terms of
foreign-policy commitments, was the charge that the bases were a
serious loophole in the nation's customs barriers. The proposal to
collect customs on all imported goods for both private and military use was one of the maximum demands in the Moroccan counterproposal of 1957, and the customs problem had been the subject
of especially bitter comments in the great debate of the same year.
Like many of the Moroccan demands, this proposal was inadmis-
sible to State Department and Defense Department negotiators, who
feared repercussions on other United States base agreements
throughout the world. Even while Balafrej was in office, the customs arrangement came under renewed attack in *al-Istiqlal* on September 20, 1958.

> No one is ignorant of the fact that these bases have become
> veritable open markets, where all sorts of goods can be pro-
> cured at prices infinitely lower than those on the national
> market. . . . Our taxes . . . are rendered ineffective by devi-
> ous means offered elsewhere which legalize all sorts of fraud
> against the law.

Al-'Alam, the newspaper of the old-guard Istiqlal, used the issue to attack the Ibrahim government, speaking of customs-free im-
portation "contemptuously" passing under the nose of the customs
inspectors and asking whether this was not another vestige of colonialism based on prior Franco-American agreements.

It was Bou'abid, however, who saw in the existing customs situation a means of getting additional money from the United States.
On his orders, Bensalem Smili, director of customs, ordered supplies
to the bases to be held up in Casablanca until a satisfactory customs
agreement was worked out. To American military authorities, it
looked as if the final stage of the Moroccan pressure on the bases
was at hand; automobiles and other goods were held up in American embarkation ports, and the marines, ready for the worst, halted
transportation of their dependents to Morocco. The tactic, however, was sophisticated blackmail, not blockade. Embassy negotiators met with Economic Ministry officials, and Moroccan customs
inspectors were placed at the gates of the bases to make a list of
traffic into town, from which to calculate a retroactive lump-sum
customs payment for all goods imported into Morocco since 1956.
In July, 1959, the Morocco-American commission agreed to a single

payment of $10,000,000 in lieu of customs for fiscal year 1960, thereby avoiding the establishment of a precedent.

An incident within this incident serves to show the complexity of the situation. The naval base of Port Lyautey, following President Eisenhower's appeal for a people-to-people program on overseas bases, had established an effective working arrangement with Moroccan officials connected with the base—including customs inspectors—through personal contacts, formal mess dinners, joint activities, and friendly services. Yet the benefits of this approach were limited. Decisions were still made only at the highest levels, and local initiative and freedom of action were possible only to the extent that they passed unnoticed by the decision-making elite. Two days after the customs inspector at Kenitra had assured the commander of naval activities at Port Lyautey that the Casablanca customs case would not affect existing operations in Kenitra, he was obliged to return to the base and admit that, under orders from Smili, there was little he could do but comply with the ministry's directives.

The last in the 1959 series of incidents, involving an embassy attempt to seek agreement on an allied matter, showed the impossibility of coming to any substantial agreement on the bases. In mid-1958 the Balafrej government had accepted a special grant-in-aid of $10,000,000 "to improve Morocco's capacity to defend the principles of the United Nations Charter." Bou'abid rose to criticize the political implications of the loan and to point out more pressing economic needs of the country; Balafrej protected his position in face of the first argument by replying that there would be no mention of mutual security to endanger the principle of nondependence. The loan agreement signed the next year provided for an immediate payment of $15,000,000 for support of the equipment budget, but the Ibrahim government did not take the same precaution with formalities as had Balafrej. The aid was announced as part of the mutual security funds. The old guard leapt to the attack, first in *al-'Alam* and then in *al-Istiqlal*, the usual order of airing political grievances first in the Arabic-, then in the French-, language press. On August 8, 1959, in mordant tones, *al-Istiqlal* questioned:

> Does that mean that this amount is the price for the American bases in Morocco? The Government drowns in deep silence everything connected with the evacuation of American forces from Morocco. . . . All this profound silence confirms that

American dollars have sealed the lips and appeased the Moroccan Government, may God forgive it.

In all the attempts of the American negotiators to come to
terms with the Moroccans, the end result was a worsened situation
and increased political pressure through organs of public opinion.
The summer of 1959 was a time of weakness for the Ibrahim government because of pressure from many other quarters. Under fire
for delays in fiscal and electoral matters, Ibrahim was summoned by
the king in mid-1959 to resign, but his optimistic view of his own
position led him to refuse successfully. His heavily criticized position pushed him to look about for easy, popular successes while the
opposition sought explosive popular issues with which further to
undermine the government. A threat of direct action was clearly
present in an *al-Istiqlal* editorial, "From Bizerte to Nouasseur,"
which appeared on July 4, 1959:

> It was not the few rifles of the meager Tunisian Army, it
> was not only the able maneuvering of Bourguiba which per-
> mitted victorious battles against imperialism, it is also and
> especially the mobilization of the people who were tightly
> associated with the progress of negotiations as well as with the
> battle of evacuation. Thus, the adversary knew that behind
> Bourguiba stood an entire population, alert, ardent, ready to
> fight. . . . Does [the government] minimize the support of
> the popular forces of the [Moroccan] nation or does it fear
> them to the point of disdaining them when it claims to wage
> the battle of evacuation?

THE THIRD STAGE

When the last stage of the base negotiations opened in the fall
of 1959, the atmosphere surrounding the question had so limited
choices that many decisions were already made; the problem was
to ratify them. The final stage shows two very different moves to
ratify.

The limitation of choice was severe. The heritage of Balafrej
and Boucetta, which equated solution with evacuation, was confirmed by the experience of 1959; no matter how it was presented,
no base agreement was possible in the current atmosphere. In fact,
as *l'Avant-Garde* was to point out in October, 1959, even a Moroccan-American accord stipulating the conditions of tenure in the
interim before final withdrawal would have been an impolitic measure, for it would have admitted the legality of the bases. In this
atmosphere, talks over secondary aspects of the status of forces was

superfluous, and under Ibrahim the work of the special commissions was discontinued, with substantive talks on the bases limited to occasional brief contacts between Yost and Ibrahim which confirmed the impasse on the allowable delay before evacuation. The pressure of the press, in context of the three-year deadlock, had convinced both Ibrahim and the king that the only acceptable way out was an American declaration of withdrawal.

To the premier and foreign minister, pressure for such a statement was immediate. In the last half-year of his administration, Ibrahim skillfully kept his government in power by riding on the crest of one event after another. Sometimes, such as the later visits of President Eisenhower and King Hussein or the meeting of the Arab League in Casablanca, which could not take place in the absence of a government, reasons of state prestige gave him a gratuitous reprieve. Other times, crises had to be sought on the basis of popular issues.

It was in search of such an issue that Ibrahim left for Washington and the United Nations in October, armed with imprecise views on such popular topics as Palestine, Algeria, French atomic tests, and the American bases and with instructions from the king to get clarification of the last point. In the tradition of the king's visit in 1957, talks with Eisenhower and Secretary of State Christian Herter were carried on with diplomatic cordiality and vagueness. Ibrahim's proposal for an evacuation in two years was rejected by the Pentagon, as it had been during the past two years, and American proposals for a longer delay ran up against Ibrahim's need for a popular success to bring home. As the talks necessitated a joint communiqué, however, the State Department drew up a brief statement along the lines of all earlier pronouncements on the question, confirming "the confidence of the two parties that an agreement would be found which would be in the interest of the two countries. . . . Negotiations will continue in Rabat, in order to arrive at an agreement as soon as possible." Lodged in the text of the communiqué was the statement that "the [American] proposals concerning withdrawal . . . reflect continuing recognition by the United States of Moroccan sovereignty over the American bases."

Ibrahim had found his issue. In his airport statement on November 3, he claimed to bring back an American recognition of Moroccan sovereignty over the bases and an agreement to the principle of evacuation; out of the blue, he added a promise to fix an evacuation date by negotiation "in the two weeks to come." In a political sense, victory was present; the activist press took his declarations at their word and prepared to look for an early final solution to the question.[27] A few opposition observers saw more clearly. *An-Nidal*, a short-lived paper of the Liberal Independent leader Rashid Mouline, aimed one of its piercing editorials at the premier on November 7, 1959: "We were prepared to applaud our Foreign Minister if he had come back carrying a time-limit for the evacuation of American troops. But he has not succeeded in doing that." The paper pointed out the fact that both evacuation and sovereignty had already been admitted and that the continuation of negotiations per se was an empty claim.

The warm welcome accorded to Ibrahim and his much publicized proclamations strengthened his political position. But both the criticisms and the attempt to make a precise pledge out of a general communiqué completed the process of public commitment in which the elite had been boxing itself since the beginning of the negotiations. The final element in the limitation of choice was provided; the government committed itself to obtain an agreement on evacuation before the end of the year. But, by the same process, it had lost its bargaining power in deciding the only remaining question—the delay in withdrawal—at the price of losing the badly needed popular support it had so carefully courted.

The ambassador saw the situation in a similar light. The time was not only propitious for a solution; it was propitious for the most favorable solution since 1957. The second American proposal, presented by Yost in September, 1958, as a result of the ambassador's appeal to Washington to break the deadlock, had contained not only recognition of the principle of evacuation but also lowered the delay in evacuation to seven years, although it had not satisfied Balafrej's desires for nonutilization or inactivation of the bases. With the approval of the Joint Chiefs of Staff and the National Security Council, the air force then decided, in September, 1959, on a unilateral policy of withdrawal within five years.[28] In his October visit to the United States, Ibrahim was presented the same five-year offer, coupled with other details. Ibrahim was not interested in Balafrej's ideas on utilization, but, as seen, he stuck to his two-year limit. If the American offer was to have its full effect in the situation of November, 1959, therefore, it would have to be accepted over the head of Ibrahim and be based on fewer than five

[27] See *at-Tahrir*, October 31 and November 3, 4, and 7, 1959; *al-'Ahd*, October 30 and November 4–5, 1959. (Columnist Mohammed Nasser wrote, "This is a man!")

[28] *Times*, September 13 and October 31, 1959; *al-'Ahd*, October 13, 1959. Yost had gone back to Washington in early June for consultation.

years—to save face for the Moroccan negotiator—in order to get more than two.

The occasion for such negotiations was appropriately provided by the December travels of President Eisenhower, which had Rabat as the last stop. Initiative for a final solution at this time appears to have come from the Americans, who were aware of the king's desire for an agreeable termination of the affair. Talks between the ambassador and the king prepared the way for the meeting between the two heads of state; during December the embassy worked on the preparation of a communiqué. Neither the embassy nor the Palace, however, was unaware that, as a result of Ibrahim's promises and the obvious opportunities provided by the president's visit, the meeting was regarded by the press and public opinion as the occasion for a base settlement. On the first day of December the Moroccan government asked that Eisenhower arrive at Casablanca instead of Rabat. Although there was an element of convenience in having a nearby airfield at Nouasseur capable of taking the president's two Boeing 707's, the reason was more strongly political. The city was the scene of labor unrest and newspaper attacks on the government and the monarchy and the stronghold of the activists' four-month–old political party, the National Union of Popular Forces (UNFP). The king wished to show his strength in even his weakest spot. The choice of Casablanca, however, further increased the pressure for an agreement on the bases. After some strictly Moroccan negotiations, the governor of the city, the Ministry of Labor, and the organizations of labor and management all called on the population to greet the heads of state with festivities, and several thousand tribesmen from as far away as the Atlas were brought in by truck to provide loyal local color.

Both sides prepared their followers for a base agreement to come from the president's visit. *Ar-Rai al-Amm,* the UNFP daily, pointed out (December 20 and 24, 1959) that an evacuation date was prepared for by the visit of Ibrahim to Washington in October. *Al-'Alam,* the organ of the Istiqlal, indicated that a general settlement was anticipated in the king's visit to Washington in 1957, when Balafrej was in office.[29] In reference to incidents marring the

---

[29] *Al-'Alam,* December 18 and 22, 1959; *al-Istiqlal,* December 19, 1959. It was at this time that the last incident before the agreement took place. Some Moroccan merchants had bought surplus aircraft engine oil and had watered their cooking oil with it. Chemical products in the oil caused widespread cases of paralysis, termed "meknesitis" because the cases were concentrated in the Meknes region. The merchants were eventually sentenced to death in a pathetic trial that culminated the pitiful affair and revealed local business ethics. In the mean-

president's later trip to the Far East, an embassy member remarked, "We were obliged to come up with an agreement to save him from a Japanese-type welcome."

The president and the king met for an hour and twenty minutes of closeted conversation. They talked of many things, as the communiqué related. There was no negotiation in the usual sense of the word; the communiqué was read over by the two heads of state and accepted as prepared.[30] In the last paragraph, it contained an agreement to evacuate over a four-year period, with no restrictions on the use of the bases during this time. The base negotiations, which had never really taken place, were over.

Epilogue

Subsequent implementation of the United States decision was similar to the previous problems of the decision-makers. The communiqué of December 22 provided for the evacuation of the inactive base at Bensliman by the end of March, but even in this there were problems. A month before, Bou'abid, profiting from his position as acting premier and foreign minister in Ibrahim's absence, made a long and pointed press statement insisting on the bilateral character of the evacuation. In fact, the French were caught in the middle by their tenacious adherence to legality; on February 3 they had announced to the Moroccan Government that they would cede to Morocco the land of the base, which they held by the 1950 agreement that Morocco did not recognize. The subsequent remission of the radar posts at Mechra Bel Ksiri near Kenitra and Beni Mansour near Berkan involved the same problem. Since the sites were shared by the French and the Americans, the American withdrawal left the French in charge, and the intervention of a third party before Morocco took over incited the press. As a result, the American post at the shared Rabat-Salé airfield was directly handed to the Moroccan Army in a smoother ceremony.

Other diverse elements that had been involved in the negotiation were present during the evacuation. The principle of nondependence, which in Ibrahim's speeches became "more than a principle: a program," remained the guideline of Moroccan foreign policy. The Base Workers' Labor Union, which saw the issue in

time, however, party papers took the United States to task for complicity in the affair, pointing out that, if the bases were not in Morocco, the whole thing would never have happened. Particularly sharp commentaries are found in *loc. cit.* and *al-'Alam,* April 27, 1960.

[30] The prince unexpectedly attempted to insert some commitment on Algeria and couple it to the base question; this prolonged the conversations beyond the allotted time and delayed the scheduled departure of Eisenhower.

terms of its own interests, shifted its line and clamored for increased
lay-off benefits. The press began to find the agreed delay excessive
and, on the death of the king in 1961, started another campaign
for accelerated withdrawal until a firm word from the new king,
Hassan II, cut it short.

The major result of the agreement was to shift the limited
choice from the Americans to the French and Spanish. Following a
slogan of Ibrahim's, the king proclaimed that "1960 is the year of
evacuation," and pressure was first directed against the French to
follow the Americans. Moving toward a step never taken against
the American bases, the prince declared in early May that it was
time for a concrete act, such as a blockade, as had occurred unoffi-
cially in southern Morocco in 1958. On September 1, 1960, the
French evacuation agreement was signed. It provided, in greater
detail than the American agreement, for withdrawal in stages from
all operational bases by the fifth anniversary of independence and
from all training bases by the end of 1963. The agreement was
negotiated on the Moroccan side by the prince, and his two-week–
old reign as King Hassan II benefited from the success of the first-
stage evacuation of all army bases on March 2, 1961. By September
30, 1961, all French units were withdrawn from air bases and
flight schools at Khouribga, Fez, Agadir, Meknes, and Marrakesh.
The naval complex at Casablanca was evacuated on February 8,
1961, and the last base, the naval air base at Kenitra, was handed
over to Morocco ahead of schedule on May 1, 1962. On September 1,
1961, without any negotiated agreement, the last Spanish bases in
Morocco were also evacuated, although the troops were only withdrawn to the Spanish enclaves of Ceuta and Melilla, which Morocco continues to claim.

A sequel to the Morocco-American base agreement of 1959 was
negotiated between King Hassan II and Pres. John F. Kennedy during the king's visit to Washington in late March, 1963. The joint
communiqué of March 29 reaffirmed the American intention to with-
draw from the bases by the end of 1963, but it also opened the way
for Morocco-American cooperation in converting the bases to
Moroccan use. American forces on the remaining bases were gradually reduced during 1963, and Ben Guerir was evacuated by July 1.
The bases were handed over to the Moroccans on January 1, 1964.
Facilities are left intact. Nouasseur was to be converted to an industrial complex, commercial airport, and dental-training center;
Sidi Sliman to an agricultural center and the site of agricultural
transformation industries; and Ben Guerir to a training and main-

tenance center for civil aviation. Arrangements appear to have been made to retain use of the naval communications facility at Sidi Yahya for a limited time.

CONCLUSIONS

Decision-making in foreign policy in Morocco, as seen in the example of American base negotiations, is personal and partisan. Its machinery is simple, its agencies are few, and, instead of the institutionalized mechanisms for channeling and transmitting public opinion into a regular role in decision-making, the relations between the deciding elite and the public are direct, inchoate, and often crude. The public usually has more fixed thoughts and less knowledge about foreign affairs than about any other aspect of governmental activity; unless public opinion is provided effective institutional outlet and inlet to the acting agencies of foreign policy, there is a gap between these agencies and mass opinion which the latter can close only by rioting, striking, or editorially throwing poisoned pens. This gap and the communications difficulty in bridging it also tempt the elite, in or out of power, to please the people with slogans and popular successes. The leaders emerge from this process strengthened when they need popular support on simple, direct issues, but, as long as the government has an opposition, it is also limited in the choice of possibilities and issues from which to decide.

1. Moroccan leaders in the early years were decision-makers in search of a policy. American newspaper accounts often enjoyed pointing out that neither side was in a hurry to find a solution; the major reason was that Morocco, in its general foreign affairs as in its approach to the specific question of American bases, was looking for a general policy within which to fit details, rather than risking incoherent foreign relations by building up a policy from disparate details. In this, Moroccan foreign policy was far freer of *ad hoc* arrangements than was evolution of its government.

The criticism has been made that a base agreement would have been possible during the early period, with the accompanying implication that the agreement would have been just as favorable to the Moroccans, the Americans, or, perhaps, both as was the final solution. In what sense is this true? It is certainly correct that, if all the secondary points—customs, jurisdiction, post office, and so on— had been agreed to on the Moroccan terms, an agreement could have been signed before the assembly session of November, 1957, and with the support of the king. The price would have been extraordinarily high, and there is nothing to indicate that the final *delay* in *evacuation*—neither of these issues having been discussed under Balafrej—would have been any shorter. A two- or three-year agreement would have confronted the bases with a decision on evacuation at roughly the same time as the question was actually decided.

Balafrej actually made no decisions on the base question—not even the decision to refuse American offers, toward which he remained merely vague and curious. He was too busy with such other things as French relations, Spanish relations, Maghreb unity, and his great, unexploited success, Tarfaya, within the ministry and as governmental leadership and party unity outside the ministry. He may or may not have consciously decided to reject the second American proposals of September, 1958. His political position was far too weak even to live off fabricated crises as Ibrahim was to do a year later, and Bou'abid would undoubtedly have blocked any positive decision either in the council or by calling up his resignation six weeks earlier. In many ways Balafrej did not decide foreign policy; he tended it and watched it grow. In the early period of negotiations, America was the potential buyer of an agreement that Morocco would not offer; Morocco was passively looking for a general sales policy. In the later period, it was Ibrahim who was the buyer of evacuation and the United States who offered, at a price compatible with established general policy.

Ibrahim's decisions, too, were few; he decided not to concern himself with the question of nonutilization, a negative if important decision at best, and he decided to use the bases as a political issue. The king's single decision—to accept the American offer himself, without passage in the Council of Ministers where Ibrahim and Bou'abid sat—was in part only procedural. It was a move filled with the king's usual diplomatic skill, for Ibrahim could not disown the agreement because he benefited from its happening during his administration.

2. More than any other aspect of governmental work, the decisions of foreign affairs were in the hands of a small, isolated elite. There was no delegated authority. The system had its most serious effect in slowing the operations of the government. Since all matters of decision had to come to the attention of the minister or secretary of state, problems could be solved only one at a time, with the waiting list growing longer and longer. As problems waited their

turn, their susceptibility to influence from outside incidents and political pressures increased, making the solution more difficult or the choice more limited.

The personal element of limited competence was reflected in the negotiators' experience with some of the side issues. There was a chronic lack of coordination between the ministries, made worse by the inability of other ministries to make decisions in the absence of their minister. Public Works employees at Nouasseur transporting Dallas huts given by the base to the ministry were not let out the gate until the customs inspectors could check with the chief of customs, Smili. Ammunition piled up at bases abandoned in 1960 because no rail clearance was given for its evacuation; Public Works officials not only prohibited shipment but also discouraged contact with the minister because they considered it hopeless. The minister was called and gave immediate approval. The incidents could be retold in many other forms.

A basic lesson in these incidents is that the American efforts to be friendly on the people-to-people level were worthless. The frequent aid the bases gave to annual flood victims in the Sebou River valley or the rapid and massive aid given to the victims of the Agadir earthquake was a problem for the minister of the interior or defense or public works and had no effect on the foreign minister's thinking; the help bought not one day of reprieve for the bases, nor did the United States economic or military aid, a political matter so complicated that it had no effect on the base question. The only contact at the popular level that had a wide effect was the economic impact that the bases had on nearby towns, especially on the USBA workers; these groups muttered among themselves over the ill effects of withdrawal, and the base workers saw the buttered side of their bread clearly enough not to become leaders in the fight for evacuation. Any program designed to win over friends would have been effective in keeping the bases for the Americans only if the targets of the program had been the ministerial level and the leaders of the opposition. The pasha of Berreshid or the supercaid of Kenitra, who were helpful in many small ways to the bases near them, would not risk their positions to attempt to influence the larger question of withdrawal, especially since they knew it was useless.

3. The most significant element in the decision-making process, as it involved American base negotiations, was the decisive role of public pressure. The specific effect of this element in continually constricting the choices of the deciding elite has been frequently

underlined; it should be noted that this public involvement was on a higher level than the "street" of the Middle East. In this type of society, however, public pressure must not be taken to mean the substance of grass-roots opinion, but rather the forms of mass reaction—demonstrations, press statements in the name of popular symbols and of the people, party pronouncements—manipulated by political leaders and a partisan press through the use of national slogans. Non-dependence was such a slogan. It was flexible and popular, and its role was as important in establishing a bridge of communication between the decision-makers and the masses as it was in giving vague substantive guidance to the makers of foreign policy.

In fact, non-dependence was only an extension of independence into the field of a newly sovereign nation's foreign policy. The king owed his political leadership to legal authority supported by his popularity as a symbol of Moroccan independence. Because of the crucial relation between independence and foreign policy, he was especially vulnerable—in his own mind—to articulate nationalist pressure in this field. When a year and a half passed without results, the situation changed from one in which the 1950 agreement was regarded as illegal and subject to renegotiation to one in which the bases themselves were considered a heritage of the French protectorate and an insult to Moroccan sovereignty. Total independence must, therefore, involve evacuation of American as well as ex-protectorate troops. The king never made plain the criteria by which he decided when the opposition was sincere or justified in its use of the banner of independence and when the danger of his being outflanked on the issue of independence was real or, on the other hand, when he could afford to ignore or firmly oppose this type of pressure; these criteria appear to have been purely subjective.

The opposition's use of popular pressure, made possible by the fact that they, too, had access to symbols, shows the unfortunate mingling of partisan politics with foreign policy that is so common in newly independent nations. Essentially the base negotiations were channeled by domestic rivalries, internecine strife, and the need for popular political success. The American bases became a political football, and the important decisions—both negative, on what could *not* be done, and positive, on when something *had* to be done—were made in an atmosphere of public pressure according to domestic political exigencies.

So much has been made of the constricting and committing nature of these public "decisions" that the question must be asked, "How decisive were they?" A discerning answer puts Moroccan decision-making on foreign policy into its proper perspective. Public pressure was as decisive as the elite felt it was. The decision-makers still made the decision, but their choice was whether to accept the public commitment. Such a decision was most often unconscious and was conditioned by the individual's image of his position. The king, as seen, felt himself a prisoner of his nationalist popularity and sometimes went beyond his personal policy choices to maintain it. The foreign ministers courted popular or partisan support and were trapped by their attempts to appear attractive. All were apprentices to their own sorcery, and their decisions to maintain this position were their ultimate criteria in their decision-making in this incident.

THREE

The Army will always work in silence;
it will remain faithful to its oath
and motto: My God, My Country, My King.
—Moulay Hassan

MILITARY PROBLEM
Organization of the Army

Military organization in Morocco posed a problem to decision-makers that was slightly different from other questions. Whereas in other cases there was little question as to which office was competent to handle the particular matter, in military affairs no such agreement was present. Because of this uncertainty, military organization was accomplished under the influence of two factors, the actual military operations and the political fight for control of the army. Operations brought to light military needs and even pertinent solutions to questions of size, territorial organizations, and unit specialization. Politics combined with the inertia inherent in the system to block these solutions—and even to hinder other programs, such as conscription—which political forces had suggested and agreed on. Military decision-making was thus unusually complicated, and its complexity is fully apparent only under the light of a day-to-day examination of happenings.

The effect of outside events, too, was more important than in any other question. In the diplomatic problem outside events were caused by forces related to the issue at stake, and in education external influences constituted the situational context for decision. But the Moroccan army was organized under the blows of unrelated incidents, that is, incidents whose causes had no relation to army organization, even though their occurrence had an effect on the military. The efforts of the prince were devoted to dealing militarily with these incidents, to defeating his critics' programs, and to keeping control of his armed forces; he was left with little energy to put his own ideas in force until events compelled him to do so. His opponents, on the other hand, had only enough power to slow down implementation of the prince's program; in the process, they put forward their own ideas, but their power was not sufficient to push them through. With both sides busy neutralizing each other, events were left to play a large role in shaping decisions.

Still occupied by an 85,000-man garrison of the French army and a 60,000-man garrison of the Spanish army in the northern zone, newly independent Morocco had no troops of its own. Yet the March declaration of independence stated: "His Majesty Mohammed V, Sultan of Morocco, has a National Army at his disposal. France lends its assistance to Morocco in setting up this Army." The intention was clearly future. One of the first tasks of the king's government in asserting the sovereignty of the nation was to establish and organize the Royal Armed Forces (Forces Armées Royales) —the FAR.

The background of the FAR was varied. Traditionally, designated tribes had supplied the majority of the armed forces as part of their allegiance to the king and in return for certain tax and land concessions. The uncertainty of this system was one of the major reasons for the sultan's invitation to French protecting forces in 1912; once the protectorate was established, the French and Spanish supplied the military arm of the government. Moroccan soldiers were incorporated into special units of the protectors' armies and, at the time of independence, about 50,000 were stationed in the metropoles and in French and Spanish possessions throughout the world, including Morocco.

The relation of these diverse components to the FAR was not formally settled until 1960, and it continues to play an integral part in some of the problems of the army. The type of army to be established was another question treated in the same way. Was the FAR to be small or as large as the protectorate forces? Was it to be a professional force or a popular army, grown out of the resistance struggle? Was it to be based on national conscription or on volunteer forces? Was it to be a military organization, or was it also to serve as a construction brigade? All these questions were posed and quickly decided in early 1956. Yet none of them was to remain decided, and in the coming years all were again called into question during the evolution and operations of the FAR.

Yet in 1956 speed was important. The army had to be established quickly for many reasons. The demands of prestige and sovereignty and the necessities of defense and security gave the creation of the FAR priority; the presence of a war next door, with both sides—the French and the Algerian FLN—capable of exercising military pressure on Morocco, was as urgent a reason to form the FAR as was the obligation to exercise effective police power at home. Finally, the FAR would replace two undesirable elements in Morocco—the French and Spanish armies and the Army of Liberation—by absorbing some of their members and all of their functions.

FORMATION

With the independence agreement signed on March 2, 1956, in Paris, both King Mohammed V and Premier Bekkai were able to turn their attention to implementing details. Military discussions began the first week after the King returned from Paris; in accordance with a letter annexed to the March declaration, Bekkai met with Maj. Mohammed Oufqir and Capt. Driss ben 'Omar, Moroccan officers in the French Army, and Colonel Costantini, director of the French High Commissioners' Military Cabinet, on March 13 to discuss the establishment of a national army. This commission was to decide such basic matters as the choice between a standing and a conscripted army, the mission of the army, its finances, and its officer corps. The following day Bekkai telegraphed the French Defense Ministry to release the French Army's highest ranking Moroccan officer, Brig. Gen. ben Hammou Kettani, from his enrollment in the Center for Advanced Military Studies in Paris in order to participate in the work of the commission. An enlarged military commission was constituted among interested ministers and ranking Moroccans in the French Army; the presence on the committee of Ministers of State Ahmed Reda Guedira, 'Abderrahim Bou'abid, Driss Mhammedi, and Mohammed Cherkaoui and Vice-Premier Mohammed Zeghari, as well as the premier, the crown prince and the king, meant that defense was the essential occupation of the government during the following week.

On March 22, the committee decided on a *dahir*, which, signed by the king, created the first military institutions—the Ministry of National Defense and the General Staff.[1] Guedira, who had previously been charged with negotiations, was named defense minister. His new job was essentially a continuation of his former duties

[1] *Dahir* No. 1-56-096 of March 22, 1956.

specifically applied to the establishment of the army; his favorable reputation with the French, his close acquaintance with the prince for over a dozen years, and his position as an independent political figure in the Istiqlal-dominated cabinet made his choice a logical one. Political logic and royal desires determined the selection of Prince Moulay Hassan as chief of staff. The king's desire to preserve the useful tradition of a *royal* army, his aversion to putting it into the hands of an Istiqlali, and the lack of prestige and nationalist reputation of Kettani, the ranking military officer rumored for the post, all left the way open for the appointment of the prince. In addition, Moulay Hassan himself wanted the job and so told his father. The long working session of the committee ended with acceptance of both the king's nominations and the committee's draft instructions for negotiations with the French; with adjournment, decisions on the army passed into the hands of the prince and his minister.

The plans for a national army called for a 20,000-man force to be known as the Royal Armed Forces, with the king as commander-in-chief. In keeping with the haste already shown, the king set the 'Id as-Seghir, the three-day Muslim feast to begin about May 12, 1956, as the first formal parade of the FAR. The first activity therefore was essentially diplomatic. Guedira, accompanied by Kettani and Captain Nmichi, left for Paris immediately following his nomination and began negotiations with Alain Savary, French secretary of state for Moroccan and Tunisian affairs, and Maurice Bourgès-Maunoury, French defense minister.

The prince accompanied Mohammed V to Madrid to conduct independence negotiations with the Spanish government. Article 3 of the protocol signed on April 7 was parallel to the French text and protocol of March 2: "The Spanish Government will lend its assistance to the Moroccan Government for the organization of its own Army. The present status of the Spanish Army will remain in operation during the transition period." In Spain the prince and Lt. Gen. Mohammed bel Qassem Mezian, Spain's highest ranking Moroccan officer, discussed the Spanish Moroccan army units. Moulay Hassan then went with Guedira to Paris for further negotiations, and the Moroccan delegation returned to Rabat in April.

The prince announced the results of the first round of talks by predicting a 15,000-man army "not on paper, but on foot" by May 14; Guedira added, "We have obtained not only the complete agreement of France, but also its assistance." [2] Guedira also an-

[2] Mohammed V, *Réalisations et perspectives* (Rabat: Ministry of Information and Tourism, n.d. [1958]), pp. 59–60; *PM*, April 25, 1956.

nounced the Spanish government's declared willingness to put its Moroccan troops at the disposal of the prince. The pair returned to Paris on May 3, accompanied by the military commission headed by Kettani, to work out final details for the transfer of units, including equipment valued at $40,000,000 and especially the repatriation of the Moroccan officer corps. They attained agreement four days later in an atmosphere of cooperation unhampered by political controversy and returned to Rabat on May 8. The negotiations had been roughly divided according to competence: Guedira handled the groundwork, Moulay Hassan took the active lead in final arrangements, and Kettani with his commission worked out the military details.

In terms of the 'Id as-Seghir deadline, the mission was a success. The entire 14,000-man Royal Moroccan Army and its 200 vehicles were reviewed in the *meshwar* (courtyard) of the Palace on May 14, 1956, by its commander-in-chief before a crowd estimated at 200,000. The parade consisted of ten infantry battalions of five companies (French *goumiers*); one infantry battalion of three companies (French *tirailleurs*); two infantry battalions of three large companies (Spanish *mehallas*); one cavalry battalion of three troops; and one armored group comprising one armored squadron of seventeen fourteen-ton armored cars and one armored squadron of seventeen fourteen-ton tanks, one artillery group of three batteries of four 105-mm. howitzers each, one engineer battalion, one mule company of two platoons, one signal detachment, one transport company, and one logistic group. The units were all under strength, the dress was ragged, and the uniforms were diverse, but the army was there.[3]

The haste necessary in establishing the FAR, however, left a number of questions unanswered. In the process of setting up the parade, nearly all problems had received only temporary solutions. Their continuing nature alone was sufficient to provide the substance for decision-making over the next five years. In most cases, however, these problems were to be complicated by the rapidly changing nature of their context and by the peculiar but recurrent fact that external events repeatedly intervened to force decisions or block those on the verge of being made.

The actual transfer of personnel, as agreed on in Paris, had been effected in the week before the parade. Units of *goumiers* (French-commanded troops who had seen action in Tunisia, Italy, France, Germany, Indochina, and Algeria as well as in the pacifica-

[3] *Les Forces Armées Royales* (Rabat: Ministry of Information, n.d. [1957]), p. 15. *Monde*, May 14, 1956.

tion and the maintenance of order in Morocco), arrived from their posts throughout Morocco for the change-of-command ceremony at Nkheila on May 10. The *goumiers* were largely Berber, usually with a family tradition of military service and often even from the tribes that had formerly filled the sultan's armies.[4] They had been recruited by their commanding officer and, if he was good, they were personally loyal to him; there had been little enlisted turnover, although an increasing if small number of desertions took place during the Moroccan resistance. Most *goumiers* had undergone a long, agreeable, and secure association with the French Army, were rugged soldiers, and had received good infantry and guerrilla training, although their sense of maintenance and their mechanical, literate, and technical development were extremely low. The *tirailleurs*, who often had even longer experience in regular infantry units, were similar in status. Generally the units were transferred intact.

The immediate task imposed by the goal of a 20,000-man army, the deadline for which was postponed by the king to the end of the year, was first to expand the number of troops. An appeal by the government resulted in 2,000 five-year enlistments in June, 1956, with little difficulty; at an Istiqlal youth rally on March 26, Moulay Hassan had cried out, "Will you sign up in the Moroccan Army, that Moroccan Army that I have the honor of directing with His Majesty the King?" and 20,000 boys and girls answered, "Yes."

Another source of troops still had to be dealt with. It was only after the formation of the FAR that full attention could be given to the Army of Liberation (AOL), although it had been an object of concern for some time. The first action of the military complement to the resistance antedated the king's return from Madagascar by only a month. By March, 1956, controlled from its headquarters in Nador and Tetuan in the Spanish zone, it had established its hold over a zone of insecurity which encompassed the Rif and the Middle Atlas, cutting vital lines of communication to the south at the Zad Pass and to the east at the Taza Gap. The guerrilla army, no bigger than 3,000 at this time, operated under a strict hierarchical organization with three grades of *qaids* (officers). Many of them had served in the French Army, and guerrilla successes and growing nationalism brought increasing desertions, encouraged by a special section of the AOL under Mahjoubi Ahardan, a former officer in the French Army and the defense minister in 1961. Formed by the French,

[4] According to personal estimates in 1960, Berbers made up over 80 per cent of the troops, half of the officers commissioned before independence, and a few of the officers commissioned afterward.

trained in World War II, and hardened in guerrilla warfare in Indochina, the leaders were experienced but not schooled, and their troops were little more than tribal patriots fired by nationalism.

On February 7, 1956, before the Great Mosque of Casablanca and a month later in his independence address, the king made pointed reference to the AOL in his call for a return to order and national unity. But the political stand of the AOL complicated the situation. Like the Bolsheviks of 1917, it looked to "world revolution": the liberation of all French North Africa. It was suspicious of the new regime, in which it saw political leaders trooping home from abroad to head a political and governmental apparatus which, from the mountains, looked little more to the guerrillas' liking than earlier groups of "moderate nationalists" under the protectorate. The AOL looked for positive recognition of the losses it sustained during the bitter Rif fighting. Finally, it considered the solemn declarations of independence mere banter as long as the details were not negotiated and the civil and military representatives of France withdrawn.

Behind all these political attitudes lay the fact that the AOL—like the Algerian ALN—considered itself the national army, born of the independence struggle, equal in value with the nationalist groups who had already received recognition as political parties. In this it received the agreement of the resistance, whose opinion of the parties was similar to that of the AOL. Even in 1960, 'Abderrahman Yusufi, president of the Association of Resistance and Liberation, called the AOL "the authentically Moroccan army" and regarded the FAR as "a French creation to permit the dissolution of the AOL." General Kettani, on the other hand, regarded the AOL as illegal or, worse, nonexistent, claiming the FAR was the only legitimate national army.

Following the king's admonition, party leaders were dispatched to Tetuan and Madrid to attempt further contact with AOL chiefs and gain their submission to the king. The envoys' efforts to reinforce the position of the party in the government by obtaining recognition as the predominant element in the independence movement canceled any hope for agreement with the AOL. Even the matter of allegiance to the king remained unresolved.

Between March 7 and 18, 1956, however, offensive guerrilla operations were sharply reduced, and tracts signed by the Army of Liberation announced that the king's plea had been heard. The military silence was the immediate signal for all parties to claim that it was their control over the AOL that brought about the cease-

fire. Politics were proving more powerful than war; the Berbers'
hand was forced. On March 29, an official announcement from the
Moroccan Resistance Movement and the Army of Liberation denounced "the wave of appeals sent out by the political organizations
or groups of impostors which lead international and Moroccan public opinion to believe that they control the Resistance and the Army
of Liberation"; it recognized the authority of the sultan "to whose
command we submit" and announced "the provisional cessation of
military operations, although the Army of Liberation will keep its
positions until Moroccan sovereignty is entirely liberated." On the
following day, thirty *qaids* of the AOL "General Staff," clad in
anonymity and a newly adopted uniform to symbolize their dual
clandestine and military nature, appeared before the king and the
prince, offered them a submachine gun and a sword (respectively)
and "our homages, and . . . our indefatigable attachment to his
person, his throne and the sacred cause of the country." The group
also presented their political aims and discussed for the first time
their integration into the FAR.

Just as the partisan political atmosphere was the major deter-
minant of the AOL decision to declare its allegiance to the king, so
the same party rivalry was to force decisions from the other side
and finally bring about the integration of the AOL into the FAR.
The complexity of the problem, however, was evident in the announcement that it could be decided only by the king. To the relief
of many, especially the French Army and the new Moroccan Army
units, the month of May passed with no decision made, and AOL
members were watching, not marching in, the FAR's first pass-in-
review on the 'Id as-Seghir.

The obstacles to a decision were essentially a hardening, as
time passed, of the complications which characterized the situation
before March 30. From the military side there was out-and-out opposition, headed by Kettani. It stemmed in part from professional
concern, in part also from the fact that most of the new troops of the
FAR were the units which had borne the brunt of AOL military
attacks and nationalist criticism. The last battle of the Twenty-fifth
Goum took place on March 6, 1956, against the AOL attack on Ain-
Leuh, and another unit of the same forces had met the first offensive against Immouzer des Marmouchas on October 1, 1955. From
the Army of Liberation, the attitude was equivocal. Its claim to be
the army of Morocco was only partly compatible with integration
into the Moroccan Army. At the same time, it also publicized itself
"a North African army. Consequently, as long as Algeria is not free,

we will not parade in Rabat." Even 'Allal al-Fassi had made it plain in a speech at Cairo that "the Army of Liberation will retain its present status until the settlement of the negotiations between France and the Arab Maghreb."

The AOL was not idle after the cease-fire. It hindered authority without replacing it. In a situation where the local administration of the protectorate was discredited, the French Army politically tied down, and the new local authorities only unsteadily installed in their posts without benefit of effective liaison and backing from Rabat, the Army of Liberation was strong enough to ensure chaos. Actively adopting the self-appointed role of security forces, the AOL occupied posts abandoned by the French Army, exercised police functions, and collected funds for the resistance in the areas where the political parties were traditionally weak. Between April and June the situation rapidly degenerated from scattered insecurity to characteristic anarchy, and bitter French observers saw the beneficial work of the protectorate dissolve in a regional return to the *bled as-siba* (historic dissidence).

The problem was partially recognized by the AOL and the resistance, which on May 18, 1956, issued a declaration denouncing the groups which had sprung up under the name of the two organizations and had proceeded to extort funds or stir up troubles. Although thereby implicitly acknowledging the ineffectiveness of AOL "security forces," the two groups also agreed to cease their own collection of money and to prohibit resistance, but not the AOL, members from bearing arms. Immediately, the AOL increased its security activity, controlling all French and Moroccan traffic and confiscating arms. Local authorities and security forces were either ordered or intimidated into not interfering. Belatedly, the central government acted, sending instructions to all governors to collect all illegal arms; since arms permits were normally held by Frenchmen rather than by Moroccans, this measure was the first attempt to control AOL activities, as well as those of irregular terrorist bands. The Army of Liberation and the resistance joined this effort with another declaration in which it included AOL members in the arms interdiction, as well as forbiding any money dealings (presumably not commercial), including the acceptance of gifts. Citing the specific desire of the king, the AOL announced it was suspending all activity and was turning over the security of the country to the central authorities. The declaration was made in agreement with the Interior Ministry and was proclaimed by the minister.

During the three months following the March 30 audience with the king, continual attempts at negotiation with the AOL were encouraged by the palace. Such Istiqlal leaders as Mehdi ben Barka, also of the resistance, and 'Allal al-Fassi; provincial governors, particularly Ahardan of Rabat, Hajj Fatmi ben Sliman of Fez, and Mohammed ben 'Abdelkhiari of Taza, and especially the AOL "general," Dr. 'Abdelkrim Khatib, were used as intermediaries to negotiate with the guerrillas. These talks, however, made little progress, since they attempted to solve all details before any formal act of integration was agreed on. In Cairo on June 24, 1956, among a number of other statements which appeared more far-reaching than the situation actually warranted, Moulay Hassan predicted that the guerrillas would be integrated into the army or the gendarmery when he returned. In fact, the situation needed a serious shock to bring forth a direct order from the king and to force a decision on integration first, with attention to details afterward.

On June 27 near Fez, 'Abbes Messa'idi, former head of the AOL officer training school at Nador and now in charge of the local AOL sector, was assassinated by a rival guerrilla group. The insecurity of which the AOL was partially the cause had turned against its own leaders. The circumstances of the incident are still obscure. One interpretation says that a band favoring unrestricted AOL support of the FLN killed Messa'idi for his integrationist views; the other claims that Messa'idi was removed as part of the Istiqlal drive to control the AOL. Whichever the case—and both are credible in the circumstances—the guerrilla groups in the Fez and Taza sector were infuriated by the attack, and, unsheathing their arms, they prepared to descend on the two provincial capitals and eventually march on Rabat. Moulay Hassan, in Rome seeing the pope, returned to Rabat on the day of the assassination and received orders from the king to negotiate immediate integration. The prince went immediately to Fez and dispatched a commission on June 28 to make the entire Rif circuit between Taza and Fez, contacting groups of the AOL. The prince kept in continual telephone contact with the king and on June 30 returned to Rabat with the commission to report to a limited cabinet meeting composed of the king, the premier, Foreign Minister Balafrej, Security Director Mohammed Laghzaoui, Interior Minister Mhammedi, Guedira, and Ahardan. Units of the month-old FAR were rushed to Taza, and a news blackout imposed. On July 2, the prince, Mhammedi, and Laghzaoui joined Dr. Khatib and flew to Fez, where they were met by another AOL chief, 'Abdullah ben Ahmed ben 'Ali Senhaji, and then landed at Nador. They were joined by Governor

Ahardan and Governor 'Abdelkhiari and drove along the top of the Rif to Talamagait on the "toboggan road" just inside the former Spanish zone between Tizi Ouzli and al-Huceima. There 1,000 AOL men and officers representing some 5,000 troops, swore ". . . by Almighty God to be faithful to the religion, the country, and the King, to obey only the orders of the King, supreme head of the FAR, and to execute scrupulously the orders of Prince Moulay Hassan, Chief of Staff of the FAR." The integration was formally accepted. It had occurred so rapidly that it was only a week later, on July 8, that the AOL and resistance were able to meet and issue a proclamation acceding to the decision.

The details of actual integration began the day after the formal oath. On July 3 and 4, the king and Moulay Hassan met with the AOL "General Staff," uniting Ahardan, Khatib, Senhaji, Brahim Manouzi, and Mohammed Kharbouchi, as well as about 200 lesser chiefs. This group spoke for AOL sectors in the Rif and in the Middle Atlas south of Taza. At the same time, guerrillas from the region south of Rabat under the command of "Colonel" ben Miloudi arrived in the capital. It took a special trip by the prince to rally the remaining sectors. On July 23, 1956, accompanied by Khatib, Moulay Hassan met "Colonel" al-Amrani at Amizmiz in the High Atlas south of Marrakesh and negotiated the integration of his troops.

With the crown prince carrying out his direct order, the king lent his prestige to certain problems connected with the situation. On June 2 he had shown his concern with one of the major grievances of the AOL by making a radio appeal for public aid to the Rif. Once authority was established, the king surrounded himself with his ministers and his military staff and made a triumphal voyage across much of the Army of Liberation's territory in the Rif and Middle Atlas. On July 6 in the forests of Souissi, Mohammed V held his first pass-in-review of "integrated" AOL troops, some 500 Zemmours from ben Miloudi's sectors.

A significant problem soon arose in the process of integration, however. The original numbers had swelled with the success of the AOL, with its less rigorous turn of activity, and with the promise of secure employment that membership in the integrated AOL now implied. The men of Talamagait represented about 5,600 Riffis, of of whom 2,000 appeared in Rabat on July 3, 1956; the rest came on three special trains three weeks later. Some 4,000 more swore allegiance to the king on the plateau of Ajdir, with another 300 joining them at Ifran during the king's mountain tour. Five special train sections brought in more from Berkan, Ahfir, and Oujda. By the end of July, 10,000 guerrillas were assembled in and about the capital, occupying educational institutions closed for the summer. By zeal and force of habit, some of them continued their police functions in Rabat, scolding drunks, correcting careless veils, and generally helping the city police.

Although the king had put off his trip to Madagascar, set for July 27, to attend to the AOL and other problems, these affairs, as well as the sudden appendectomy of Moulay Hassan, postponed regulation of the AOL police-guerrillas until August. Meeting in interministerial council with the prince, Guedira, Mhammedi, Public Works Minister Mohammed Douiri, Agriculture Minister Ahmed Nejjai, and Laghzaoui on August 29, the king called for immediate action on the band of permanently unemployed and placed the council in permanent session. An integration commission of Khatib, Ahardan, and other AOL leaders was also set up to screen candidates. Estimates placed the number that could be integrated into the FAR at 3,000 to 4,000; the figure was stretched to about 5,000 at the end of 1956. Not all of the 10,000 guerrillas expected military jobs. Many were content to return home with "reserve commissions" as formal recognition of their services.

Outside of a special segment of the Army of Liberation integrated in 1960, there has been practically no more recruiting since 1956. Since a military career offers great security in a land where unemployment is a problem and a military uniform offers high prestige in a society with a fighting tradition, applications for enlistment have consistently exceeded the need. For the few post-1956 enlistments, the French system, whereby the commanding officer is his own recruiting agency, continues. Enlistments are for five years and are renewable, with a high re-enlistment rate. Medical examinations (including X rays) and occupational questionnaires are used, but there are no clinical or aptitude tests. Enlisted training is also accomplished by the individual units. Contrary to the structure of the officer corps, therefore, the enlisted age pyramid is top-heavy; units below the company level are often placed under the command of noncommissioned officers.

The need for officers was crucial. In May, 1956, Moulay Hassan set a goal of 1,000 commissioned and 1,000 noncommissioned officers that was not to be filled until 1960. Forty-two former officers in the French Army had been presented to the prince in a ceremony two weeks before they met their troops and three weeks before they took their oath before the king; sixty were on hand on May 14.[5] The officers were an elite group—aristocrats, Francophile, frequently sons of merchants or of pashas and caids who had occupied their tribal posts with the favor of the protectorate and who were in a position to give their sons the education necessary for the officer corps. The nationalism of the officer corps was expressed in a firm, conservative loyalty to the king and a dislike for politics. They spoke French among themselves, and some had French wives; there was little turnover in their ranks. Because of these characteristics, they could perpetuate the established and successful relations between the French officer and his *goumiers*, based on loyalty and caste.

Officers of the Army of Liberation were sent to the training camp at Bensliman (Boulhaut) for six months of instruction in military and civic duties, including reading and writing. Ninety officers and noncommissioned officers were graduated on May 18, 1957, and many of them were given reserve commissions.[6] The touchy problem of equivalent grade was solved only by reducing most AOL *qaids*—many of whom had been only noncommissioned officers in the French Army—to second lieutenant, with a few first lieutenants and one captain, a system which usually amounted to a demotion of one grade from the AOL rank. Twenty-eight officers were finally integrated into the FAR.

The situation in 1956, therefore, not only imposed a great demand for more trained officers—with the realization that these officers would be young, would lack practical experience, and would create a highly distorted age pyramid and a highly differentiated caste structure—but also put command into the hands of noncommissioned officers or French officers on loan to the FAR. However, even the noncommissioned officers, although experienced, were scarcely trained for command. Between 20,000 fighting men and the General Staff there was, for all practical purposes, no Moroccan

---

[5] The account in *Réalisations* (Mohammed V, *op. cit.*, p. 60), which says that "200 Moroccan officers were ready" is a gross exaggeration, based on the number enrolled in the various academies and not ready until the next year. Cf. speech by the prince (*PM*, May 15, 1960).

[6] Ben Miloudi and Senhaji were prominent among those who received reserve commissions, whereas another group was named to posts in the local administration. Ahardan, Senhaji, and later Mohammed ben 'Ali Zerqtouni and Mohammed ould 'Omar Amidou were named governor of Rabat, Nador, Ouarzazat, and Oujda, and others were appointed caid, pasha, and supercaid, predominantly in the northern zone. Many of these men, including all four governors, subsequently lost their posts for malpractice of some kind.

liaison, service, or command. This artificial structure was to have repercussions in future military operations. In 1956, however, France, Spain, and Morocco made efforts to supply both permanent and temporary remedies to the problem.

The May 7 agreement stipulated that "France will place at the disposition of His Majesty the technicians and officers necessary to form the officer corps of our Army. They will sign individual one-year contracts with the Moroccan government, will wear the uniform of the Royal Moroccan Army, and will be subject to its command." A Bureau of Military Assistance to the Royal Army (BAMAR) was established to coordinate supplementary military personnel assistance. In July Morocco asked for 200 French officers and 900 noncommissioned officers as instructors; the final number of Frenchmen in Moroccan uniform in both categories for 1956–1957 was 745. This number remained constant until 1960, for the increased number of French specialists needed to set up new units had offset Moroccan replacements for French instructors in the infantry. Rotation, retention, or replacement is decided for each French officer by his unit commander and the General Staff. Such technical units as artillery and engineer battalions have been under French command, with junior Moroccan officers in assistant command positions; it was not until the beginning of 1960 that a Moroccan had a command position in the Engineer Battalion.

One of the largest instruction jobs the French undertook was the staffing of Dar al-Beida, renamed the Royal Military Academy. The academy, founded by Marshal Lyautey in 1918 in a former imperial palace near Meknes, had trained the Moroccan officer corps in the French Army. Since independence its eight-year program has been compressed into ten months for the rapid formation of an adequate-sized officer corps for the FAR. Instruction includes history, geography, language, military, and physical training, with the program entirely under French tutelage. In the summer of 1956, over 600 applications were received for the school, about 100 of whom were accepted, although the normal class capacity had been only seventy-five.

Because the French had agreed to staff the Royal Military Academy, they also provided the instruction for a new noncommissioned officers' training school that was set up by Maj. Driss ben 'Omar at Ahermoumou in 1957. Based on a one-year course and a normal capacity of 200 students a year, the school trained noncommissioned officers of the Royal Army, graduating 240 by mid-1957. In recent years Ahermoumou has turned to direct training of candidates picked by competitive examination from civilian life for noncommissioned rank.

Finally, agreements with the French and also with the Spanish filled the gap in officer ranks most substantially by opening the national military academies at St. Cyr (Coetquidan) and Toledo.[7] About 200 officer candidates, chosen from 1,400 applicants for accelerated programs beginning in July and August, 1956, in each school, returned after a year to form the largest group of officers. Some, however, remained in France to take specialized advanced training.

As a result of training at the Royal Academy, Ahermoumou, St. Cyr, and Toledo, by mid-1957 the FAR had some 500 officers and one-sixth of its 1,500 noncommissioned officers trained, out of a total 30,000-man army.[8] After two years, continued use of the three academies and other specialized schools provided a total of 884 officers and 3,722 noncommissioned officers to 25,841 enlisted men, for a total army of 30,447. The officer-soldier ratio was still about half of the French figure for comparable units. In terms of numbers, however, it was an impressive job, and training and *esprit* made it even more so.

MISSIONS AND OPERATIONS

Moroccan history and French precedent have given the Royal Army a dual military mission of external defense and internal security; from the French Army it also inherited a mission of social work.[9] The mission of the FAR has been frequently alluded to by the king and the prince, but only rarely stated. The clearest of the infrequent declarations was made by the crown prince in 1959: "The Army . . . pursues its double mission, consisting of the establishment of security and the safeguarding of Independence, and also of extending constructive assistance on the social level." The relation of

[7] A few also went to Egypt and Iraq during this first year, but their experience was richer in propaganda than it was in training, and the experiment was not repeated. Compare the Moroccan experience with exchange teachers from the Middle East, described in the chapter on education.

[8] There were 514 members of the 1957 officers' graduating class, named after Mohammed V; 830 (including noncommissioned officers) in the 1958 class, named after Moulay Ismail (fifty-three of them from Dar al-Beida); and 161 in the 1959 class, named after Lalla 'Aisha.

[9] In Paris Ambassador 'Abderrahim Bou'abid declared, "The FAR has the prerogatives and the mission of the French Army in Morocco" (*Monde*, September 16, 1956). The mission drawn from Islamic tradition, that of the *jihad*, is, of course, no longer likely.

these missions is political and hence constantly changing; it is a function of both the decision-makers and the events surrounding the army. Thus the king has called the army "the most sure guarantor of national independence and dignity, and the best safeguard of the integrity of our territory." In October, 1956, the army was to accomplish its first major mission—ensuring internal security after the Meknes riots of that month.

However, decisions to conduct operations pursuant to the mission of the FAR also resulted in changes in the organization of the army. These changes, designed to make the FAR a more effective instrument, were debated and made or blocked in a partisan atmosphere that was tantamount to continual re-evaluation of the mission. In the final analysis, too, this debate on mission was also a personal battle for positions of control, for, as long as military decision-making was in the hands of the Palace, the mission of the FAR would be clearly subject to the royal will. The complexity of the debate about the mission of the FAR can be seen by an examination first of the operations, then of the organization, of the army.

The army's role in the Meknes riots of October, 1956, was more an occupation than an operation. The FAR arrived late, did little, and, through no fault of its own, left the European colony feeling insecure. The weakness, however, was not so much that of the FAR as a military group as the lack of decision-makers when the highest command was absent. The absence of the king, the prince, and the prime minister on a diplomatic trip to Tunisia created the conditions for slow-moving action, probably in the same measure that it created the conditions for the riots.

When the news of popular demonstrations over the French kidnaping of five Algerian rebel leaders on their way from Rabat to Tunis reached Interior Minister and acting Premier Mhammedi, he allowed all governors and mayors full police powers to deal with the situation. The massacre in Meknes began on October 23, when the head of the municipal guard (a former AOL "colonel") was shot while enforcing order; French troops received permission to cordon off the European quarter, but FAR reinforcements did not arrive until a day later.

In the middle of a diplomatic crisis with France and a political crisis over a falling government, the three governmental leaders rushed back to Morocco and met with Mhammedi and Defense Minister Guedira on October 25. The prince and the king then received the General Staff. The result, announced the following day in the name of the king, was the appointment of Maj. Driss ben 'Omar as governor of Meknes province. With characteristic vigor, the officer announced,

> I am charged with re-establishing order and security whatever the cost, and to punish the guilty. I will fulfill my mission or leave my head. If I do not have enough troops, I will have others come in. I will make no distinction between French and Moroccans.

Other troops did raise the number at his disposal to two battalions, and close cooperation with the French Army was possible. The arrival of Major Driss ended attacks in the city; units of the FAR, like the French Army, were stationed in villages and plantations throughout the *bled,* although security was not established until over a week later. Army troops were also used throughout the northern part of Rabat province by Ahardan. Rapid trials were provided a month later by a retroactive clause hastily added to the Code of Military Justice, providing for courts-martial in areas under military government. Several rioters were judged and given light sentences.

The FAR had a very important connection with the Meknes riots. After the initial excitement had died down, it became apparent that the instigators of the massacre were primarily Algerians and that some unintegrated elements of the Army of Liberation were the leaders of the attacks and pillaging in the *bled.* Although units of the AOL had not yet been integrated into the FAR, the action plainly showed that the FAR was not to be a revolutionary army, but an instrument of order within the country—even where the Algerian revolt was involved.

Meknes showed the need for fast action at high levels, and the government has never since been caught unaware. In all probability, there was a more immediate effect. It is reported that, when, on his return, the king asked Guedira where his units were, the defense minister who had been appointed to conduct negotiations did not know. In the second government, formed two days after the king's return, Guedira was minister of state for information, and Mohammed Zeghari, an old, loyal trouble shooter, was named defense minister.

The specific lessons gained in Meknes were almost immediately applied in the Tafilalt. As a political incident, the dissidence of the governor, Brahim Zedki Addi ou Bihi, is a striking example of polit-

ical intrigue and social adjustment in a country coming of age; as
a military operation, it was an effective show of force.

Since the replacement of Lahcen Lyoussi by Istiqlali Driss
Mhammedi as interior minister in May, 1956, relations between the
ministry and its highest local agent in the Tafilalt province had
fallen to insubordination and sullen silence. Appointed by Lyoussi
and sympathetic to his traditional views of state relations in which
allegiance is owed directly to the sultan without any identification
with his government, Addi ou Bihi refused to accept the Interior
and Justice Ministries' appointment of caids, police, and judges
to his bailiwick.[10] His enmity was all the more aroused because
just at that time the Istiqlal was using all means to increase its
control over internal administration as well as political government
posts. Addi ou Bihi planned to arrest Mhammedi when the interior
minister and Justice Minister 'Abdelkrim Benjelloun came to inspect
the province.

The governor was a provincial lord; as one of his hesitant
supporters later remarked, "Since it is impossible for anyone to dis-
obey Addi ou Bihi, I agreed to take up arms. . . ." [11] In fact, the
governor said, "The King and the throne are in danger" and did
begin distributing rifles.[12] On January 17, 1957, the king left the
country on a Mediterranean cruise, leaving the "endangered throne"
under the crown prince. Within twenty-four hours, the governor
had arrested the judge and police chief of Midelt, locked up the
police, and taken over the Post, Telegraph and Telephone Building. Sympathizers in adjoining Fez province were alerted, and roadblocks, guarded by dissident groups, were set up along the single

---

[10] Lyoussi and Addi were both accused of frequent contact with the PDI, and
Lyoussi was called a "PDI man" at the trial of Addi. But their outlook was
certainly much closer to the founders of the then clandestine Popular Movement,
and the Popular Movement leaders vaunted Addi's virtues at his death. Lyoussi
certainly played a double role in the affair and, according to Addi, was the
instigator of the revolt. During the trial and the Rif revolt, he fled to his tribe,
which refused him, and then escaped with Palace help to Malaga, with the army
not too close on his trail.

[11] Testimony of Sa'id ben Hussein Lyoussi at Addi's trial. The witness was
caid of Bouleman, not even within Tafilalt province.

[12] According to testimony at his trial, the governor told French General Divary
at Ksar as-Souq that he was permitted to arm the tribesmen from Marrakesh to
the Beni Ouarain and so received 7,000 rifles. When the king left on his cruise,
Addi spread the word that he was fleeing the Istiqlal, and the stage was set for
the revolt. In the trial it was never clear whether Addi believed this story on
Lyoussi's say-so or whether he was simply seeking an excuse to do away with
the Istiqlal, although it seems that the latter motive was clearer in Lyoussi's
actions than in Addi's.

artery of communication from the north.[13] That night the premier called the post office at Midelt with a message for the governor: "The order is given to His Excellency Addi ou Bihi to evacuate the Post Office and reopen communications, to remove the roadblocks and open the roads, and to come immediately to Rabat."

The prince, acting as commander-in-chief, ordered two under-sized battalions of the FAR south from Fez on October 19 after a cabinet meeting. Forced to take the Bouleman bypass because of snow, one battalion waited at Bouleman while the other went on to meet the rebel force blocking the road south of Itzer. The governor of neighboring Ouarzazat province, Capt. Mohammed Medboh, tried to reason with Addi ou Bihi and failed; the king's aide, Col. Moulay Hafid, also told Addi ou Bihi to let the army through, and Crown Councilors Moulay Larbi al-'Alawi and Lyoussi were sent on a conciliatory mission, to no avail.

Continued opposition, therefore, led the prince to order Addi ou Bihi to be replaced by Maj. Mohammed ben Larbi, head of the military cabinet of the king. In his statement, read over the radio by Lyoussi in the local Berber dialect and by Moulay Larbi in Arabic, the prince also offered the *aman* (amnesty) to followers of the governor who would rally to the government. The FAR battalions marched the next day, arriving with few incidents and no combat in Rich and Midelt, where Major ben Larbi and Captain Medboh disarmed the population. Addi ou Bihi retreated to the family castle of Kerrando, near Rich, where he received the prince's envoys, General Kettani and Royal Cabinet Director Mohammed Awad, and agreed to go to Rabat under *aman*.[14] The prince himself made a tour through the cities of the Tafilalt in January a week after the governor had been replaced.

The delicate position of the army was clearly shown during Addi ou Bihi's trial by General Kettani's testimony concerning the *aman*.

> The mission of the Army is sacred, since it has the responsibility of defending Moroccan national territory and maintaining national security. His Majesty the King has not only advised us but ordered us not to spill a drop of blood unless

[13] Lieutenants in the FAR played a role in warning Rabat, although Lyoussi had the Palace ear and played down their reports (*al-'Alam*, January 19, 1959).

[14] After two years of waiting, Addi came to trial, was denied the *aman* because it was not given by the king, and was condemned to death. The Supreme Court denied his appeal on July 8, 1960, and he died of dysentery in prison on January 30, 1961.

it be in self-defense. . . . I understood that if I did not promise [Addi ou Bihi] the *aman,* it would have been difficult for
us to eliminate the rebellion without bloodshed, and therefore the nation would have been exposed to danger.[15]

The decisive action of the prince and his radio appeal destroyed
the dissidents' unity and permitted a bloodless military operation.
In the process, the army followed rules that were to become doctrine
and accomplished its first truly national action, for it unseated loyal
—if misguided—followers of the king for the sake of the authority
of the national government.

The military operations of the FAR in Agadir and Tarfaya
provinces can be divided into three types of exercise, one leading to
the other and each having its own effect on the organization of the
military establishment. In 1957, the FAR made its first appearance
in strength in Agadir, drawn by the need to limit the Ifni war; decisions here were routine and a natural product of the situation, although the late and limited installation of the army in this region
was a result of the lack of available units and the impotence of the
army against local bands, not a result of the weakness of the military command structure. In 1958, FAR units moved across the Dra
River to take possession of newly acquired Tarfaya, the former
Spanish protectorate of southern Morocco; the expedition began
with haste and mismanagement and ended in a series of face-losing
encounters with the Spanish Army. To its credit, the FAR learned
its lesson, which led to important changes. During the next two
years, there was uneven progress toward the establishment of security
in Tarfaya, both through the installation of a military network
and through periodic campaigns.

The two infantry battalions that make up the normal complement of Agadir province were based at Inezgan, near Agadir,
at the disposition of the military governor; they had only limited
effectiveness in this territory. The only permanent unit in the surrounding desert was the small group sent to share the French garrison at Foum al-Hassan in 1956 by order of the king. When war
between Spanish troops and the *mujahidin* (holy warriors) of the
southern Army of Liberation broke out in Spanish enclave of Ifni
on November 23, 1957, the prince sent two additional battalions

---

[15] *Al-'Alam,* January 23, 1959. Things might have been otherwise if the *aman*
had not been offered. In testimony, Addi said, "Nobody arrested me and if I
am here it is because I came on the promise of the *aman* by General Kettani.
By force, neither I nor any of these people here present would be here." This
is doubtless true.

of infantry and an artillery group to Agadir. For the first time the army moved south of the provincial capital, through Tiznit and Mighleft, and took up positions about the enclave, from the latter post at the north Atlantic corner of the enclave down to Goulimim. Its mission was to protect Moroccan territory against Spanish invasion from Ifni—hence at the same time affording the Ifni rebel groups a safe haven for regrouping. Because the rebels generally succeeded in keeping the war on Spanish territory, the FAR saw little other than anti-aircraft action. For the first time, however, the Moroccan military doctrine allowing only defensive fire was applied to an external enemy by order of the prince, who was acting as king during his father's absence. There also appears to have been a secondary mission of weeding out members of the local tribe, Ba Amran, from the other elements of the southern Army of Liberation and disarming the latter, for by the end of the war the FAR had disarmed 400 *mujahidin* and cleared Bou Izakarn and Goulimim of their AOL camps. Hence the war both forced and allowed the army to occupy several hundred square miles of its own territory, but in the process the AOL was pushed south to create further incidents across the Dra River, Morocco's southern boundary at the time.

Following a Spanish threat to carry the Ifni war to Agadir [16] and the increased pressure from Mauritania and Spanish Sahara, where the joint Franco-Spanish "Operation Swab" in February, 1958, had forced AOL groups north toward Moroccan territory, the king talked with Saharan groups at Mhammid and Ouarzazat in early March, 1958. On his return to Rabat, he called together the High Committee of National Defense, including the prince, the premier, and the interior and defense ministers; it was the defense minister, Istiqlal leader Ahmed Lyazidi, who on March 3 announced the reinforcement of the southern garrison in Goulimim and Bou Izakarn by two infantry battalions and the entire armored contingent—three squadrons—of the Royal Moroccan Army.

Thus, when Tarfaya was given to Morocco by Spain less than a month later, troops were already on hand to occupy the new province. At midnight of April 10, 1958, in accordance with the Hispano-Moroccan agreement signed at Cintra, Portugal, an enlarged, combined infantry-engineer battalion of 1,000 men under Major Oufqir,

[16] Although fighting about Ifni dwindled away in early 1958, the war scare in Agadir caused a battalion of five 105-mm. howitzers to be brought to the provincial capital in December, and the Kasba, a fifteenth-century fort on a 650-foot mountain, was closed to tourists and occupied by the army as an observation post.

the king's aide-de-camp, crossed the Dra on the unknown road to
Tarfaya town (Villa Bens). A ceremony was planned for the following day, to be attended by the prince, five ministers, General Kettani, General Mezian, who had formerly commanded the Canary
Islands as Spanish governor-general, and the new governor of
Tarfaya, 'Ali Bou'aida. At the end of the first day's march, however,
the column of Oufqir found itself faced with a Spanish armed force,
for the road to Tarfaya dips south across the border of Tarfaya into
Spanish Saqiet al-Hamra. Trapped in a maneuver undertaken without reconnaissance or intelligence and frustrated in its highly publicized ceremonial rendezvous, the army was obliged to camp in the
desert and construct thirty miles of difficult road on the Moroccan
side of the border.

The next day the prince arrived in Goulimim with Maj. Driss
ben 'Omar, the trouble shooter of Meknes, accompanied by another battalion and on April 12 occupied Hassi Tantan in Tarfaya
province, from which the first aerial and field reconnaissance efforts
were made. Lyazidi arrived with fresh instructions from the king,
and Moulay Hassan, Lyazidi, Majors Oufqir and Driss, and
Governor Bou'aida conferred on the proper political strategy and
military tactics to hold the province. Tantan was quickly built up as
a supply base, using the installations which had not been destroyed
by the withdrawing Spanish Army. Meanwhile, as the prince and the
minister returned to Rabat for consultations with the king and
Major Driss commanded work on the Tantan base, the first scouts
of Oufqir's column came within six miles of Tarfaya town.

New difficulties set in. Supplies of gasoline, water, and even
parts had been stocked on the basis of mileage measured on a map,
not on the basis of the actual conditions of terrain. In addition,
Spanish forces had systematically destroyed the deep wells necessary
in the desert area up to the *medina* of Tarfaya town itself. The
column suffered logistic and mechanical breakdowns and was
obliged to call on the French Army to salvage some of its vehicles
in the desert. Only on April 17, 1958, did a motorized company
under Oufqir enter the red mud walls of Tarfaya, Saint Exupéry's
"outpost of desolation," where the Spanish Army remained en-
trenched behind barbed wire in the few "modern" buildings. The
medina well had been filled with rubble, the airfield plowed, and
the simple supply port enclosed in the barbed-wire confines of the
Spanish base. A month later Spain announced the withdrawal of
its 1,500-man garrison, and during the last week in May the evacuation was completed.

Although it had been a short, frustrating, and embarrassing military operation, the occupation of Tarfaya provided many lessons for the military decision-makers. It was one of the most striking examples of the impetuousness of the crown prince and was undertaken without adequate planning and reconnaissance. It showed the extreme weakness of the army in logistics, and it demonstrated the need for serious and extensive installations, including the construction of roads and bases throughout the entire Saharan section, for effective security and defense of the southern region and frontiers.

During the next two years Tarfaya was practically governed as a military province.[17] Much work was needed. A chronic low ceiling and a damaged airfield made air communication unsure, and the state of the desert track made land travel less than a touristic adventure. The need for work on communications installations was therefore evident when the prince finally arrived, in July, 1958, with the ministers of interior and public works, representatives of the Health, Telecommunications, Agriculture, and Habous Ministries, and General Mezian, Col. Moulay Hafid, and Major Oufqir. The necessity was intensified the same week when, in Rabat, an agreement was signed between the government and the Ente Nationale Idrocarburi (ENI) of Italy for exclusive research and exploitation of the hypothetical petroleum deposits in Tarfaya. Beginning in mid-1959 to install themselves throughout the province in little compounds picturesquely named after major Italian cities, ENI groups depended on the FAR for protection against local thievery and AOL raids. The main ENI truck park was established next to the army base at Tantan. The first tasks of the FAR were the construction of wells and airstrips at Tarfaya and Tantan, improved track to Tarfaya, and finally a road linking the bases to Goulimim. Next in priority was the construction of bases at Tantan, Tizgui Remz in eastern Tarfaya, and Tarfaya town.

In the beginning of 1959, additional internal and external problems began to arise. Reqeibat tribesmen crossed the eastern frontier of Tarfaya in February and made a foray at Tizgui Remz. Two companies were flown in from the north to Tantan, but raiding parties continued to disturb the population, even making exactions in kind and in money. The clash of local tribes with nomadic groups

[17] Tarfaya had its own governor, 'Ali Bou'aida, until 1960, when it was placed under the governor of Agadir province, and then again after 1962, when it was placed under the governorship of the colonel in charge of the Agadir military region. The supercaids of the two districts, Tarfaya and Tantan, have been army officers.

rallying or fleeing from the south necessitated a trip by the governor
to Rabat in early February and a visit by the prince in March with
Defense Minister Mohammed Awad to make local contacts, hear
grievances, and settle disputes. Until the disturbances reached major
proportions, however, and came to the attention of the king—as at
Mhammid in March, 1958—no serious action was taken. On May
27, 1959, the king visited Tiznit and Goulimim for the first time
since independence and spoke to the authorities about local conditions; AOL chiefs from the Saharan area were present, and a delegation from Tata told of raids on its region. As the king was speaking,
a Reqeibat group from Saqiet al-Hamra made a serious attack on an
army column some hundred miles to the south, outside of Tarfaya
town, and carried off several civilians. On the royal party's return
to Agadir on May 29, without going any further, the crown prince
called together his staff and rapidly decided on a "massive installation" of the FAR in Tarfaya.

As a result, the three Moroccan paratroop companies were flown
to the border the same day, and Tantan and Tizgui Remz became
the headquarters camp for two battalions whose component units
were spread over the entire province in small posts and patrols. A
company of camel corps was stationed in Akka, Tantan, or Goulimim, as the occasion demanded. Units of the Engineer Battalion
worked at great disadvantage on the local camps, having to import
all materials from the main engineering base at Kenitra; the camp
at Tarfaya was not completed for three years, but the base at Tantan, finished in the summer of 1960, had barracks and supply areas
designed to support two battalions and provisions for a third. The
Engineer Battalion, one of the smartest in the FAR, had completed
its jobs in regular succession since the taking over of Tarfaya, but
the internal pacification and border control missions of the infantry
and other units were only slowly accomplished under the impetus
of serious incidents that brought the problem to high-level attention.

As a political phenomenon, the events of the Rif in the winter
of 1958–1959 are a large-scale repetition of the incidents of Tafilalt
twelve months before; the newly independent state was in serious
danger of having its governmental and social ways thrown back
more than a century to the time when division between the *bled
as-siba* and *bled al-makhzen* characterized the differentiated power
of the sultanate. The Rif dissidence was the largest problem ever
handled by the FAR, yet it was an operation in internal security, not
external defense. Since it was the first coordinated military exercise
in which army units took part above the company level, there were

important mistakes and important lessons. Logistics, mobilization, and organization were shown to be inadequate, the dual command which still existed in the former Spanish and former French zones had to be abolished, and—given the size of the country and the size of its army—a more flexible plan of dispersal was shown necessary in order for the FAR to fulfill its mission.

The Rif dissidence was a protest against modernism, changing cultural patterns, the Istiqlal, and neglect from Rabat. It was limited to the areas which were most deeply involved in the activities of the AOL in 1955–1956, and it frequently concerned the same people. Its beginnings were connected with the AOL and its political successor, the Popular Movement. On the third anniversary of the October 2, 1955, uprising, a group of former AOL members, including Dr. Khatib and former Governors Senhaji and Ahardan, dug up "Colonel" Messa'idi from his grave in Fez and carried him to Ajdir to put him to rest among his fellow warriors in an AOL cemetery. The demonstration got out of hand, the police intervened, and several Popular Movement leaders, including Khatib and Ahardan, were jailed. Within a short time, the Beni (tribe) Ouriaghel about al-Huceima on the Mediterranean; the Gzennaya, Marnissa, Senhaja, and Targuist tribes, and the Beni Touzin in the Rif north of Taza; the Beni Ouarain south of Taza; the Ait Seghrouchen and Ait Youssi in the Middle Atlas; and the Zemmour tribe in Rabat province had in whole or in part taken to the hills, again in armed revolt.[18]

Immediately the gendarmery and the Mobile Mokhazni and Auxiliary Forces were sent to control the uprising, but the task proved too great. As normal means failed, the king called a Council of Ministers, including the prince, and appointed Majors Hammou and Chebli respectively governor of Rabat province and military assistant to the secretary general of Taza province. An army battalion with mountain artillery and mules was sent to reinforce the two battalions of the Auxiliary Forces near Oulmes, where AOL "Colonel" ben Miloudi had taken refuge with his band. Army orders were to encircle, avoid open combat, and await the expira-

---

[18] The facts that the Beni Ouriaghel were the tribe of 'Abdulkrim al-Khattabi, Riffi leader of the 1920's, who died in 1963 exiled in Cairo; that the Ait Lyoussi were the tribe of Lahcen Lyoussi who was soon to flee the Addi ou Bihi trial in Rabat; and that the revolt took place in the area of former Spanish control and of the strongly pro-Algerian AOL all suggested that 'Abdulkrim, Egypt, Lyoussi, Spain, and the FLN were at the root of the trouble. Of these forces, only Spain had any hand in the dissidence; despite its denial (*Monde*, October 31, 1958), it appears to have supplied arms to the tribesmen.

tion of a surrender ultimatum on October 23. In a light exchange
of fire, ben Miloudi was seriously wounded, although the hardy
fighter walked about for three days until he gave himself up for
medical care.[19] The backbone of the dissidence among the Zemmour, in the home territory of Ahardan, was thus destroyed, although army units remained in the area, and scattered encounters
took place through December.

In the Rif, the fortunes of the FAR were less favorable, and in
Rabat and Tangier spokesmen for the dissidents talked of the tribesmen's coming down from the hills and capturing the government,
as had been threatened in June, 1956. The difficulty of the situation
was compounded by political troubles at the top level. Lyazidi,
defense minister in the homogeneous but factional Istiqlal government, had been very active in his post, seeking to increase the party
power in a sector that had always been under direct Palace control.
Confronted with the Berber dissidence, Lyazidi demanded a free
hand until a decision of the cabinet and the king on October 25,
applied by the High Committee two days later, gave him full
powers of military government over the Riffi provinces, including
authority over the movement and disposition of army units. The
king, however, retained the power, to be given only by written order,
to authorize army intervention in any sector.

Armed with authority, Lyazidi visited Oulmes, Tahala, Aknoul,
and Ajdir to ascertain the grievances in these disinherited regions
of the country. On his return, the king and the prince, meeting in
cabinet on November 3, decided to place the Taza province under
Captain Medboh, a Berber who had been governor of Ouarzazat
during the AOL and Tafilalt incidents, of Nador after Senhaji,[20]
and of Rabat after Ahardan. Army reinforcements were also sent to
the dissident sectors. At the same time, an appeal drawn up by the
premier in the name of the king was broadcast in Berber to the Rif,
and on November 11, 1958, a delegation of fifty Riffi leaders were
received by the king and Balafrej to discuss grievances. Civil measures, such as the sending of Lyazidi and a royal commission of investigation to Taza and al-Huceima to collect more grievances,
were taken during the same time, and on November 30 Ahardan
and Khatib were released from prison.

The same day that the king received the first Riffi delegation,

[19] He was freed from the hospital in September, 1959, without ever facing trial.
[20] Senhaji himself was leading the dissidents near al-Huceima. Al-Husein al-
Ayachi, the replaced governor of Taza and a former graduate of Dar al-Beida,
was publicly exonerated and returned to the governorship when the government
changed at the end of the year and Medboh became telecommunications minister.

however, more serious troubles arose to disturb effective military and political authority. Party factionalism, which had weakened the country's political leadership, broke into the open, and the government soon fell. The new cabinet, constituted on Christmas Day, was dominated by the Istiqlal's left-wing faction, which was even more disliked by the Berber tribesmen, and the dissidence broke out with renewed seriousness, the nation manifesting its own disunity in a reaction to the disunity of those who governed it.

As new unrest spread in the Rif, the prince reasserted his control of military matters. He found his staff ignorant of the operations, with the Supply Staff officers out of touch with transportation units, the Intelligence Staff officers out of touch with the field, and General Mezian incommunicado in a hospital in Tetuan. Leaving his staff in Rabat and shunning the northern units of General Mezian, the prince took personal command of operations, immediately relieving at least one officer for weakness in the face of the enemy.

The prince met with the king in the Council of Ministers and then in the High Committee of National Defense on January 3 to discuss operations and two days later, before leaving for the field, held another series of meetings with his staff, the king, the premier, and the interior minister. The renewal of armed revolt prompted the king to drop leaflets and make a radio appeal in Arabic, Berber, French, English, and Spanish to the rebellious areas, offering pardon and an ear for their troubles if the rebels would return to their villages by noon of January 7; for those who did not, a "cruel punishment" was being prepared, he said, quoting the Quran. Designed to separate the dissidents from the merely discontented, the ultimatum was largely successful. Before the end of the period of grace, nearly all areas had returned to order except for fractions of the Beni Ouraghel under Haji Salem Amezian, of the Gzennaya under Mess'oud Akjouj, and of the Beni Ouarain under ex-Caid Moha al-Ahsen ou Haddou, totaling about 5,000 in all.[21]

In the first days of the year, the prince planned to land at the airfield of al-Huceima, located at nearby Ain Zoren, to show his mastery over the rebellion. Instead, his plane was greeted by small-arms fire from the field, and the prince was forced to establish headquarters in Tetuan, on January 7, and to undertake a full-scale operation against the rebels surrounding al-Huceima, "the Isolated."

A major operation was finally begun. In the preparation of an

---

[21] There was also a slight flare-up in Rich, where Addi ou Bihi's sympathizers protested against Addi's trial in Rabat.

amphibious and air-borne assault on al-Huceima, commercial air-
planes, local fishing boats, and a British ferryboat in the Straits of
Gibraltar were pressed into service along with the royal yacht and
the few FAR aircraft. From all over Morocco nearly 20,000 of the
army's 28,000 troops were called north from wherever they might
be—at least ten of the eighteen battalions, plus most of the cavalry
and field artillery. They were formed into three columns; one under
Major Oufqir in Nador was to move west, and the two others were
to move from the south and southwest under Majors Driss and ben
Larbi. Another mopping-up operation moving eastward along the
Rif ridge among the Ghomara tribe was carried out by the Auxiliary
Forces and Mobile Mokhazni. Oufqir's column was the first to reach
al-Huceima, on January 12, 1959, but the dissidents simply moved
back into mountain areas where there were no roads, tracks, or
trails. During these operations, the king maintained ultimate control of military operations; in a prohibition that was probably more
tactical than total, he forbade offensive use of gunfire and allowed
the army to use its weapons only for "legitimate self-defense" as it
moved in on the enemy.[22]

A week after the relief of al-Huceima, the prince moved his general headquarters to Fez, and on January 23 he sent his troops in
the Rif on a final mopping-up operation against the bands of
Amezian and Akjouj between Aknoul and Targuist.[23] Even this
operation went on for at least two more weeks. It is interesting to
note that, largely because of pledged loyalty to the king and prince,
effective military indoctrination, and traditional love of fighting,
the Riffis integrated into the FAR fought their dissident brothers
without hesitation and in good discipline.

The installation of the prince in Fez permitted attention to the
Taza sector of operations, where dissident elements among the Beni
Ouarain were still holding out. Major Driss, head of the nearby
noncommissioned officers' school at Ahermoumou, was put in charge
of the operations. On January 22, two of the five battalions which
had been standing by south of Taza moved against partisans of

[22] As the prince explained, much more poetically, in a newspaper interview,
"His Majesty the King (God glorify him) told me to use forbearance, but this
must not reach the limits of weakness, and to employ firmness which cannot
be called injustice. . . . He explained that the inhabitants who are still hiding
in the mountains are there for reasons of fear but not rebellion. . . . The question of opening fire concerns His Majesty the King exclusively, with the exception of self-defense situations" (al-ʿAlam, January 10, 1959).

[23] Amezian fled to Spain and was sentenced by military tribunal to life at hard
labor; Akjouj and other lieutenants received ten to six years in prison (PM,
July 4, 1959).

Moha ou Haddou. The caid himself had previously sent his son to the prince, promising to comply with the January ultimatum in exchange for a written *aman* from the king. Told by the king to wait for a propitious time to surrender, he gave himself up on February 3, 1959, in order to serve as an example for Amezian and Akjouj. With his surrender—and with his *aman* respected—the dissidence south of Taza gradually melted away. It was not until the situation in the Rif was under control that the king convened the High Committee of National Defense to hear the prince's report. Order of the Day No. 4, commending the FAR for a job well done, was not given until February 13.

Immediate results of the Rif operation actually occurred during its course. On January 26, 1959, the prince recalled to active duty 3,000 of the 4,000 men who had been discharged for budgetary reasons during the past two years. Forming them into three battalions, he stationed them in al-Ksiba in the Middle Atlas, Ahermoumou, and Fez. By the end of the year, two of the battalions were disbanded and their troops reassigned to other units in order to bring them back to strength. From 1959 to the Congo affair, six out of the twenty-one army battalions were stationed in the Rif, and two more were nearby at Fez and Meknes, the largest concentration of forces anywhere in the country; these battalions were usually broken down and spread into small outposts, as was being done in Tarfaya.

The army's response to the outbreak of dissidence in March, 1960, showed better preparedness, although operations dragged on for nearly a month because of bad weather and the king's counsels of prudence. The operation was much smaller than the Rif, with two battalions facing 200 to 250 men, or ten-to-one odds. The tactics employed had points in common with the Rif operations—the use of a surrender ultimatum, the king's rule against offensive firing, and the necessity of carrying out operations in the most rugged terrain against a dug-in enemy. The tactical lesson learned before al-Huceima was reflected in a doctrine for operations in a rebellious area, set down by the prince and providing for a three-stage action: (1) encirclement without firing, (2) small-arms fire from positions, (3) full campaign with fire and movement. Usually the ultimatum has been presented at the end of the first stage.

The political history of the dissidence of the supercaid of Beni Mellal, Bashir ben Thami, is more complicated than any previous dissidence. A member of one of the rival urban terrorist groups during the resistance, ben Thami was rewarded with an administrative position in the radical heart of the country, Beni Mellal in the

Tadla plain. There he was a supporter of the activist government
of Premier Ibrahim and was also suspected of complicity in an al-
leged plot against the prince, discovered by the security forces in
February, 1960. When Beni Mellal Police Commissioner Mohammed Akbali appeared to be on the trail of the plotters, they shot
him and took to the hills. The following day, an interministerial
council of the king, the crown prince, the premier, and the defense
and interior ministers decided to call out the army, and two battalions were moved from rescue work in Agadir to Ouawizaght in
the Middle Atlas. Ben Thami had planned his moves and had
stocked up on cigarettes, medicine, and munitions, but not on food.
The band overcame three posts of gendarmes and took refuge in a
section of the Atlas even more rugged and roadless than the Rif.

In cooperation with other security forces, the FAR, under the
command of Colonels Chenna and Moulay Hafid, surrounded the
area and on March 22 delivered a twenty-four–hour ultimatum,
threatening to use all the Royal Army's 105-mm. howitzers, which
had been assembled for the occasion. Some of the partisans surrendered, others were shot or captured on their way to join the
fight, and the army continued to keep the remaining band in a
restricted area while slowly tightening its circumference. Living as
bandits in the territory of the 3,000-member Ait 'Abdi al-Kousser,
the rebels could not be openly attacked until early April, when the
army ordered the Ait 'Abdi and neighboring tribes to regroup
away from their villages. This maneuver brought half of the rebel
band to surrender and allowed the army to move in. Ten days later,
his feet swollen from the snow, ben Thami surrendered to the army.
A week later his lieutenant, Caid ben Hamou, was also captured by
the army, who had been obliged to use their weapons on ben
Hamou's band, aiming for the rebels' legs. But ben Hamou soon
escaped from prison and was not recaptured until May 27, 1960.
Cautious tactics in the entire affair had slowed operations but permitted successful accomplishment of the army's mission without the
damage to the countryside that had marred the earlier larger operations in the Rif. The howitzers were never used.

Two other missions of the FAR deserve mention, although both
were carried out under somewhat curious circumstances. In the defense of the frontier—usually considered a primary role of a national army—the FAR's role was unclear, its enemy was ambiguous,
its numbers were inadequate, and the frontiers themselves were
highly in question. The Moroccan military establishment has never
had any organizational concept of border defense zones nor any

operational plan for the defense of the frontiers, and, the one brief time when the danger of an attack on the country from without appeared serious—in May, 1958—there was more discussion in government councils over resort to civilian brigades than over a deployment plan for the army. During the first two years of independence, the border was completely open from Oujda to Foum al-Hassan.

The FAR reached the eastern border only in mid-1958, when combined and related pressure on the French Army to evacuate its forces and fear of the military rumblings in Algeria brought about the stationing of token forces in Oujda province and the closing of the border during May and June. At the same time, the Army of Liberation announced in one of its rare interviews that it was responsible for Moroccan border control.[24] Of the four armies in the frontier region, it was never clear who was the ally of whom, and on different occasions each army was engaged in combat with one of the other three.

The army forces stationed in Oujda province were scattered along the frontier in company-sized or smaller units, based on former French outposts such as Ahfir (Martimprey du Kiss), Berkan, Oujda, Bergent, Bou Arafa, and Figuig, and in Tafilalt province at Boudenib, Ksar as-Souq, and Rissani. The frontier ran over 350 miles from the Mediterranean to a point south of Boudenib, where it was roughly traced even if only partially recognized, and again that distance to the elbow of the Dra in the south, where the land was unmapped and the border untraced and unrecognized. In a wartime situation with four more-or-less hostile forces, it would have taken an army larger than the entire FAR to seal the border and support the garrisons.[25] In fact, only small garrisons were available. Half a year after the French withdrawal from the east, the two provinces were garrisoned during the Rif operations by one battalion each, plus a troop of cavalry, a company of camel corps, and two artillery units. A year later, two battalions were permanently based at Oujda and one at Ksar as-Souq, with the camel corps unit stationed at Rissani. Even at this time, when greater effectiveness of French operations in Algeria increased the number of Moroccan border incidents, the three infantry battalions were sector-type

[24] The AOL occupied Figuig when the French Army evacuated it in July, 1956, well before the FAR moved in. The AOL here was made up of unintegrated groups from the Rif AOL, loosely coordinated with the Algerian Army of National Liberation and the southern AOL.

[25] In modern defense problems, the United States Army counts one division of 13,700 men, including logistic support, for a ten- to fifteen-mile war front.

units, adapted for garrison duties, not intervention-type battalions with, supposedly, more select personnel and mobile equipment.

The organization of the forces was based on the province, as it was throughout the country. In the abortive plans for a territorial organization drawn up in 1959, there was provision for the creation of a zone with headquarters at Oujda, but it was also to include Nador and Taza as well as the Oujda provinces, with the Tafilalt attached to the zone commanded from Meknes. Thus even in the project under consideration, there was no provision for a border defense zone. The military infrastructure remained based on the Fez-Meknes-Rabat-Casablanca axis both in project and practice; there were no facilities of logistic support near the border to back up frontier defense. Only in the south, where the military situation and Moroccan foreign policy coincided to require an active military policy, was there any alteration of the central logistic structure in order to support effective army operations. Along the rest of the border, when a choice was to be made, the deciding elite always found the exigencies of internal security more pressing than the ambiguities of border defense.

The social mission of the army has been of great and growing importance and of particular significance when viewed in connection with the prince's dominant role in military affairs. The general idea of the army as a leader in the new nation's economic and social expansion was expressed by the king during the formation of the FAR, when he called it "the vanguard of all activity." But it remained for the prince to implement the idea in individual operations and to incorporate it into the concept of the army as an element of royal—and princely—power. For the social mission was a means of associating the military in the work of the nation; it was an attempt to overcome criticism directed against the army from activist and "popular" quarters and to smooth over any bad feelings left by the army after its internal security operations.

The brief campaign in the Tafilalt in early 1957 was followed by energetic action by the Engineer Battalion and other army units to smooth over some of the social problems in the region. In February the French commander of the Engineer Battalion was charged by the king and the prince with preparation of work to combat threatening famine in the Tafilalt through reconstruction of the ancient irrigation system. For two months army units worked to open underground conduits, clear irrigation canals, build irrigation dams, and dig wells and reservoirs in the poverty-stricken valleys of the Ziz and Gheris rivers north and west of Rissani.

The social ramifications of the army's presence in Tarfaya have already been noted. The construction of the base at Tantan brought increased employment to this destitute region of the country; the Engineer Battalion also carried out construction and sanitation work for the benefit of the local settlement and in late 1960 turned to building communications facilities linking Tantan with Goulimim to the north, Plage Blanche to the west, and Tarfaya town to the south.

Following the extensive campaign in the Rif, military units stationed in the mountains helped local inhabitants reconstruct houses and schools damaged in the fighting, provided transportation for social service teams, and cooperated with Public Works in the construction of a road across the Rif linking Aknoul to Talamagait via Tizi Ouzli, for the king's good-will tour; unfortunately the road was never paved, and it was washed away in the next winter's rains. In Tarfaya and the Rif, it was the Engineer Battalion that was most active and successful in fulfilling the army's social mission.

Other instances of social activity were independent of any military action. Immediately following the Tafilalt project, the army aided in work on the Unity Road between Taounat and Katama across the Rif. A massive force of volunteer youth labor had been initiated by the king and supported by the Istiqlal in an effort to harness national enthusiasm and combat unemployment through the construction of a road between the northern and southern zones. To this symbolic unification of the two zones, the army supplied food, camp sites, transportation, communications, and quartermaster services. The action was particularly politic, for it allowed the army to associate with one of the most imaginative and popular projects of the government, highly approved by the social wing of the Istiqlal. Unfortunately, as at Tizi-Ouzli two years later, the road was allowed to erode and was of little use to the FAR in its Rif campaign of 1958–1959.

Less spectacular projects formed the yearly substance of the army's social work. Infantry units supplied and participated in such diverse activities as the establishment of machine tractor stations (Operation Plow), reforestation (Operation Tree), annual anti-locust campaigns in the Sahara, establishment of field kitchens in urban centers during Ramadan, distribution of milk in the *bled,* as well as the use of medical officers among the population, the enrollment of army units in the anti-illiteracy campaign, and the preparation of barracks for use as schools. In many of these activities, the army aided the Ministry of Health, of Public Works, of National

Education, and of Agriculture and the National Community Chest. A final perennial activity of major importance, involving both engineers and infantry, was the rescue work during the winter floods in the Gharb.

The largest army operation in fulfillment of the social mission was the occupation of Agadir after the earthquake of February 29, 1960. Within twenty-four hours of the midnight catastrophe, army units were in the ruined resort town; the king placed operations under the direct authority of the prince, and three days later three battalions of the FAR were in Agadir, with more on their way. Engineer and infantry garrison units made up these forces; the mobile, elite units remained north of the Atlas, vigilant to fulfill their internal security mission if necessary, although when Bachir ben Thami's dissidence two weeks later posed just such a necessity, it was from Agadir that the required troops were drawn. Operations in Agadir encompassed rescue, medical, burial, sanitation, police, construction, supply, and feeding functions. They were directed within the military command by Colonels Driss and Oufqir, the veteran leaders of past security operations. When criticism arose from French and Moroccan quarters against the haste of decisions, the slowness of work, and the lack of coordination both between and among the deciders and the workers, all ministerial activity was brought together in the High Commissariat for the Rebirth of Agadir, also under the direction of the prince. With the notable exception of the engineer units, however, the FAR's effective role in the reconstruction of Agadir was limited to police duties and emergency disaster assistance, showing, if anything, that on a large scale the army was not "the vanguard of all activity."

ORGANIZATION

The FAR had come of age in its police action in Meknes in October, 1956. The ministry of Guedira, appointed for the diplomatic task of negotiating the FAR into existence, was ended by the event that cut diplomatic relations with France and showed the need for an army as an organ of order, not just a diplomatic symbol. The king selected Mohammed Zeghari to clear up the mass of administrative details necessary to the organization of the FAR, a job that was the logical domestic successor to Guedira's preliminary attention to the foreign aspects. More than any other member of the cabinet, the defense minister occupied the post of advisor to the king on administrative affairs within his competence. Organizational and operational matters were again put under the direct supervision of the prince after the Meknes incident, and, when they did not receive his personal attention, they continued to run on their own between crises, under the routine hand of the General Staff along the lines laid out by the prince.

The army was dispersed only gradually throughout the country. Location depended on the number of troops and camps available. Hence, it was not until the end of 1956, when the AOL was schooled and integrated and the former Spanish units were at least nominally amalgamated, that the numbers of the army were even theoretically sufficient for dispersal over an area larger than California. Dispersal, however, also depended on the evacuation of military sites by the French and Spanish troops. When Major ben Larbi brought his army units to the Tafilalt in early 1957, for example, they were the first Moroccan troops in the region, and he did not completely take over the area until the French evacuated their red-mud compound at Ksar as-Souq a year and a half later. Important for the organization of the FAR was the fact that, in taking over the French posts, it inherited a territorial organization of strong points and centrally located troop camps, created for the pacification of Morocco. These army installations were spread in such a way that they ensured the control, not the defense, of the country. The greatest concentration of forces was located along the Casablanca-Rabat-Meknes-Fez-Taza-Oujda line of communications and in the principal centers of the northern zone; the interior of the country was well policed, and the geographic installations inherited from the protectorate went well with the army's mission of internal security.

Less appropriate was the absence of territorial organization to go with the physical distribution of the army. Unlike the French, who had integrated their civil and military organization of the country by placing the military units under chiefs of the regions hierarchically responsible to Rabat, the young nation had neither the personnel, politics, or predilection for this type of centralism. Although the FAR was roughly organized as an oversized division, it lacked any command above the battalion level, largely because of a lack of qualified officers. With battalions in the hands of captains and companies commanded by lieutenants, there were simply not enough officers of quality and rank to go around after the General Staff was filled. The personnel problem was further complicated by the fact that some officers were named to such administrative posts as governor and therefore were too occupied to hold military command. The politics of the new country, however, decreed that such

exceptions did not make the rule, for the simple make-up of the
civilian and military echelons made their cooperation difficult. Between the French-trained, authoritarian, conservative officers and
the partisan, often radical, nationalistic governors there was little
in common.

Furthermore, the desires both of the nation and its leaders
acted against any civilian-military cooperation or organization on a
territorial basis. Separation of powers, a reaction to protectorate
abuses, removed many police powers from the governors and other
administrators, and even the hasty provisions for military government left operational control in the hands of the king and the
prince. The two deciding members of the military hierarchy always
wanted this so, for they saw in their army, properly controlled, the
most effective support of the throne. Improperly commanded, it has
a potential for insurrection. The command and organizational
characteristics of the FAR, then, as decided by the king and the
prince, were dual: (1) an absence of regimental or divisional command but a direct line of authority from the chief of staff to each
battalion commander and (2) an absence of territorial organization
into military districts but simply the posting of battalions and
smaller units throughout the country. From the beginning, the
army, in its organization, emplacement, and command, was suited,
by accident and design, for the task of preserving order when internal security problems outgrew the resources of the Interior
Ministry.

Party Pressures

The problems of administration and organization were
crowded by political problems from the beginning of Zeghari's
ministry. During the governmental reorganization of October, 1956,
Balafrej presented to the king an Istiqlal slate of ministers, including Ahmed Lyazidi, then undersecretary of economy for commerce, in the position of defense minister.[26] The king refused, and
Balafrej had to leave the Defense Ministry in the independent
hands of Zeghari. After failure to capture the ministry, the party
tried another way of winning over the FAR—infiltrating its membership.[27] This approach, too, was a failure because of the army's

[26] Lyazidi was formerly a French Army officer of the same graduating class
as Kettani and was rumored to be the party choice for first defense minister
(*Monde*, March 7, 1956).

[27] Douglas E. Ashford was told that the Builders of Independence, the Istiqlal
youth group which worked on the Unity Road, joined the FAR in large numbers, presumably in 1957 ("Political Change in Morocco" [Ph.D. thesis, Princeton
University, 1960], pp. 893 f.). If this was true, they were quickly brought under
control.

very nature. For former soldiers of the French Army, the tradition of discipline and the apolitical atmosphere worked well against political infiltration; officers were respected and in turn watched their troops for partisan activity. For former troops of the AOL, the Istiqlal was unwelcome and, in fact, too late, for there was an active "AOL Veterans" organization doubled by partisan infiltration by the Popular Movement long before the party appeared in public; even as late as 1960, the party of Khatib and Ahardan was the most active political organization, although still fully loyalist, in the ranks of the FAR. Former troops of the Spanish Army were possibly most susceptible to Istiqlal penetration. Among the officers, it was only the young who had partisan susceptibility, and they were watched by their elders, indoctrinated by the Training Staff officers, insulated from the troops and finally given undesirable assignments if they persisted in their partisan ways. Party pressure became strong enough, however, that in May, 1957, the prince made a number of statements emphasizing that "the Army should keep out of politics," a declaration that could be interpreted by the Istiqlal as both a warning and a reassurance.[28]

Another opportunity was presented to the party in the following months. When the resumption of relations with France called for a new ambassador to Paris, Zeghari, the king's handyman, was chosen for the job, again leaving leadership of the Defense Ministry open for political maneuvering. Lyazidi's claim was pressed and had priority, the alternative being the abolition of the post or its demotion to the level of its tasks. The king assigned an interministerial commission made up of Istiqlal Public Works Minister Mohammed Douiri, Zeghari, and Lyazidi the job of defining the minister's role, particularly in relation to the chief of staff, and of examining the possibility of making the job an undersecretaryship of state attached to the premier or king. In the meantime, on September 13, 1957, Lyazidi received his portfolio, and the position was defined by the man who occupied it.

Lyazidi attacked his job with a "completely new concept and orientation," as *al-Istiqlal* had predicted he would. He sought to solve problems of territorial organization and composition, change the structure of military decision-making, and bring the army under civilian control. He entered his office speaking of "a national army," [29] thereby further alienating the General Staff, who thought the phrase a slur on their past patriotism. It is not likely that he

---

[28] Speeches to the AOL graduation class from Bensliman and at first anniversary of the FAR (*Monde*, May 16 and 19, 1957).

[29] *Al-Istiqlal*, September 21, 1957.

favored the plan current in some Istiqlali quarters, that of replacing the crown prince as chief of staff with General Mezian, head of the northern zone units and wedded into high party circles, but the rumor had to be publicly denounced soon after Lyazidi took over,[30] and attempts at political proselytizing within the FAR continued. Although the interministerial committee reported its inconclusive disagreements about the same time, Lyazidi also prepared a *dahir* on civil control of the military, which was based on greater powers for the defense minister and which was vetoed by the king.

Constant party pressure in the government to broaden channels of military decision finally resulted on November 9, 1957, in the publication of the *dahir* creating a permanent interministerial council, the High Committee of National Defense, composed of seven ministers whose competences properly reflected the FAR's threefold mission. The committee was placed over the minister, attached in an advisory capacity to the king, and convened by him. Not long after its creation, it was consulted on the events of Ifni, although its only contribution appears to have been that of furnishing a public corridor through which the prince had to pass to receive the king's approval for his proposals. As an attempt to confront and unite the duality of military leadership found in the chief of staff and the minister, the committee was ineffective. To the extent that it operated at all, it continued to act as an information agency and not a decision-making body or a national security council.

Lyazidi did, however, use the committee meetings as an occasion to announce military decisions, instead of leaving the opportunity to the prince. After having thus built up his office, he was in a position to request successfully the committee and the cabinet to grant him full powers to handle military operations when the Rif dissidence broke out at the end of 1958. Alienated from the prince and blocked by the General Staff in his programs for reform of the military organization, Lyazidi was an ineffective operations coordinator; when the government resigned in the middle of the dissidence, he was an inviting political scapegoat for heavy criticism over mismanagement of the operation.

One stillborn reform was in the field of territorial organization. Lyazidi realized the serious need for a regional structure, tactical command, and logistic network for the FAR. Here, too, a partisan

---

[30] *Monde,* October 11, 1957; *PM,* October 11, 1957; *Times,* October 12, 1957. Mezian's wife's sister was the wife of an 'Alami, one of the party's financial backers.

element was not lacking; party leader Mehdi ben Barka demanded a "national defense policy based on the executive branch" with forces of order that were "an agent of execution of the Government and of its regional representatives." [31] Lyazidi proposed two systems of organization during his period of office, one under which each province would constitute a military district with army units under the control of the governor and a second in which seven military districts were provided for with the army still under civilian control. Both were blocked by the General Staff, which feared the political consequences of civilian control and which thought the army too small for such a detailed organization.

In this matter the prince agreed with his minister, although he continued to dislike having any of his officers in command of large units. Several times since the creation of the FAR, Moulay Hassan had put forward the idea of territorial organization, only to be sidetracked by the need to shift troops, first to Tafilalt, then to the south, then to the Algerian border. Although the interval between each of these incidents might appear sufficient to install a territorial command, there were many nonmilitary and often even nongovernmental problems that diverted the prince's attention during these intervals. Only when incidents disrupted the plans did the need for a broad and organized distribution of military forces again become apparent. With the danger passed the emergency, and the organization was never accomplished. The army lacked the ability to reform while operating; its command lacked the initiative to reform while not operating. Despite Lyazidi's attempts, when the Berbers took to the hills in the end of 1958, the army was still directly responsible, unit by unit, to headquarters in Rabat, with no military district, no subordinate command, and no ability to converge rapidly on the trouble spot.

The draft was another of Lyazidi's reforms that met defeat. More than in the case of territorial organization, the impetus was political. Despite an Istiqlali as minister, attempts at politicizing the officer corps were effectively ended by a *dahir* forbidding affiliation with any political movement.[32] Party leaders, particularly from the restive left wing, therefore, sought new ways of exerting party influence not over, but within, the army. The March, 1956, decision to establish a professional rather than a conscripted army

---

[31] *Al-Istiqlal,* May 18, 1958.

[32] *Dahir* No. 1-58-011 of May 27, 1958. *Al-Istiqlal,* August 16, 1958, admitted that the FAR was one institution of government over which the party had no control.

had been made by military leaders without consulting the Istiqlal. As products both of the *ancien régime* and the French colonial army, Moroccan soldiers and officers were open to criticism for their nonnational origins. By 1958 Istiqlal activists, allied with the resistance who regarded the AOL as the national army and the FAR as a usurper, now sought ways to create a national army, and ben Barka, the Istiqlal left's most articulate spokesman, welcomed the appointment of Lyazidi as the chance for "an essentially national policy." [33] Part of this policy would include a purge of the pro-French officer corps and a dismissal of the French military advisors and officers on loan, and part would involve civilian control over the military. But a major segment drew its inspiration from another resistance movement, the French Resistance of World War II, which thought of a nation in arms, a popular militia, a national army which would give body to a skeletal professional group of military administrators. The idea was scarcely radical, even in the mind of such outspoken—and later imprisoned—proponents as left-wing editor 'Abderrahman Yusufi and was akin to the existing system in Switzerland or earlier ideas in the United States. The key to this concept was a selective service system.

Lyazidi's idea arose against this background, although he did not fully identify himself with his left-wing party colleagues. Far from reducing the army to a skeleton, he sought to achieve a national army through the association of a national service with the existing military organization. The role of this parallel national service would correspond to the triple mission of the army by increasing or releasing available troops for border defense and internal security and by "participating in the economic and social life of the nation." It would also release into civilian life both a ready reserve for emergency recall and, even more important, a chosen group of youths who had been given rudimentary on-the-job training in a profession. The Lyazidi plan provided, in the first stage, for a selective group of volunteers to be called up by contingents until an annual level of about 10,000 was attained. Neither budget nor training facilities would permit service for all eligible youths nor even accommodation of all anticipated volunteers. Training was to include four months of military and two months of specialized instruction, after which the volunteer would be given a mobilization billet and a reserve status and could be recalled for military service, special tasks, or additional training. The second stage, to

[33] *Ibid.*, September 21 and October 5, 1957.

follow when improved facilities were available, would lead to the formation of labor battalions, similar to the Israeli Nahal, with partial military training and also public service to aid in the army's social mission. Both stages involved service parallel to, not integrated into, the FAR.

Already benefiting from the political pressure from the left, Lyazidi also gained the support of the prince. But it was not enough. The divided and beleaguered government of Balafrej, attacked from without and fighting within, never was able to pay much attention to the proposed draft. In May, 1958, when Algeria rocked with the revolutionary transition from the Fourth to the Fifth Republic and a sympathetic reaction from the French forces in Morocco was feared, the High Committee of National Defense authorized a draft of 15,000 volunteer workers from the Unity Road to be installed in Oujda, Tafilalt, and Ouarzazat provinces. Unarmed, the volunteers were to be assigned ordinary police and patrol duties, to free armed forces for military action.[34] But the crisis slowly died down before the government was able to effect the measures necessary to implement this call. The Lyazidi plan died the same death. Rather than being openly blocked at some stage of the legislative process, it simply did not have the momentum to overcome government inertia and supersede more pressing legislation. When the Riffi Berbers added the last straw to Rabat's burdens, there was no national service to aid the FAR in its task or to replace army units called to the north. It was only by ironic coincidence that the army was carrying out an operation that was both the most genuine reflection to date of its national character and, like the Tafilalt operation, a defense of partisan as well as national interests.

The atmosphere of internecine rivalry that sapped the government's effectiveness, accounted for its fall, and contributed to the neglect of the Lyazidi plan was also evident in an incident involving the activists' use of direct pressure when their criticisms were ignored. As Lyazidi, of the Istiqlal old guard, translated activist demands for a small professional army plus a national military service into a plan for a national service corps plus an army of unchanged dimensions, Economics Minister 'Abderrahim Bou'abid, a leader of the activists, attacked. He criticized the FAR for taking money necessary for economic projects, called it a "parade army,"

[34] Three battalions of the FAR were also temporarily sent to the border (*ibid.*, May 25, 1958).

and in the latter half of 1958 wiped out four battalions by cutting the defense budget.[35] Lyazidi resigned, and only the king's refusal kept him at his post and postponed a governmental crisis. Thus, when ten battalions were needed to meet the Rif dissidence, the FAR was at its lowest size, reduced by the government it was called out to defend.

The period of political control was a debilitating experiment for the Royal Moroccan Army despite the clearsightedness and energy of the defense minister. The prince was to a large extent eclipsed in the making of significant decisions on Army organization, but partisan factionalism and military opposition kept his political replacement from enacting any effective reform. Lyazidi's ministry was climaxed by a national disaster, which effectively showed up all the unremedied weak points of the army organization, including the additional weak points created during the past year. The political atmosphere had defeated a political attempt at military decision-making.

Party Reforms

The army was returned to the prince's control by the nomination of the king's cabinet director as defense minister. Mohammed Awad took an active part in the work of his ministry, but military matters returned to the hands of the prince, beginning immediately with complete control over the Rif operations. The Rif, which had disrupted Lyazidi's projects, brought home many sharp lessons to the prince. The most immediate reaction was the recall of 3,000 of the 4,000 troops dismissed by Bou'abid's budget cuts, but the economics minister, who retained his post, exacted a heavy price. On February 5, 1959, Lyazidi's draft plan received the Council of Ministers' approval in principle. Once the formal vote was taken, Bou'abid blocked the plan in its details, which Awad had been instructed to work out, and for a year the draft made no progress. In his budget message in mid-1959, the economics minister announced that the cost of a draft, as conceived, was too great for the state to bear. Rarely has one man so dared to block the combined wishes of the Moroccan king and cabinet.

One positive lesson of the Rif which translated itself into ac-

[35] A good summary of the attitude was given by Bou'abid in the 1958 National Consultative Assembly budget debates: "We are thus forced to make a choice. . . . Everything cannot be done at once: the constitution of an army and police forces whose number still grow, the massive and accelerated enrollment of youth in school, and the application of a policy of economic development. We must choose . . . productive activities" (al-Istiqlal, April 6, 1958). At this time, fear of a repressive police was not yet a factor.

tion concerned army units in the former Spanish zone. After negotiations by General Mezian and the prince in mid-1956, 10,000 Moroccan auxiliary forces of the Spanish Army were transferred to Morocco and officially received into the FAR. There were seven infantry battalions, two cavalry battalions, and a single artillery battalion made up of an anti-tank and an anti-aircraft company. The troops were put under the control of General Mezian, who was given the title of commander-in-chief of Royal Armed Forces in the northern zone. All command passed through his headquarters, including that of former Spanish battalions operating in the southern zone, and he alone reported to headquarters in Rabat.

The amalgamation of former Spanish with former French units began in the year of independence in principle, but by the time of the Rif, only two infantry battalions were partly reorganized on the Franco-Moroccan pattern. The way of Spanish military life brought other problems: the officers were sedentary, used to family life, and, because of low pay, usually had a civilian job to make ends meet; they also were less well educated, their troops less well trained, and had no battle experience in comparison with the units of the southern zone. The results became clear in the Rif, when command and troops showed themselves inadequate to meet the challenge. When the Rif operations were ended, the former Spanish battalions were spread throughout the southern zone by order of the prince, and all military positions in the north were occupied by former French infantry battalions, other specialized services, or by the newly recalled battalions. General Mezian was relieved of his command and brought to Rabat to join General Kettani in the post of military advisor, with the title of inspector general of the FAR.

The prince instructed his minister to complete the job of amalgamation and do away with the distinction between former French and former Spanish units. Details of the operation, which was quickly completed by mid-1959, were worked out by Awad. He no longer reorganized the former Spanish units, but rather mixed their troops on the section level with former French soldiers, roughly in a ratio of one to two, to form new battalions. The school at Bensliman through which the AOL had passed in 1956–1957 was used to retrain and educate units when necessary. A military commission presided over by the prince oversaw the operation; the orders were his but the details came from the minister.

Another major effect of the Rif was to bring up again the question of territorial organization or a reasonable substitute. The dissidence had shown that either an army of the magnitude of the protectorates' was necessary in order to operate on a strong-point organization or that another arrangement was needed, based on fixed territorial units supplemented by mobile reserves. The French protectorate had maintained a territorial organization with almost six times as many troops as independent Morocco had available, and there was no question of increasing the size of the FAR. The minister humbly excused himself for recalling the three additional battalions when he presented his budget of 1959, and the bad economic year imposed even tighter restrictions on Bou'abid than he had imposed the year before on the army. The Spanish, on the other hand, had adopted the other alternative, mobile as well as garrison units. A consideration besides the budget now made the prince less attached to a pure territorial organization: the northern zone had been organized as a territorial unit with an intermediate command and had failed badly in action. The prince had been considering a static and mobile division of forces for a number of years, the idea being rather classic in military organization; plans were made in early 1959 and were finally written into the budget in March.

> The missions of the Army demand the distribution of troops throughout the entire territory, with a powerful, mobile, maneuverable mass being kept in reserve, to intervene at the desired points. In terms of organization, this should mean the constitution of territorial forces made up of infantry units, permanently located, lightly armed, under the authority of a decentralized command, and also of forces of intervention of all types, with their own means of transportation and communication, with modern arms, maintained at the disposal of a command on the national level. The former would have the job of training reserves and could be partially composed of draftees, while the latter, which should at all times be ready for action and which require more specialists, would be entirely manned by career soldiers.[36]

Following the ratio conceived by the prince, seven units were designated intervention-type battalions and were stationed in Tetuan, Rabat, Meknes, Fez, Ouezzan, Casablanca, and Hajeb, in mobile readiness for a Rif-like emergency. In the beginning their difference from the other fourteen battalions was difficult to see; the table of organization and equipment remained essentially the same, an almost identical reproduction of a French battalion with twenty-five officers and almost 1,000 men. But when the FAR was able to afford

[36] Introductory Note to the Defense Budget (*PM*, April 2, 1958).

new military equipment, it was first given to the mobile battalions, who also gained something of an elitist reputation. In reality, however, the actual strength and even organization did not always attain the projected figures.

The second part of the reform, which envisaged tying the idea of territorial organization to the distribution of static sector-type battalions ran up against the same obstacles as the old concept of territorial organization. The prince foresaw all security forces—army, gendarmery, Auxiliary Forces, police—united under one regional command, but there was no decision on who the commander should be. The General Staff favored the plan only under conditions of military, not civilian, control; the government favored the reverse. Even the prince remained wary of an intermediate command; the army revolt which toppled the throne in Iraq the previous year left an indelible mark on the Moroccan royal family, and the prince is said to have remarked on one occasion, "Here there will be no generals' and colonels' revolt as there was in Iraq, because I do not give command [of troops] to my generals and colonels." Even by 1959, there were not enough senior officers to take the command of military districts. As can be seen in the military operations, the able officers—Oufqir, ben Larbi, Driss, Medboh—were repeatedly used for the most diverse tasks; beyond these men and the General Staff, there were no other commanders available.

Despite these differences and difficulties, plans for a territorial organization seemed to move slowly forward in 1959. An early plan compressed Lyazidi's seven zones into five districts coincident with the army's communication zones: a northern district centered on Tetuan, an eastern district centered on Oujda, a southern district centered on Marrakesh, a central district centered on Meknes, and a coastal district including Kenitra, Rabat, Casablanca, and Bensliman. By January, 1960, Awad had drawn up a new proposal which simply grouped the administrative provinces into six military regions—Rabat included the provinces of Chawia and Beni Mellal, Tetuan included the provinces of Tangier and al-Huceima, Meknes was combined with Fez and the Tafilalt, Oujda was grouped with Nador and Taza, Marrakesh was combined with Ouarzazat, and Agadir was grouped with Tarfaya. In many areas, this new grouping would have resulted simply in the restoration of the regional system of the protectorate. With the designation of mobile battalions, the garrison battalions were left in position throughout the country, based on Tantan, Tizgui Remz, Tiznit, and Inezgan in the south; Marrakesh in its district; Kasba Tadla in the Rabat district; Midelt and Ksar as-Souq in the Meknes district; Taza, Nador, and Oujda in the east; and al-Huceima, Targuist and Xauen in the north. The decision to adopt these districts had been made by the prince when, in the beginning of March, 1960, the FAR was called to Agadir and then in July to the Congo. Any hope for a territorial organization was again postponed. It was only in October, 1961, after the prince had ascended the throne, that a territorial organization was put into effect. Morocco was divided into six military regions—Rabat, Fez, Meknes, Marrakesh, Oujda, and Agadir. The result was a complete return to the 1948 divisions of the protectorate with two exceptions—the partition of the former Spanish zones among Oujda, Fez, and Rabat regions in the north and Agadir in the south, and the grouping of Casablanca with Rabat in order to control the restive urban industrial belt.

A third item in the prince's military reorganization was inspired by the political situation of 1959 rather than by the Rif. The sharpening partisan conflict, heightened instead of assuaged by the split of the Istiqlal in January, 1959, called for security forces of reliable effectiveness. Of more direct danger to the prince than intraparty rifts was the new boldness with which the activists attacked the royal institutions, especially the army and the prince himself. The first open attack was voted—but dared not be immediately published—by the third annual congress of the National Union of Moroccan Students (UNEM), a radical-dominated organization.[37] Meeting in Tetuan, it echoed Bou'abid's criticism of the "parade army" but also called for civilian control, purge of "anti-national and anti-popular elements," reduction of the military budget, removal of officers with foreign ranks,[38] and the institution of a universal military service "to allow military training of the people." The same criticisms were made with such great vehemence at the next convention that the moderate members of the UNEM denounced the attack and protested their loyalty to the king; the daily organ of the activist National Union of Popular Forces (UNFP), *at-Tahrir,* which printed the criticisms, was confiscated several

[37] The motion was finally published in *al-Istiqlal,* August 12 and 23, 1958. For denials and corrections, see *Vigie,* August 6, 1958. A UNEM delegation visited the king and proclaimed its loyalty to him, although through the charges and countercharges it was not clear whether it represented the minority or whether the motion had been passed against the majority wishes (*Monde,* August 10, 1958). Even the Second UNEM Congress was not complimentary to the FAR (*al-Istiqlal,* October 5, 1957).

[38] General Kettani, for example, continued to hold rank in the French Army.

times, and its editors were finally jailed.[39] These attacks aroused deep feeling among the officers of the FAR. Captain Medboh resigned from his political post of telecommunications minister, where he had been placed by the king during the Rif dissidence to give the Riffi Berbers a seat in the government, and asked the king to put him back into uniform so that he could show his loyalty to the FAR and the throne.[40] Officers on training missions in France returned to Morocco to rally to the FAR under attack. A delegation of officers led by the prince expressed their indignation against the attacks in a special visit of loyalty to the king. Yet the criticisms continued, slightly subdued, in *al-Tali'a* and *l'Avant-Garde,* the Arabic and French weeklies of the UMT. As *at-Tahrir*'s jailed editor 'Abderrahman Yusufi explained, the criticisms were made so virulently because this was the only means of affecting decision-making; the purpose of the attacks was to make the king and the prince aware that there was, in fact, a problem.

The attacks had the opposite effect. For some time the prince had been considering the idea of a small, mobile, elite shock force, under his orders and stationed near areas of potential activist agitation. There were to be five units, about the size of a company and composed of the FAR's best soldiers. The prince announced his idea to his staff, who immediately opposed it for lack of material and officers. It also met opposition because of its mission; the officers did not enjoy their reputation as agents of repression, successors to the Senegalese who had kept order for the French. "They wanted to make war, not make better policemen."

The insistence of the prince prevailed, however, with urgency added by the purely nominal state of the distinction between the intervention-type and sector-type battalions. The first Light Security Group (GLS) was formed in time for the 1959 Feast of the Throne. Filled with officers and men hand-picked by the prince and the General Staff on the recommendation of unit commanders, it was an oversized but heavily armed company, with nine officers and 250 men organized into a weapons platoon and three rifle platoons.

[39] *At-Tahrir,* July 31, 1959; *PM,* September 28, 1959. On December 2, 1959, the defense and education ministers filed a libel suit against *at-Tahrir;* issues for December 4-5 and 14-15 were confiscated; the paper was seized on December 16, and editors Basri and Yusufi were arrested on the same day, to be pardoned by the king the following 'Id al-Kebir.

[40] Minister of Education 'Abdelkrim Benjelloun, of Justice Mohammed Bahnini, of Defense Mohammed Awad, of Health Yussef ben 'Abbas, of the Interior Driss Mhammedi, and of Public Works 'Abderrahman ben 'Abdelalli resigned as well, but the king refused their resignations.

These groups were later enlarged to company-sized detachments. Individual detachments were commanded by first lieutenants, with over-all command by Captain Boulhimez under the prince, and over-all headquarters at Rabat. It was principally Casablanca and Rabat, the two centers of industry and government in Morocco, that were the areas of operation of the GLS. The new units were not ordered to Agadir, but at least two of them were among the forces sent by Morocco to the Congo, even though the chances of their being needed in Morocco were by no means small.

The fourth item of military reform fell by the wayside. It is likely that the prince was aware that the FAR had no specific logistic service, although it is certain that his General Staff was unaware of the inadequacy of the FAR's infrastructure. There is no supply corps, no logistic service outside of the General Staff (G-4), no battalion logistic section, and no logistic concept adequate to deal with the problems raised by the size of the army, the extent of its territory, the diversity of units and terrain, and the demands of its operations and missions. A transportation group at Ain al-Harrouda (Casablanca), a quartermaster company at Rabat and a depot at Salé, ordinance facilities concentrated at Casablanca and partially under civilian and French management, a medical company at Casablanca under French command, and the Engineer Battalion under French command at Kenitra comprised the diverse but concentrated logistic units. Field commanders handled logistic matters for their own units. The only area which had any logistic organization was the south, where the presence of an ordinance maintenance facility at Goulimim and a logistic base at Tantan showed that the profits of the Tarfaya expedition were honored at least in their own region. A better developed infrastructure would go hand in hand with territorial reorganization; however, neither the thinking of the prince nor, apparently, the training of his advisors had led the decision-making elite to consider the need for a nationwide logistic system.

A final consequence of the Rif operations was to revive the conscription issue. The impetus was probably felt most strongly in the government through the activists' pressure on Premier Ibrahim, one of their sympathizers. Universal service was not only part of their concept of a national army, but also represented the only broad access to army ranks for their adherents. They were joined in their desire for a draft by the old-guard Istiqlal of 'Allal al-Fassi, whose first program resolution after the party split included a call for obligatory military service. The prince agreed with these gen-

eral ideas, and Awad returned to Lyazidi's dossier to restudy the
national service. It was not until a year after the Lyazidi plan had
been first presented for cabinet approval by Awad and sidetracked
by Bou'abid that a modified version was ready for cabinet discussion. An eight-month voluntary service was to be instituted, integrated into existing units of the FAR. In order to avoid its being
simply a refuge for the unemployed, a vague and complicated arrangement for accepting a fixed percentage from various socioeconomic classes was considered, although such details as filling
short categories or actually determining the number from each
class were not decided and proved an obstacle to cabinet approval.
A further obstacle lay in the size of the permanent core; the activists spoke in numbers as low as 1,000 whereas pro-army leaders
asked for 15,000 to 20,000. Although plans were announced for a
10,000-man draft to be in effect by the summer of 1960, with future
annual totals to be set by the defense minister after consulting with
the premier, it was never made publicly clear whether the recruits
would be draftees or volunteers.

Toward mid-1960 occurred a series of events which placed
army organization—and with it, the draft—into a new context. As
far back as December, when the editors of *at-Tahrir* were jailed for
criticizing the throne, the army was alerted for a showdown with
the activists, but it never came. On February 15, an extreme activist
"plot" to assassinate the prince, Security Director Mohammed Laghzaoui, and Istiqlal leader al-Fassi was discovered; another aim of
the group was, according to an Istiqlal party analysis, to "set newly
promoted officers against older officers of the General Staff by making [the former] believe that it would be possible for them to be at
the head of the national Army if they succeeded in eliminating
their chiefs." [41] The details and even the existence of the plot were
somewhat conjectural, although the subsequent wave of arrests
was not; it was more significant, however, that the officers' loyalty
remained intact, the plot was handled exclusively by the police,
and, except for the minor operation in Beni Mellal, no army units
were needed to keep order. A similar situation occurred during the
elections on May 29, when all army units were alerted for possible
disorders but none was needed. To some extent, the mere presence of
the army had become enough to keep down disorder, but it was
also evident that the activists were more ready to bark than to bite.

During these events, the government's position also changed.
Ibrahim told newspapermen, in a singular reversal of traditional

[41] *Al-Ayam,* February 21, 1960.

roles, "The Government has found its most precious support in the personality of the King, the FAR and the Auxiliary Forces" after the termination of the Rif dissidence.[42] In May, 1960, however, Ibrahim was replaced by the king as premier and by the prince as actual head of government. No longer was the activist faction represented in the often embarrassing position of authority, nor was there a defense minister to challenge the position of the prince at the head of the armed forces, for the Defense Ministry was attached to the office of the vice-premier. In this situation, the official estimate of the relation of the throne, the army, and the government was much different. Said the prince:

> The mission for which the forces of order have been created is in the last analysis subsidiary. . . . It is not the soldiers of the FAR . . . who assure the maintenance of order, but a single man: His Majesty Mohammed V.[43]

At another time, he explained, "I will not govern sword in hand. But I will govern with my sword at my side, so that it may be known that we are not weak. After all, Khrushchev does not use his sickle for cutting." [44] In this context the role of the army demanded some rethinking. Like the operations in the Rif, the rescue operation at Agadir was the first of its type to be carried out above the company level. The size of the operation alone encouraged the prince to air his concepts of the army as a social force, and the shortcomings at Agadir plus the new relation between the army and the government suggested another series of reforms in military organization, just as the operations in the Rif had done. The prince announced that in the army's role in Tarfaya and Agadir "the name 'Army of the People' finds justification," and he spoke of the army's purpose as "civil and social above all," emphasizing the possibilities the FAR offered for professional training and citing the economic activity stimulated by its demands on the nation's production.[45] In telling of the aims of his government, he announced that the first draftees resulting from a new conscription *dahir* would be ready to parade on the Feast of the Throne in the fall of 1960.

A new look was directed at the military establishment, with an eye to the complete reorganization and integration of the FAR, the gendarmery, the Auxiliary Forces, and the police into a coordinated

[42] *PM*, March 25, 1959.
[43] *Ibid.*, July 9, 1960.
[44] *Ibid.*, June 10, 1960.
[45] *Ibid.*, May 15 and July 2 and 9, 1960.

unit reflecting the new role of the security forces. An interministerial committee composed of the prince, the ministers of interior, finance, civil service, and telecommunications, and a representative from the Defense Ministry, was established to study the problem. As in the relation between the national service and the professional army, the social role of the FAR was to enhance, not replace, its security mission. The army was to be a source of technical and professional competence, "susceptible of assisting and complementing civil administration in case of emergency." Army officers would be appointed to more administrative posts, "according to the needs and the cadres which we have at our disposal"; [46] in fact Colonels Oufqir and ben Larbi and Major Medboh were appointed director of national security and governors of Oujda and Casablanca. In this over-all re-evaluation, the issue of national conscription was lost, and no draftee or volunteer trainee marched with the army in November.

The broad re-evaluation did not go far, however. Within the week after the prince had outlined his thoughts and the committee was formed, the United Nations appealed for security troops to go to the Congo. Between July 16 and 19, in the fastest response ever registered by the FAR, a complete battalion was flown to the United Nations command. Between July, 1960, and withdrawal for political reasons in January, 1961, 3,700 of the best Moroccan troops, including light security groups, most of the General Staff, and such specialist units as signal and parachute companies, were stationed in the Congo under Colonel Driss. General Kettani was named deputy commander-in-chief of the United Nations Forces and was charged with organizing and training the Congolese Army. The Congo gave the FAR helpful training in security operations and in implementing its social mission. The absence of the best troops and officers, however, meant the end of attempts to reorganize the army until its return from the Congo.

CONCLUSIONS

The patterns of military decision-making involve the interaction of three distinctive elements: (1) a firmly established royal authority intent on preserving its position in the military domain, (2) a military group that was the country's most direct heritage

---

[46] *Ibid.*, July 8, 1960. Guedira had earlier favored a high commissariat of the FAR and of National Defense, attached to the king, a solution close to that adopted between May, 1960, and June, 1961, when Ahardan was named defense minister; see *La Deuxième crise ministérielle* (Rabat: n.d. [1958]), p. 22.

from its colonial past, and (3) a series of external events involving peripheral elements which posed problems and provided a mobile situation in the context of which the deciding elite was obliged to manipulate its military forces. Several of these patterns of action are significant.

1. The major decision-maker in military matters was the crown prince, whose role consisted of laying out the major lines of action which others implemented. The prince rarely concerned himself with particulars, and, when he did, it was with a characteristic impetuousness that was occasionally regrettable. The defense minister in administrative matters and the General Staff in routine military details followed the orders of the prince. These civilian and military agencies provided for the day-to-day continuity of military life, but their actions were strictly routine and did little to prepare for foreseeable emergencies or to show initiative. The sporadic nature of the prince's interest meant that even long-range problems touching the establishment of an effective army were to be treated with bursts of energy and periods of inattention. The king's role in these matters was one of residual control, with a few rare but imperative directives which reinforced the prince's role and goaded him to goad others into action.

2. The goal of the prince, as he often proclaimed, was to make the FAR an element of stability in the nation. Translated into the context of politics and power in the nation, this implied the maintenance of the army as an element of order and loyalty behind the throne, accomplished by keeping it responsive to the personal orders of the prince. To the extent that the prince and the king represented the same element—which they did at least in military matters before 1961 and in physical being after 1961—this goal benefited both the system and institutions of government and the two leading personalities. This policy may appear to suggest, however, that the prince molded the army as an element of personal support against the king during the king's life or in the favor of the prince after his father's death. The former interpretation would be applicable only in the case of a policy difference in which the army could have been used or invoked to support the prince against the king; in fact, such an event never took place despite the two men's differences in approach and personality, but in so using the FAR the prince would have been attempting to divorce army loyalty to the king from army obedience to orders from its chief of staff. This was contrary both to the oath of the army and to its prevailing attitudes. Although the prince was generally popular with the army, it fol-

lowed him because those were the king's orders. The second interpretation is partially probable, although in view of the prince's actions and the king's untimely death, it appears incontrovertible
that the prince conceived of the FAR as a supporter of the system—
of the king and of himself—as much as a future guarantee to his
claim to the throne. When the prince became the king, the army
followed him because it knew him, because he was the king, and
because his views of government echoed the army's own nonpartisan but very political thinking.

3. The nature of decision-making had a peculiar relation to
the events which made up its context. Although choices were consciously made, the necessity of a choice was frequently forced by an
event, choices—or lessons—were suggested by events, or choices
were blocked by subsequent—often unrelated—events. This threefold impact of external events on the decision-making process seriously narrowed the freedom of choice in almost all cases and was
aided by the system of government itself. The forcing of a decision-
maker's hand reinforced the sporadic nature of the prince's and
king's attention and the constant nature of subordinate units' inattention. The habit of ignoring pressing problems made the problems and the lessons all the more acute when they reappeared. Most
significantly, the limited number of competent government personnel who could give their attention to a particular problem in a new
state meant that external events could be potent decision-makers
merely by blocking unimplemented decisions. In a positive sense,
things appeared just to happen, as an actor follows a natural course
or seizes whatever means are at hand. The pattern of alternating
attention among pressing problems may have been a heritage from
the French system of government under the Fourth Republic, but
it was more likely a native pattern common to other spheres of
governmental activity. The prince and the Council of Ministers
were too often distracted, and there were so few competent senior
officers that decisions had to wait. The military goal of the prince
and his penchant for personal favoritism also limited the number
of officers, for it encouraged inaction among the military; overly
dynamic officers might invite suspicion.

4. The opposition was ineffective in inserting itself into the
decision-making process. Political forces first tried to infiltrate the
army and failed. They then tried to win or take over the officer
leadership and failed. The deepest penetration into military matters occurred when the Defense Ministry fell to a political leader,
but he was prevented from effective control by military foot-drag-

ging and by the highly politicized atmosphere in which he operated and to which he finally fell victim. Political control was also
attempted through the High Committee of National Defense,
through the Council of Ministers, and through the budgetary control of the Economics Ministry; even during 1959 under the activist-
dominated government, none of these agencies was effective in
imposing its decisions on the army. Public criticism of army organization and management in the activist press and in the National
Consultative Assembly was as influential as any other activity.
These attacks brought about little except the occasional imprison-
ment of their authors, but they did make the deciding elite conscious of another point of view and usually hardened their already-
made decisions. Within the officer corps, there was unshakable
loyalty to the king. There was complete discipline under the prince,
although he was a lesser object of reverence and admiration than
was his father. Among the older elite of the corps, apolitical obedience was a part of the military code; the danger to the prince of his
"colonels and generals" was not the same as it was in Iraq. The
young officers, who formed the mass of the officer corps, were slightly
more susceptible to political infiltration, although their family
backgrounds and training were not usually conducive to radicalism.
Promising young officers were taken up and accepted by the older
elite. The overwhelming majority of the lieutenants who entered
the FAR after 1956 were serious if youthful and loyal to the system
of military decision-making.

FOUR

The agrarian revolution required two centuries in Western Europe; it cost eight million deaths in the Soviet Union. We do not want to wait so long nor act so brutally.

—Mehdi ben Barka

ECONOMIC PROBLEM
Agrarian Reform

Every year in the Speech from the Throne, the king has declared that "the farmer remains an object of constant concern for us." Although the subsequent details in the speeches are usually few, agriculture has been one of the areas in which the king played an active role in determining, blocking, and making policy. In so doing, he worked with other political forces in the country. His influence was one of moderation, but the other forces—although themselves restrained—forced his majesty to act. One side of the relation of forces is particularly evident in the early demands for agrarian reform and the king's land distribution in 1956 and 1959.

THE KING'S DISTRIBUTIONS

Agrarian reform was a natural corollary of the two years of urban resistance and rural terrorism that brought independence; taking land was mild compared to taking lives or the legal sovereignty of the country. Since the most conspicuous of the large landowners were either *colons* or "feudals" who had enriched themselves during the protectorate, it was even patriotic to expect a settling of accounts after independence.[1] The naïve euphoria which

[1] Six thousand Europeans owned a little less than 2.5 per cent of Morocco's land, the majority of which was acquired between 1912 and 1932. An estimated 7,500 Moroccans own 4 per cent of the land; these are the large landowners,

119

accompanies the birth of so many new countries and which was expressed in Morocco by servants' and tenants' threats to *colons* and city-dwellers that tomorrow all "this" would be theirs was merely a popular expression of the spirit behind agrarian reform. This feeling was expressed inchoately and individually in the *bled,* where, of course, it was most relevant. In the cities, it found more organized and even doctrinaire formulation among the growing proletariat. Even the choice of words is instructive. The National Council of the Resistance called for a "reform of the agricultural system," including "distribution of the lands of the feudals and the big landowners to the *fellahin* [farmers], the disinherited, and the needy and the restitution of stolen lands" and "the rationalization of tribal and public lands under an obligatory cooperative regime" as well as development and mechanization. The National Council of the Moroccan Labor Union (UMT) called for "an agrarian reform, and the exploitation of tribal, public, feudals' and traitors' land through cooperatives." [2]

The National Council of the Istiqlal party also called for agrarian reform, although it clearly defined the term to mean only seizure and distribution of collaborators' lands. In fact, neither in the crash program of 'Abderrahim Bou'abid nor in the Agricultural Subcommission's report, both given before the Extraordinary Party Congress in December, 1955, was there any mention of agrarian reform. The reason lay in the composition of the party. In addition to the urban elements of the resistance and the UMT, there were many large landowners among the leadership of the party; to them the concept of agrarian reform was an anathema. Before independence agrarian reform programs were proposed and discussed within party circles, and in early 1956 the government made studies of nationwide changes in ownership and extent of farm property.[3] The item of paramount importance to Istiqlal leadership and mem-

---

although the term "feudals" is more opprobrious than exact and in current usage refers to those who acquired land by questionable methods during the protectorate. See I. William Zartman, "Farming and Land Ownership in Morocco," *Land Economics,* XXXIX, No. 2 (1963), 187–198.

[2] *Al-Istiqlal,* August 24, 1956. The Communist party also asked for expropriation and limitation of holdings during 1956. Pressure for confiscation and land reform was also strong from the PDI during 1956 and 1957.

[3] One of the most comprehensive of these was "rediscovered" in *al-Istiqlal,* September 14, 1957. It was made in early 1956 by a French technical advisor in the government and called for reapportionment to stem the rural exodus, regroupment of apportioned property (with no specified regime of ownership), and establishment of a controlled relationship between the rural population and production.

bership alike, however, was party unity, and the best the party leaders could do was to agree on reforms limited to groups connected with the protectorate. But another characteristic of the times was a conciliatory attitude toward France. During the first half year of independence, *al-Istiqlal* was full of protestations of amity, the king spoke well of the former protector, and Franco-Moroccan official relations were probably better between March and October (when they were broken off) than ever after. Public virulence against the *colons* was, therefore, discouraged pending further developments, and agrarian reform was further subordinated.

The Istiqlal, however, had also asked for distribution of a small category of lands that were eminently suitable for immediate action and unhampered by political conflicts because they were seasonally under water. Under the Napoleonic Code, variable marshes (*merja*) belong to the state. Drainage of some of those lands located in the Gharb had long been discussed; some of the land was colonized, and other plots were cultivated by bordering tribes despite the recurrent danger of disastrous floods. The area in question was small compared to the possible scope of full agrarian reform, but, when it had been presented by the minister of agriculture, it caught the interest of the king because it symbolized the hopes for land reform and headed off presssure for a more radical program. The king appointed an interministerial commission to investigate the availability of land appropriate for distribution, and the Council of Ministers approved a *dahir* setting forth the principles of distribution.[4] At the mouth of the Sebou River, marshland which already had been prepared for drainage by the construction of a canal during the protectorate was selected by the minister of agriculture, a large landowner in the area. The ministry divided it into tracts that provided an acceptable income with the possibility of savings and modernization. In September, 1956, in time for the preparation of the winter wheat crop, the king distributed 125 plots to the members of the Mnasra tribe living on the land. The *fellahin* were to rent for nine years, with an option to buy after three. They were given a book of obligations imposing conditions of tenure, including full and immediate exploitation. The king also used the occasion to define his concept of agrarian reform, which consisted of a "better distribution of land" and a "modernization of techniques of exploitation" in order to "accelerate yield and production." A week later, the same process was repeated in the Triffa

[4] *Dahir* No. 1-56-127 of August 27, 1956. Conditions of the distribution are given in the interministerial order of September 13, 1956.

plain.[5] Here some effort was made to approximate the nationalist exigencies of redistribution, for, although no land was confiscated, the beneficiaries were chosen from the Beni Snassen living in Oujda who had suffered during the resistance as members of the Army of Liberation.

The move was a political success, for the wave of public demands for agrarian reform fell into the general channels outlined by the king and was washed of its radicalism. Moderation was further ensured by the succession to the ministry of Hajj 'Omar ben 'Abdeljalil, a Fassi landowner, in the second government and by the demotion of the ministry to an undersecretariat of state, occupied by the young, moderate Istiqlali 'Abdelhafid Kadiri, in the third government. Economically, the program was often a failure. Par-

TABLE 2

LAND DISTRIBUTIONS IN 1956–1957

Date		Location	Land	Acres	Lots	Size	Regime
September	1956	Gharb	public (merja)	5,500	125	35–50 acres	private
September	1956	Triffa	public	2,150	145	7–22 acres *	private
November	1957	Triffa	public	2,650	191	7–22 acres *	usufruct
November	1957	Gharb	public	6,500	153	35–50 acres	usufruct

* Five hundred acres for the Experimental Station of Bougriba, 175 acres for the model village of Aklim, and 625 acres of forest for communal use.

ticularly in the Gharb, an attempt to modernize agriculture through controlled distribution met with opposition and inertia from the local tribe, who, because of the confused status of ownership, felt that the public lands on which they had always worked and lived were theirs. Furthermore, in most places, there was no attempt to follow up distribution with guidance and modernization. In the Triffa, success was limited by the absence of controls on the farmers and by the fact that they were city dwellers chosen for political reasons. The first drawback was dealt with by 'Abdeljalil the following year in the Triffa and the Gharb by leasing the land in usufruct,

[5] The recent inauguration of the Meshra' Homadi Dam on the Moulouya River had opened up irrigation possibilities for 125,000 acres in the Triffa project; the *dahir* was No. 1-56-126 of August 27, 1956, followed by an interministerial order of September 13, 1956. The king's speech in the Triffa was similar to that in the Gharb (*al-Istiqlal*, September 21, 1956; *Monde*, September 21, 1956; Mohammed V, *op. cit.*, pp. 137–139). A typical book of obligations, for use in the Triffa, is found in the interministerial order of February 7, 1958.

as the protectorate had done, in order that the book of obligations be respected.[6]

Raising agriculture to the level of a ministry at the end of 1958 put it into the hands of the Marrakshi agricultural engineer, Thami 'Ammar. Once again, pressures for agrarian reform arose, goaded by a minister who prepared *dahirs* on expropriation and was supported by his premier. In such a situation, the king again undercut the opposition (in the strange case of Moroccan politics in 1959, an opposition that was part of the government) by enacting a facsimile of its program. Although this rarely satisfied the opposition, it brought scattered action. In the latter half of 1959, therefore, the king asked his minister to prepare more land for distribution. He visited the Tadla to set up the agricultural community of Sidi Jaber, north of Beni Mellal, where some *gish* land farmed and claimed by the Ait Arba' had been attached to the Beni Amir-Beni Moussa irrigation office pending final disposition.[7]

New twelve-acre lots were grouped into ten-lot units of production to facilitate communal utilization of machinery and equipment, according to a formula worked out by the ministry's Rural Engineering Division on the basis of a pre-independence project. Twenty-four lots were reserved for resistants, ten for homeless families from the previous winter's dissidence in the Rif, and the rest for candidates chosen by the governor from among landless natives of the Tadla who had an aptitude for farming, a good police record, and a large family. The *fellahin* were granted only usufruct, as under 'Abdeljalil, for which they paid a small and regularly decreasing percentage of the harvest to the state. The allocation of the land to five different crops was required by a type of book of obligations.

By combining and improving on elements of the 1956 and 1957 distributions, a more successful program was created. The hand of the ministry was evident in the units of production, which employed a collective formula designed to overcome the weaknesses of individual exploitation in the northern distributions. The king again took the occasion to redefine agrarian reform to include "renovation of agriculture and distribution of land," with accent

[6] Ministerial orders of November 27, 1957.

[7] There are 500,000 acres of *gish* (army) lands granted in past centuries to certain tribes as payment for military services. In the case of the Ait Arba', this land was owned by the state but had been held by the tribe in usufruct although the Ait Arba' claimed ownership. Partial recognition was paid to the Ait Arba' claim by choosing members of the tribe to receive the lots, for which the governor was criticized from other quarters.

on collective exploitation, "which guarantees private property and gives satisfactory results"; later in the speech, agrarian reform and distribution of lands were defined as separate issues, and in his address even the minister minimized agrarian reform. In his policy of doing a little so that critics would say less, however, both the king and his minister announced further distributions for the fall of 1959.

About 45,000 acres were specifically cited as part of the lands that the Royal Commission had discovered to be available; this very determination removed any hope of a general distribution of

TABLE 3

LAND DISTRIBUTIONS IN 1959

Date	Location	Land	Acres	Lots	Size	Regime
July 1959	Tadla	public (*gish*)	4,140	287 *	12 acres	usufruct
November 1959	Gharb	public	2,120	89	25 acres	usufruct
November 1959	Tetuan	public	1,120	140	1–25 acres	usufruct
November 1959	Meknes	public	1,300	44	15–30 acres	usufruct
November 1959	Fez	public	480	20	18–25 acres	usufruct
November 1959	Agadir	public	180	25	7 acres	usufruct
November 1959	Doukkala	public	1,060	34	30 acres	usufruct
November 1959	Haouz	traitors' †	2,440	97 ‡	22 acres	usufruct
November 1959	Haouz	traitors' †	495	18 ‡	28 acres	usufruct

* One hundred thirty acres for farm building, twenty-four acres for communal orchard, and thirty-five acres for agricultural center reserved for communal use in production units.

† Thirty-three thousand acres provided for distribution by *dahir* of July 20, 1957, and government announcements of August 20, 1958, and November 12, 1959.

‡ Thirty-five acres for an agricultural center and 230 acres for canals and roads reserved for communal use.

public lands. The promised October deadline had just passed when the king paid his visit to Sidi Qassem and Marrakesh. In the first city, an agricultural center of the Gharb, 293 farmers received lots totaling 5,020 acres in four provinces. There is no indication that the lands had been confiscated. The *fellahin* were chosen from landless farmers with large families in the region; the farmers agreed to farm the plots themselves, not to overtax the land, and to maintain its fertility; a third of the plots in each region was reserved for former resistants. Again, only usufruct was granted; the ministry was to advise on the choice of crops and methods, and a book of obligations was imposed so that the land could be taken back if the farmer did not fulfill requirements. The state also supplied seeds, fertilizer, and modern equipment and encouraged the beneficiaries to group in agricultural cooperatives "to awake in them the spirit of enterprise." Without so much as lip service to "agrarian reform," the king defined agricultural policy as that of distribution, mechanization, and the establishment of cooperatives.

A week later the king was in Marrakesh, distributing public lands to farmers in Marrakesh, Agadir, and Chawia provinces. Although the lots in the latter two provinces were unspecified public lands, the land in the Haouz had a more significant history, for it was part of 37,000 acres owned by Hajj Thami al-Glawi, the pasha of Marrakesh who was instrumental in the deposition of the king in 1953. Despite the fanfare, the distribution was an immense disappointment, for it involved not even one-tenth of al-Glawi's former domain. The rest remained theoretically confiscated but actually continued to be administered by the Glawi family, farmed by the methods of sharecropping that were traditional to Morocco. Except for the 115 benefiting *fellahin,* who now had legal usufruct to the land, the distribution was only a meager symbol of the minimum nationalist demands. The conditions which covered the usufruct were similar to those imposed in the previous distribution in the north. A sliding scale of rents was applied, with a book of obligations, and a strict allocation of crops was required.

With 18,500 acres of the Royal Commission's findings on public land available for redistribution still unallocated, the Council of Ministers decided to allocate the Glawi's and other declared traitors' lands, beginning with an additional 15,000 acres to be divided among 1,000 families at the end of 1959.[8] But after the initial distributions in November, the ministry turned to more ambitious programs and prepared to present its agrarian reforms in the coming five-year plan; the king turned his attention to political problems of greater priority. The edge had been taken off the urgency of land distribution, and the year passed without any further action. It was not until after the discussion of the plan that the final distributions were undertaken. The 1960 distribution was slightly larger than the 1956–1957 or the 1959 program, although it still fell far short of disposable land schedules drawn up for the Agricultural Reform Commission of the plan—and even these were

[8] 'Ammar press conference, December 2, 1959 (*PM,* March 25, 1959; *Times,* November 12, 1959). The UNFP, 'Ammar's party, expected 75,000 acres (*at-Tahrir,* July 1, 1959). In *Bilan et Perspectives de l'action du Ministère de l'Agriculture* ([Rabat: Ministry of Agriculture, 1959], p. 15), 'Ammar attributed the slow distribution of traitors' lands to the problem of clearing titles, many of which were mortgaged.

modest in comparison to the potentially available traitors', public, tribal, and colonial land from which distributions were made. In 1960, the king distributed *merja* from Kenitra in October and from the Dkhissa tribal region north of Meknes in November. The

TABLE 4

PROPOSED DISTRIBUTABLE LAND

(Commission of Agricultural Reform, July 18, 1960)

Location	Land	Acres	Lots	Average size
Rabat	colonial	6,250	160	39 acres
	traitors'	2,000	35	53 acres
	public *	3,450	33	104 acres
Tangier	traitors'	120	3	40 acres
Fez	traitors' †	490	14	35 acres
Meknes	colonial	2,960	54	55 acres
	traitors'	290	10	29 acres
	public	1,740	48	36 acres
Oujda	traitors'	230	5	46 acres
	public	570	38	15 acres
Chawia	colonial ‡	6,170	191	32 acres
	public	1,440	38	30 acres
Jadida	traitors'	280	20	14 acres
Tadla	tribal	6,300	310	20 acres
Agadir	traitors'	550	20	27 acres
	public	2,710	72	38 acres
Marrakesh	traitors' §	375	7	53 acres
	public	3,590	100	36 acres
	tribal	750	50	15 acres

* Ministry plans in 1959 spoke of 33,000 acres of public lands ready for distribution in 1960.
† Additional 1,360 acres of colonial land reserved for tribal grazing.
‡ Additional 10,750 acres of colonial land reserved for tribal grazing.
§ Thirty-three thousand acres of Glawi lands not included.

TABLE 5

LAND DISTRIBUTIONS IN 1960

Date	Location	Land	Acres	Lots	Size	Regime
October 1960	Gharb	colonial?	5,330	?	?	usufruct
November 1960	Dkhissa	colonial?	2,400	93 *	25 acres	usufruct
November 1960	Marrakesh	traitors'	10,000	400	25 acres	usufruct

* Grouped in three agricultural units of production.

latter program marked another step in the pragmatic development of doctrine, for the twenty-five–acre farms were grouped into three units of production under ministry control in order to encourage better utilization of the land and to maintain the colonial structure. In November the prince distributed 10,000 acres to 400 families at Marrakesh, accomplishing the last and largest segment of the program.

An evaluation of the king's distributions depends largely on the direction from which it is approached. To the 2,100 *fellahin* who benefited from the program, it was an immense success, for their land was good, the conditions imposed actually assisted them if they wished to modernize their farming as required, and material assistance was also forthcoming. As a symbolic action, the program was also successful from two points of view. Twice it served to head off possible radical pressure for a large-scale agrarian reform that, in the absence of technical guidance and intensive re-education that the government was not prepared to give, would have been disastrous to Moroccan agriculture. It also served to develop doctrine—as shown in the use of a book of obligations, encouragement of cooperatives, adoption of the usufruct formula, distribution of traitors' lands, creation of units of production, choice of local landless farmers and worthy resistants, and preparation of strict conditions of exploitation—and to point the way for future action.

The success of this doctrine depended on continuing and effective counselling, surveillance, and education by the ministry, which had prepared it; the success of the program in a larger sense depended on the ministry's responsiveness to the guidelines laid down by the king. In the follow-up to redistribution, the program broke down. On the practical matter of education and surveillance, the ministry was often more interested in planning centralized control from Rabat than in developing grass-roots contact in the *bled*. A full evaluation of agrarian reform and its problems of decision-making must therefore turn to an examination of the ministry.

CONFLICTING INTERESTS
Nejjai and the UMA

The relatively moderate planks of the platform presented to the Extraordinary Congress of the Istiqlal in 1955 were largely the work of Ahmed ben Mansour Nejjai. The thirty-five-year–old nationalist landowner was a graduate agricultural engineer from the Institut d'Algérie, had been a major in the French Army until 1941, and then was appointed caid in his home area in the Gharb among the Sefrian tribe. His badge of nationalism was his deposition from this office in 1947 for too actively favoring reforms for the *fellahin;* in 1955 he was appointed first minister of agriculture. It was natural that his ideas should be shaped by his position as a large modern landowner. He was not interested in any limitation, confiscation, and repartitioning of landholdings; instead he believed that the development of agriculture depended on creating plantations large enough to support modern equipment and on inculcating a spirit of modernization in the *fellah*. These two goals were made possible and compatible by efforts to group small farmers into cooperatives. Articles written by his ministry for the party newspaper included under "Objectives concerning landholdings" only the consolidation of parceled property and the recuperation of marginal land.[9] "The agricultural crisis does not come from a lack of land but from the *fellah*'s ignorance of the value of land," he once said.

The party had originally presented 'Abdeljalil for the ministry, but he was in ill health in 1955 and proposed Nejjai instead. By the end of 1956, there was growing feeling against Nejjai among the activist wing. When the second government was formed in October, 1956, 'Abdeljalil proposed himself as a compromise candidate, no more radical than Nejjai but a more venerable figure of party unity.

Nejjai returned to the *bled* where he began organizing large and small rural landowners into agricultural unions in order to have an effective means of defending the interests of the group. Nine unions were formed in Rabat province in 1958, seven of them in the Gharb. Other farming regions followed soon after. By the summer of 1958, sixty-eight local unions claimed over 100,000 members; the locals were grouped into provincial federations and were given the buildings of the protectorate's Chambers of Agriculture, dissolved after independence. In July, 1958, the provincial federations met in Rabat and formed the Moroccan Union of Agriculture (UMA), of which Nejjai was elected president. Two months later, the king inaugurated the UMA in a grand *moussem* (harvest festi-

[9] Inheritance and purchase by poor farmers both tend to fragment property. Since Muslim law decrees that equal value as well as equal area must be distributed among heirs, lands are subdivided so that everyone may have several pieces in several places. A single parcel in Morocco is between one and two acres (Jean and Simonne Lacouture, *Le Maroc à l'épreuve* [Paris: Seuil, 1958], p. 189; Yahya Benslimane, *Format des exploitations et exploitation collective* [mimeographed report; Rabat: Ministry of Agriculture, 1959]).

val) at Souq at-Tleta in the Gharb. It was to be one of Morocco's most effective modern pressure groups.

The UMA is a remarkable organization. It has been able to remain a strong pressure group while representing the interests of both the large modern landowners—French as well as Moroccan—and the small, traditional *fellahin*. Its officers generally come from the large landowners and are elected by all the members of the local union, who appear to remain satisfied with the protection of their interests. There is no evidence of constraint on the smaller members, and, although the UMA is generally associated by position and membership with the Istiqlal party, in several of the regional groups there is a surprising degree of cooperation among members of differing political parties. The association of large and small landowners in the same organization, however, imposes the need for a common denominator for naturally differing positions and the need for solutions compatible with the needs and demands of both groups. In general economic policy, the UMA clearly favored free market competition over a planned economy. On the question of land ownership, the need for compromise worked in the direction of Nejjai's views during his ministry and against expropriatory agrarian reforms. It was for this negative reason as much as any positive one that the UMA was formed.

The UMA favors the distribution of tribal lands to private owners in order to create incentive for better exploitation and to simplify the inheritance laws so that the division of plots among several heirs will be avoided and the migration to the cities will be stabilized. Religious holdings should be bought by the state and distributed to private individuals. The Tunisian precedents in these areas are often cited. The UMA's main concern is that private ownership be increased; however, since it is a defender of both small traditional farmers and large modern plantation owners—two essentially conservative groups—the UMA often opposes rapid transformation from traditional to modern farming.

'Abdeljalil, Khadiri and Bou'abid, and the Istiqlal

'Abdeljalil's approach to the agricultural problem was similar to that of Nejjai. His speeches did not mention reforms in land-ownership, and his contacts with the *colons* were less frequent than Nejjai's, but he sympathized with modern agriculture. At a time when the Foreign Ministry and Paris were waging a bitter battle over the status of official colonization, he declared, ". . . as Minister of Agriculture, that we will never apply to European farmers measures that we will not apply to our own farmers." [10] His greatest contribution in this field was to apply the *coloniat partiaire* (usufruct system) to the distribution of public lands in order to force farmers to use modern methods and to prevent the further parceling of land according to existing laws of inheritance. Although it touched only a small number of farmers, the doctrine was an immediate step toward agrarian reform, utilizing the minister's available powers without going through the far more difficult process of revising inheritance laws.

The most important and controversial accomplishment of 'Abdeljalil was Operation Plow, an idea revived from the files of the protectorate by Nejjai but put into operation by his successor. The whole concept of a state-owned and -operated tractor rented for use on private lands was totally antithetic to land redistribution. It was all the more so because Operation Plow could very well have been used as an attempt to impose state or collective ownership, as the *fellahin* feared it would; but the king and the minister both vowed that the boundaries would be respected, and before a dubious audience the king dramatically drove the first tractor across a property line which was thereafter marked again with little piles of stones.

It took 'Abdeljalil months to convince Bou'abid, the economics minister, of the value of Operation Plow, but, when the agricultural minister left for France to consult physicians in the summer of 1957, Bou'abid had been won over. Since he became interim agricultural minister, it fell to him to inaugurate the first plowing. 'Abdeljalil, who was to return the day of the inauguration, delayed his arrival so that Bou'abid could make the opening speech and be publicly committed to the project. When 'Abdeljalil became minister of education in the third government, Bou'abid demanded complete control of all economics ministries, and the Ministry of Agriculture became an undersecretariat of state. As the authority responsible for the administration of public land, the Service of Domains of the Finance Ministry (after 1956, part of the Economics Ministry) had been a constant competitor of the Agricultural Ministry in farm matters since the early years of the protectorate. Bou'abid's "superministry" meant the predominance of industrial development over agriculture, but, to the extent that there was

[10] *Al-Istiqlal,* September 16, 1957, November 9 and 16, 1957; *Monde,* December 29, 1956. His ministry did, however, cancel a number of leases in the Tadla during August, 1957, including leases on the *gish* lands distributed at Sidi Jaber in 1959.

interest in agriculture at all, it was Bou'abid who was committed to lead Operation Plow into its second year.

The second attempt was less successful than the first because natural conditions were less favorable that year, because the technical program needed some improvement, and because the zeal of the new regime turned the operation from a voluntary into a centrally planned program.[11] Fertilizers were not always well coordinated with the types of soil; pastures were often plowed, leaving the farmer no grazing land for his sheep; the farm machinery used did not always break down the hard dry earth enough for the *fellah* to finish cultivating with his wooden plow; a reversal in 'Abdeljalil's policy made the farmers buy the fertilizer, and payment was fixed and obligatory instead of on a sliding or long-term basis consistent with harvests; and above all the *fellah* did not participate in the local committees and therefore was not properly indoctrinated to take a personal interest in the administration of the program. Farmers who were not convinced by the first year's experiment were nevertheless obliged to submit their lands for the second year. The most difficult part of the operation—the education of the farmer to the values and vicissitudes of modern agriculture— was given too little attention, and Operation Plow—the most revolutionary idea in Moroccan agriculture and one of the country's most far-sighted programs—was forced to undergo retrenchment and re-examination for the next two years.

The second year's operation had several results that were relevant to agrarian reform. Bou'abid's commitment to Operation Plow in his agricultural policy left little room for a renewed attack on the problems of land ownership. In many farmers' eyes the failure of the experiment strengthened traditionalist opposition to radical farm policies of any kind coming from Rabat. All the political forces, therefore, contributed to make 1958 unfruitful for progress in agrarian reform, as they also helped to block developments in most other fields.

The agricultural policy of the Istiqlal party of 'Abdeljalil and Kadiri—and, through 1958, of Bou'abid as well—was situated somewhere between the UMA of Nejjai, with which it was affiliated, and the UMT of the activists, which broke its Istiqlal affiliation at the beginning of 1959. It was this indecision of the party that caused its

[11] For three critical evaluations of Operation Plow, see *Vie*, March 14, 1960 (by the UMA), July 5, 1960 (by a French economist, Pierre Suisse), and December 9, 1961 (by the UMT). For some more satisfied expositions, see *L'Operation Labour 1957* (Rabat: Ministry of Agriculture, 1957); *al-Istiqlal*, September 22, 1958 (by Tahiri); and November 8, 1958 (by Benslimane).

weakness. 'Abdelhafid Kadiri, Bou'abid's undersecretary of state for agriculture and later a founder of the General Union of Moroccan Workers (UGTM) that tried to rival the UMT, was a young member of the executive committee of the Istiqlal. His ideas were heavily impregnated with traditional concepts, and so "the agrarian reform that we desire must be preceded by a reform of the system of land ownership which respects private property, in conformity with Islam." [12] Thus, to the problem of underexploited tribal lands, he suggested the "*melkization* of production," a hybrid system resting on tribal ownership, "collective and cooperative" exploitation, and private distribution of production. Colonial lands belonging to the tribes should, therefore, be neither redistributed as *melk* lands nor in usufruct, but should be restored to the tribes. Colonial lands should be recovered, although such matters as confiscation and compensation were left vague, as was the upper limit to large landholding. Public lands, on the other hand, should be distributed in usufruct to poor *fellahin*, according to 'Abdeljalil's formula.

At the other end of the spectrum was Mohammed Tahiri, Nejjai's chief of cabinet and later 'Abdeljalil's undersecretary of state for education. Tahiri, who on many questions sided with the UMT, proposed recovery of all colonized lands and also of a percentage of the increased value on irrigated lands, regardless of ownership. He favored an unspecified limitation for landholdings and strict control of production through a system of cooperatives. An anonymous author wrote in the same tone as Tahiri but with more precision. The goals of agrarian reform were social justice; increased production; the abolition of the parceling system; obligatory exploitation; and state recovery of increased value from irrigated lands, "objectives which are valid no matter what the juridical system of farmlands might be." [13] Thus, the journal looked toward regrouping and redistribution of public and private lands along with a number of serious measures for control, education, mechanization, advice, and assistance to farmers in need of credit.

It was the latter way of thinking, which was compatible with the broader projects of the UMT, that was expressed in greater detail in the soul-searching resolutions of the party in January, 1960, a year after its scission. The party declared itself against parceling, concentration of landholdings, and proletarianization of the peasants—a rather restricting list of negatives to begin with. It sup-

[12] *Ibid.*, January 23 and 30, 1960; the footnote pertains to the rest of the paragraph. *Melk* means "private," and *melkization* refers to distribution to private owners.

[13] *Ibid.*, July 11, 1959.

ported a cooperative system, as did most political groups, and the establishment of optimum land units as the basis of agricultural production, a point which was quite close to the plans of those who had just broken with the party. Although no land limits or conditions of expropriation were stated, the platform was obviously an effort to undercut the agrarian program of the activists and went beyond the attitudes of such moderate members of the party as Kadiri or Nejjai. Yet for all its detailed programs, the Istiqlal was the least homogeneous group to express an opinion on the question of landownership, and it lacked the conviction, planning, and dynamism to carry out any agrarian reform program beyond Operation Plow.

'Ammar and the Activists

Thami 'Ammar was one of the most active people ever to occupy a ministerial position in Morocco. His sixteen months in office were marked by a prodigious production of *dahirs*, most of which never won the king's seal. He carried the Agriculture, Economics and Interior Ministeries' competition in rural affairs almost to the point of a public battle. His many trips all over the *bled* were a local replica of the Dulles-like wanderings of his premier and foreign minister, 'Abdullah Ibrahim. Deeply engaged politically, he was one of the few ministers who from the beginning took a public part in the Istiqlal split that came a month after the formation of the fourth government. His agricultural activity was not foreign to his political interests; he once remarked, "The decisive part of Moroccan politics is played in the *bled*." As an agricultural technician in Marrakesh, he had observed the difficulties of Operation Plow in the Haouz region, where the lack of rain dried up its chances of success, and he was consequently opposed to the program. One of his major ideas on Moroccan farming was summed up in his often repeated phrase, "The *fellah* is hungry for land." The government that entered office in December, 1958, therefore, announced agrarian reform with a fanfare.[14]

'Ammar's program for land redistribution was contained in a number of related *dahirs*.[15] He was very aware of the dangers of a bold shock program that might cause the modern sector of agriculture to fold up and the French farmers to go back to France. 'Ammar's interest was rather to educate the small farmer in the possibilities of modernization by making land available to him under

[14] *PM*, March 25, 1959; *Monde*, March 26, 1959.
[15] For a brief outline of 'Ammar's own view of his program, see *Bilan . . . , op. cit.*, pp. 13–14.

conditions amenable to cooperative exploitation and modernization. "The measures taken for these land distributions and the conditions of seriousness and equity in which they take place should
convince public opinion of the permanent concern of the state for
social justice, and also its desire to see the local economy expand." [16]

The first *dahir* of the program did not appear until August,
1959.[17] It was a joint law drawn up by the Agriculture and Interior
Ministries ordering the establishment of a land register for all of
Morocco; a joint ministerial order followed, giving the details for
the operation.[18] Land census, however, is an arduous, intricate, and
costly process, especially if legal titles are not clear, as in Morocco.
Although it was to begin in September, not until spring of the
following year did the work get underway, after a new ministerial
order from the Interior Ministry alone established new operational
details.[19] Much of the delay was caused by tests and procedural
problems which had to be worked out by the Central Service of
Statistics, a division of a third ministry, the Ministry of National
Economy. The fact that this operation, which was so important to
the programs of 'Ammar, passed from his ministry is indicative both
of the difficulties of any reform and also of relations among the
three ministries.

A second *dahir* made all foreign land transactions subject to
review by the Finance Ministry, with the possibility of state pre-
emptive buying when it was requested by the Agriculture Ministry;
the law was actually a revival of a protectorate regulation that followed a number of highly publicized purchases of land by *colons*
in early 1959.[20] However, it left Moroccan acquisition of land un-
regulated. During the same year, further criticism was aroused by
large Moroccan landowners who expanded their property by buying from *colons* or small Moroccan farmers. Although the Agriculture and Interior Ministries proposed bills to make the original
dahir applicable to all farm-land transactions, no action was taken.
An illustration of the delicacy of any measure touching land ownership is in the preamble to the Agriculture Ministry's bill, which
stated that "it is not within the framework of the governmental
policy of agrarian reform to permit the growth of large Moroccan

[16] *Ibid.*, p. 17. Note the modern language—"social justice," "public opinion,"
"state" instead of "king," and so on.
[17] *Dahir* No. 1-59-280 of August 20, 1959.
[18] Ministerial order of August 21, 1959.
[19] Ministerial order of April 8, 1960.
[20] *Dahir* No. 1-59-287 of November 20, 1959.

landowners at the expense of the small [farmers]"; an editing hand crossed out the words "of agrarian reform."

Another group of *dahirs* was more radical and less successful. The minister continued to attack the problem of the large Moroccan landowners, many of whom held their lands as speculatory investments which then lay largely uncultivated. A bill was drawn up to permit expropriation of these lands with compensation and allocation in usufruct to small farmers who would be grouped in agricultural cooperatives and would farm under the direction of the state. Commissions of Census and Cultivation for Abandoned or Insufficiently Exploited Lands were to be attached to the governor of each province, comprising a provincial representative, a local representative of the ministry, and farm technicians appointed by the minister of agriculture. The commission was to determine whether each "large private agricultural plantation . . . was insufficiently exploited or abandoned," after which any commercial transaction involving the property would be null and void. A national commission, presided over by the premier and including the ministers of finance, public works, and interior or their representatives, a counselor from the Court of Appeals, and the minister of agriculture or his representative as reporter, would decide on the expropriations. Compensation would be paid in state development bonds and would be fixed at the market value of the land less the increased value accrued to the land by such public works improvements as irrigation.

In large irrigation projects, the minister found that instead of bringing about economic development, intensive cultivation, and rural full employment, the state improvements had further favored speculation and large landholdings. Unimplemented clauses in the protectorate's legislation allowed the state to require payment from farmers whose lands benefited from increased value following state improvements. An estimated 75,000 acres could be claimed as payment for increased value throughout Morocco. The minister, therefore, proposed to consider all farmers owning over twelve acres in debt to the state for increased value if their land was arable and irrigable (not necessarily tilled and irrigated). All property in excess of 200 acres would be confiscated, except in cases where the landowner divided or sold his lands or agreed to intensive farming according to programs approved by the ministry. Compensation would be fixed and paid in the same way as in the census and cultivation bill. A farmer owning more than twenty-five acres could pay his debt either in land, as forced expropriation, or in cash, significantly defined as "the market value of the land he would have ceded" if he had chosen to cede the land. A farmer owning twelve to twenty-five acres could pay only in cash in order to prevent reduction below the optimum size for intensive exploitation. Opposition would result in expropriation without compensation, and there appeared to be no appeal to the decision of the minister or the National Commission of Census and Cultivation. Other obligatory measures compelled farmers in the irrigation projects to irrigate at least two-thirds of their lands or pay a special tax and to adhere to a producers' cooperative if the minister so decided. Application of the law would have required an immense staff to administer against strong opposition a revolution in the irrigated sector of Moroccan farming.

In August, 1959, the Council of Ministers met and, under pressure from 'Ammar, created an interministerial commission of the interior, economics, and agriculture ministers and representatives to study the agrarian reform bills. Five days later, 'Ammar had another bill ready, providing for the creation of a national land office under the Agriculture Ministry. The office was to be charged with "recovering lands susceptible of reverting to the tribes within the framework of agrarian reform" and financing and administering exploitation of these as well as other arable public, tribal, and *habous* lands. It would be administered by a council combining the ministers of agriculture, economy, and interior, five technical assistants of the Agriculture Ministry, and three farmers appointed by the ministers of agriculture and interior. The minister of agriculture would preside and would also nominate such additional employees as the director and the secretary general. The bill contained no technical measures other than financial provisions (for the benefit of the economics minister, who was particularly economy-minded during the tight year of 1959), although "other measures envisaged within the framework of agrarian reform," such as exploitation and repartition, were promised.

In the commission's discussions that followed, there was disagreement about whether public lands should be owned or only controlled by the state. The Economics Ministry was also concerned over the heavy demands that would be imposed on its personnel. Comments were most numerous from the Ministry of Interior, which was responsible for protection of the tribal lands through its Trusteeship Office and which was in contact with the rural areas through its provincial administrators. An undated memorandum from the ministry was jealously critical of the proposed land office. It protested that competent attention and protection of property rights were already being given by the Trusteeship Office. It pointed out the proliferation of administrative agents that a land office would demand and contrasted this demand with the chronic lack of skilled technicians. It suggested cooperation between existing organizations, such as the Habous and Agricultural Ministries, to avoid the creation of a large bureaucracy. Only in the matter of confiscation did the ministry find a useful purpose for a land office.

The speed with which the bill was prepared was not equaled by great haste in discussion. There was great difficulty in just having the meetings. The interministerial commission frequently met only to postpone its meeting. 'Ammar wrote the premier on August 27 to complain of the economics minister's absence, but the following meeting of September 9, for example, was put off to September 18 because the ministers of interior and economy were not represented, then to September 23 because of the Feast of the Mouloud, then to the following day because of a meeting of the Trusteeship Council of the Interior Ministry, and then, because of the absence of the ministers of interior and economy, to September 30, when it finally met. On April 30, 1960, the Ministry of Agriculture asked the governors to reply within thirty days; by the time the letters were due, the government had fallen and with it the minister of agriculture and his projects. The comments of some of the governors, important men in the Interior Ministry, are nevertheless instructive. Although they approved of parts of the land office and the census and cultivation bills, they disapproved of the dominant position of the Ministry of Agriculture and attacked the vagueness of the bills.

> The great majority of Moroccan lands could be confiscated by the proposed procedure, which would be beyond the competence of this text and even beyond means of the Government, for outside of a tiny number of lands—most of them European—no plantation today is fully exploited. The European lands are few and also are decreasing, for political reasons which escape no one.

They also questioned the ministry's energy, which was more evident in inaugurating projects than in finishing them.

> The spirit of continuity and effective organization of the rural masses are the conditions *sine qua non* of the application [of reforms], for often the administration does not only run

up against ignorance and poverty, but also meets conscious
resistance against the alienation of the freedom to act which
is inherent in the proposed *dirigisme* and the limitation of
property.

Furthermore, expropriation was so lightly defined that it was "sim-
plified to the extreme of eliminating the judicial authority, the local
authority, and the interested party himself," and the same was true
of the process of determining increased value.

It is hard to tell whether the shortcomings of 'Ammar's measures were the result of misplaced energy and innocent omissions or
whether political purposes were actually basic to the programs.
There is no doubt that part of the agrarian reform was designed to
strengthen the Agricultural Ministry against the Ministry of the
Interior. Because of its weakness in three areas—the technical, the
partisan, and ministerial politics—the reform program was defeated.
Blocked by the Interior Ministry and weakened by vagueness of
technical details, the bills were buried in the fall of the government
of which 'Ammar was a member. But the most definitive opposition
came from the king. As the measures of confiscation were reported
in the Council of Ministers, he turned them down as being too
socialistic and incompatible with Muslim property rights. In view
of this resistance, it is more accurate to say that the endurance of
the bills was the result of the minister's tenacity, rather than to
emphasize their slow progress through the labyrinths of politics and
bureaucracy.

Pressure for a broad program of agrarian reform came from the
activist groups—the UMT and the National Union of Popular
Forces (UNFP)—who substantially backed Ibrahim's government.
Public demands for agrarian reform began reappearing in earnest
in 1959, although it was often difficult to get behind demagogic and
doctrinaire repetition of the slogan to find out what its users had in
mind. The two most common ideas were a broad confiscation of
colonial lands of all sorts and a vague desire to raise the peasants'
standard of living. A comprehensive outline was given in the UMT's
proposals presented to the Superior Council of the Five Year Plan
(CSP) for its meeting of November 23; the activists claimed the
proposals were even closer to 'Ammar's ideas than to those of
Bou'abid. The UMT demanded first a full land inventory, with the
penalty of confiscation for those who would not cooperate. All state
property, including confiscated, *habous*, tribal, *gish* lands, and
irrigated lands recovered in payment of a fifty per-cent tax on increased value should be united under one land office. This prop-

erty, totaling 1,200,000 acres, should then be made available to land-less peasants, unemployed agricultural workers, and small landown-ers willing to organize in cooperatives. No system of distribution—*melk,* usufruct, *coloniat partiaire*—was ever made explicit, and later, when the government changed and the activists were no longer in power, the UMT denounced all distributions as an escape from policy-formation. Both public and *melk* lands should be or-ganized into cooperatives based on an optimum unit of production; *melk* holdings should be encouraged to conform to this optimum size. Sharefarming was to be replaced by modern contract work.

Although this proposal is broad, it is a policy which coincided with the bills of 'Ammar. The UMT and UNFP were not only aware of the ideas of the minister; they seem also to have been cog-nizant of the king's opposition, for they presented their demands as an impersonal attack on the government while citing their agree-ment with Bou'abid and 'Ammar, a tactic frequently used when the target of the attack was the king or his too heavy hand on the shoulder of the premier. The activists also put forth complementary aspects of an agricultural program, including credit facilities, dis-tribution of fertilizer, full production planning, government sale of primary crops, and a massive education and propaganda program throughout the *bled.* All these items were certainly necessary for effective agrarian reform. Also necessary was the willingness to en-gage in a controlled political life and planned economy, as much a cherished item of the activists' program as it was an unpopular item throughout the countryside. The final element necessary for the program of 'Ammar was thus either political support or political control, and both of these he sorely lacked.

Zemmouri and the Interior

Because of the trusteeship it has exercised over tribal land since 1919, the Ministry of Interior has always been an active rival of the Ministry of Agriculture.[21] In 1959 both ministries had imaginative and independent personnel interested in reaping a political harvest from public lands. At the same time that 'Ammar was named to his position, Hassan Zemmouri, a young Berber political scientist of uncertain politics, energetic ambition, and proven competence, was named undersecretary of state for rural and municipal affairs in the

[21] It had already made a move to limit the harm caused by tribal ownership by calling for repartition every ten years instead of every three (Circular No. 2976, November 13, 1957). The ultimate goal of this reform was a usufruct re-gime for all tribal lands (*Revue des communes rurales et des municipalités,* IV [September–October 1959]).

Interior Ministry. Lines of authority were even less clear within the Interior Ministry than they were between the Interior and Agricultural Ministries, and competence in any particular affair was more often fixed by pre-emptive exercise than by legal definition. Zemmouri, therefore, attacked the problem of agrarian reform within the ministry's domain of tribal lands.

In March, 1959, while 'Ammar was discussing the king's distribution of public lands, Zemmouri presented the first program for confiscation. In May the *dahir* was sealed, although it was published two months later.[22] It provided for the cancelation of leases covering the 75,000 acres of tribal lands held by *colons* under the title of Perpetual Alienation of Usufruct (APJ) and the 33,000 acres held under long-term leases of ten to ninety-nine years. This land was owned by the tribe but had been leased at low rates for long periods by 114 European families. Between the publication of the *dahir* and October 1, the date it was to come into effect, the government was subjected to strong and conflicting pressures to work out details which had not been specified in the law.[23] The tribes demanded the return of their lands, and they sent successive delegations of *fellahin* with their knotted cloth bags to camp on the ministry's door and make their claims known. The *colons,* who knew their legal contracts were politically tenuous, nevertheless demanded compensation for the increased value of their improved land and called on the government of France to back them up. The Interior Ministry wished to maintain both the level and continuity of production and also its own control over the tribal lands; in fact, these two aims of the Trusteeship Council went hand in hand.

The Ministry of Interior's *dahir* was both specific and supple where the Ministry of Agriculture's bill was broad and strict. A commission, presided over by a member of the Interior Ministry and having members from the Agriculture, Justice, and Economics Ministries, was established to handle appeals and was empowered to decide between cancelation of the contract and substitution of a new short-term lease. The final tribunal was the Trusteeship Council, although it was also an interested party and could not be taken

[22] *Dahir* No. 2-59-172 of May 9, 1959. In fact, the measure was small; the land involved was only one-sixth of total land leased by *colons* and equal to only one–twenty-fifth of colonial-owned land.

[23] As early as the end of July, some forty tribal delegates came down to Rabat to thank Zemmouri and Bou'abid for "giving them back" their lands, an early sign of the pressure and an augur of the disappointment that the authorities had to deal with. Some of the *colons* went to Rabat and won a reprieve, but they were barred by tribesmen from retaking possession of their lands.

to court. Under pressure from the various contenders, the Trusteeship Council decided during the summer of 1959 to buy or rent the
colons' equipment, to respect the *colons'* claim to planted crops
which would mature up to the spring citrus harvest of 1960, and to
divide the lands on individual merits into three categories. The first
group of lands, incorporating 28,000 acres, was taken over by the
local Agricultural Work Centers (CT), which ran them as units for
the benefit of the tribes, using the same farm labor that the *colon*
had hired.[24] A second group of *colons* was offered three- to five-year
leases in order to give them time to liquidate their investments; the
third group simply had the leases renewed but the rent raised.
About 62,000 acres of former APJ holdings were recovered by mid-
1960. Some problems and inequities remained, such as the maintenance of production on farms that were to be liquidated and the
conflict between France and Morocco over which country should pay
the compensation, but the law was generally applied with an attempt at respect for the individual.[25]

When 'Ammar presented his ideas for a land office to the Council of Ministers, interested ministers could present counterproposals,
as was the custom. Zemmouri made a careful evaluation of Agriculture's land office, with its large budget, its legal personality, and its
possibilities for broad action in recovering land and encouraging
exploitation. Instead, however, he proposed a type of permanent
administration for land reform, to be attached to the presidency of
the council and charged with studying conditions of exploitation
and with utilizing the scattered agencies which had built up confidence in some sectors of Moroccan agriculture. The Ministry of
Interior's plan was thus less costly and more modest than that of
the Ministry of Agriculture. The bill "for the creation of a Commissariat of Agrarian Reform" was in many places a carbon copy
of the Land Office bill with differences consistent with the counterproposals of Zemmouri. The commissariat would not "recover or
acquire lands," administer tribal lands already handled by the
Trusteeship Council, or finance exploitation of recovered lands. The
membership of the Superior Council of Agrarian Reform was more
balanced although more bureaucratic than the Ministry of Agricul-

[24] Originally created as Sectors of Peasant Modernization (SMP) under the
protectorate, the renamed Work Centers were most active as administrative
agents for Operation Plow. For a good study of their purpose and accomplish-
ments in the earlier years, see Yves Barennes, *La Modernisation rurale au Maroc*
(Paris: Librairie Générale de Droit et de Jurisprudence, 1948).
[25] In the Gharb, however, colons were evicted without recourse to judicial
proceedings (*Monde*, October 15, 1959).

ture's National Commission; it united the ministers of agriculture, economy, and interior with the directors of the Agricultural Work Centers (Agriculture) and of the plan (Economy), and a commissar of agrarian reform appointed by the Council of Ministers. At the provincial level, secondary councils operated in the same way, coordinating the work of the ministries of Agriculture and Finance and CT representatives; similar councils could be set up locally.

Despite its more limited scope, its lower cost, and its greater detail, the proposal of the Interior Ministry was no more successful in the Council of Ministers than was that of the Ministry of Agriculture. To many its modesty wore the color of the UMA; that may have brought it closer to the ideas of the king, but it did not arouse the enthusiasm of the premier or his economics and agricultural ministers.

Zemmouri then began attacking the problem from other angles, just as 'Ammar had done. In the spring of 1960, he discovered the Tunisian measures of agrarian reform and instructed his associates to prepare a *dahir* based on the Tunisian laws and decrees. The wording of the old bill, the Ministry of Agriculture's bill for a land office, and the new bill for a "Secretariat for Land Reform" are all remarkably close, and the provisions for the secretariat were identical to the description of the stillborn commissariat. However, instead of the "slow and costly" method of compensation by state bonds, Zemmouri proposed the French and Tunisian method of payment in shares of a nonnegotiable state loan with limited interest and with reimbursement spread over ten to fifteen years. The property involved was "neglected" ("without habitual agricultural practices for a year") or "insufficiently exploited" ("where the land does not attain the total productivity which its agricultural vocation renders it capable"); confiscation would be decreed by the agriculture minister on proposals from the interior minister. Except for the rather broad definitions and the increased role of the interior minister, the bill was still very similar to 'Ammar's census and confiscation bill and no more successful.

An evaluation of the Ministry of Interior's rivalry with the Ministry of Agriculture is easier to make than is a comparison of Zemmouri's and 'Ammar's agrarian reform plans. The Interior Ministry's long-standing role in tribal affairs meant continuing friction with the Ministry of Agriculture and an unhelpful diffusion of authority in the establishment of an agricultural program. To say that the agricultural domain was parceled among many agencies is not to say that the Trusteeship Council was incompetent; it is to say, however, that a unification of land administration was necessary at a higher or lower level before a concerted program could be carried out. Zemmouri conceived this coordination at a high level, leaving the diffused authorities in place under an administrative secretariat or commissariat. 'Ammar proposed consolidation of all the agencies on the ground level in the branches of a land office. Zemmouri's program was less comprehensive, if a program at all; his measures, however, were no less political than 'Ammar's, and they were presented to a large extent simply to have something to offer as an alternative to 'Ammar's proposals. Politically, Zemmouri was in the weaker position for the adoption of a program. He had no fixed political association; although he was frequently in touch with the UMT, his strongest support came from the king, whose respect was not reciprocated, and from the Alumni Association of the Berber Academy at Azrou, a powerful bloc in the civil service but not in the government. Neither of these groups gave an undersecretary of state support sufficient for the adoption of a detailed program essentially outside his competence. They did, however, aid in the passage of such individual measures as the termination of the APJ, particularly where the action was such a patriotic one. By the same token, Zemmouri was politically in a stronger position than 'Ammar when the government fell in May, 1960. 'Ammar was carried away with the other activist members of the government, unwelcome in the king's new government because of the connections with the *dirigiste* group which might have made his program effective. Zemmouri, having successfully discharged his principal function—setting up communal elections—was named his successor.

THE PLAN

All these forces met and fought over the Five Year Plan. Their relation, as in the past, was more effective in blocking decisive action on a rural land program than it was in deciding on an effective reform. Work on the plan actually began in March, 1959, in the Agricultural Commission, a preparatory body for the Superior Council of the Plan (CSP). At its first meeting, three subcommissions were set up covering products and markets, agricultural distribution, and means and institutional reforms. The fact that all currents of opinion were represented on the commission and subcommissions meant that a final report was delayed until the end of 1959. The heterogeneous composition was also reflected in the report of the third subcommission, which dealt with agrarian reform and was written by Charles Zaoui, a member of the UMA and the

Istiqlal and the director of the ministry's Division of Land Conservation and Service of Topography. An early indication of the tenor of the discussion came less than a week after the first subcommission meeting, when the two representatives of the UMT boycotted the session because some of their suggestions were turned down. When the report finally appeared, it was redrafted by the Division of the Plan, who thought it should do more than merely report the internal division of the subcommission.

The Zaoui report, submitted in January, 1960, at least made clear many of the differing opinions on agrarian reform. There were two divergent attitudes, which the report called "liberal" and *"dirigiste";* one sought to develop the traditional sector through diversity and liberty, and the other questioned the value of liberty for the traditional farmer and instead advocated state intervention to improve his resources and general welfare. Agreement was registered on such past practices as the use of pre-emptive purchase for recovery, of cooperatives for modernization, and of the usufruct formula for the distribution of tribal lands. Even more important, there was also general support for Tunisian-type expropriation of abandoned or insufficiently exploited property and recovery of increased value in irrigated lands, as already provided by the unapplied *dahir* of the protectorate. The report stated:

> The mention of agrarian reform often arouses lively opposition. But if the laws on increased value were only applied, we would be in the presence of the start of an agrarian reform on irrigation projects which would appear to receive general agreement.[26]

There was, however, little clear idea of what to do with the recovered land, and there was little indication that the personnel and financial means were available to do it.

A majority of the subcommission also favored the establishment of a general land office that would combine the functions of the three ministries currently responsible for farm land. The appeal was made in patriotic terms by attributing the division of authority to the protectorate, but it stemmed from the Agriculture Ministry's representatives' desire to gain full authority as well as additional land. The report, however, was most vague on the type of organization it advocated and avoided choosing among a secretariat, a commissariat, and a land office. Sharp disagreement was evident on many

[26] *Third Commission Report* (mimeographed; Rabat: Ministry of Agriculture, n.d.).

questions. Should public land be distributed in *melk* or in usufruct? To what extent should the state intervene in the exploitation of farm land and in the structure of agrarian society? What were to be the details of colonial confiscation and compensation and the future of private colonial lands? [27] These problems, with that of conflicting and often competing ministerial authorities, were the knotty questions of agrarian reform, and none of them received a clear answer from the subcommission.

When the CSP met in August to discuss the latest draft, it heard the new economics minister, Mohammed Douiri, give the general outlines of a plan "which will enable Moroccan agriculture to double its production in twenty years." These measures involve the creation of an office of irrigation to administer all irrigated lands, recovery of "certain lands," administration of all public lands by a single agency, state control—presumably by a different agency— of the exploitation of tribal and *habous* holdings and of confiscated colonial land, and the creation of cooperative units of production. When the draft reached the council, however, it was subject to the same differences of opinion that had marked its course to that point.

On five major aspects of land reform, there was agreement and disagreement.[28] On property rights, the draft foresaw state limitation of private ownership through use of pre-emptive purchase and prohibition of hereditary partition, although state control would be limited to public, *gish*, tribal, and *habous* property. The UMA, consistent with its past stand, demanded unrestricted private property rights and full respect of possession in *melk*. The UMT went beyond the draft by demanding a limit on the extent of private ownership and distribution of excess land. In addition, where the draft proposed the purchase of private colonial lands in a program for recovery of all types of colonial farms, the UMT called for the confiscation of all colonial land, private or official, whereas the UMA appeared to protect private colonial property by warning against "measures which might harm the modern sector of agriculture."

[27] In addition to the lands of official colonization (700,000 acres owned by 1,813 *colons*), 1,600,000 acres were acquired by 4,300 *colons* as private colonization.

[28] Division of the Plan, "Note sur les principaux points de la réforme agricole exposée dans l'avant-projet débattu en session du CSP" (mimeographed notes, as are "Notes" that follow; Rabat: Economics Ministry, n.d.); see also individual positions in *al-Fellah*, December 15, 1959; Nejjai press conference, August 10, 1960; "UMA Notes to CSP," December 3, 1959, August 1, 1960; "UMT Note to CSP," August 1, 1960; "UMCIA Note to CSP," August 2, 1960.

On the eventual status of state-controlled or -recovered land, the draft supported distribution in usufruct with the possibility of state control and intervention, such as provided for in a book of obligations. The ministry proposed conditional distribution in *melk,* combined with allowance for state control on exploitation, a partial inversion of the draft proposal. The UMA repeated its demands for distribution in full title. The UMT, in a surprising application of its doctrinaire position, supported *melk* distributions under the slogan, "the land to those who work it," although outside the CSP the union newspaper went on record against redistribution and for "collective work by all landless peasants on the newly available land." [29]

On the beneficiaries of land distribution, there was rare agreement on the choice of poor or landless *fellahin* for redistributed public lands; further agreement was worked out on the choice of poorer members of the tribes as beneficiaries of tribal land division, although the system of ownership was, of course, still a point at issue. Even on the formula of cooperative exploitation, unanimity covered a whole span of differing interpretations. Dr. 'Abdelkrim Khatib, the new labor minister and one of the members of the government closest to the activist position, supported collective exploitation as compatible with the principles of Islam, but the UMA looked merely to cooperation among private owners and the UMT advocated fully collective production.[30] Finally, on the question of rural leases, the draft called for a full reform along with state assistance, although it was more specific on the evils of traditional leases than it was on a substitute regime. The UMA rejected the reform in the absence of consultation with interested parties; the UMT declared the reform impracticable unless the hold of the "feudals" was broken by a full land limitation and distribution program.

The session of the CSP neatly brought out the differing points of view of those interested in land reform, but it did this so successfully that it called into question even agreements that had been reached in the government. The two extremes of opinion were clearly represented by the UMT and the UMA. The inclusion of these organizations in the CSP was quite necessary if the CSP was

---

[29] As an example of how supposedly doctrinaire stands swayed in the wind of political advantage, *AG* said that the government wanted to give away land because it did not know what to do with it (June 25, 1960).

[30] Dr. Khatib was head of the rural Popular Movement. The movement's aims in agrarian reform were explained, by co-leader Mahjoubi Ahardan in an interview, as limitation of property, recovery of excess land, formation of cooperatives, creation of "recover banks" to compensate large landowners, and expropriation "much later in the future."

to fulfill its political role in the democratic evolution of Moroccan government. But it hampered any decision on this touchy question, showing the CSP's weakness as a decision-maker, and the attitudes expressed clearly showed the divisions in relevant Moroccan opinion.

The massive dossier went to the government during the summer of 1960. In the burst of activity that followed the creation of the king's new government, a synthesis was made in the Council of Ministers and in the Ministry of Agriculture, effecting a broad reform program. The new principles were based largely on past practices, aided by the impetus of the Division of the Plan and of the Ministry of Agriculture's staff of technicians. "Agrarian reform" became "agricultural reform" or "reform of agriculture" in the language of the acting premier—the prince—and was steered carefully between the demands of the UMT and the protests of the UMA. Lands owned by the state, including public land, traitors' land, and confiscated or otherwise recovered farms of official colonialization, were to be retained by the state under a single regime; tribal claims to their ownership were rejected. Production on land controlled by the state, including *habous, gish,* and private colonial lands with renewed leases, was to be put under careful surveillance, without any decision on the rights of basic ownership. Private owners were to be prevented from consolidating large plantations through state control on land transactions and the use of preemptive purchase, as already decreed by *dahir.* Recoverable lands fell into three categories: private colonial lands which would be bought; portions of irrigated farms owed to the state in payment for increased value without compensation; and excess landholdings, farms not declared in the land census, and insufficiently exploited land, all to be acquired with compensation. Measures of inheritance reform and consolidation of parceled holdings were to be put into effect. The immediate program would begin with the APJ, the 2,000,000 acres of public land that were already available, and the lands of official colonialization, which were the subject of continuing negotiations with France.[31] The progam of distribution and controlled exploitation was to be effected in stages, both to avoid psychological shock to the traditional farmers and because of the lack of available machinery and personnel necessary to a full and immediate program. The first stage was to involve distribution of land in usufruct, in lots of about twenty-five acres of dry-farmed

[31] *Dahir* No. 1-60-078 of June 30, 1960, annulled all usufruct of tribal lands acquired through a *dahir* of March 19, 1951; appeals were to be made as prescribed in the *dahir* of May 9, 1959, so that by now the Trusteeship Council was well established as a sort of independent regulatory commission with administrative and judicial functions.

land and twelve acres of irrigated land; after this was accomplished, the land would be regrouped into cooperatives of production to hasten mechanization. The lots could be mortgaged by the state and inherited, but they could neither be divided nor consolidated, and a book of obligations would go with each contract. There was no clear decision on the partition of modern plantations, although the question received a comprehensive discussion that clearly pointed up inherent contradictions in political, economic, and social goals.

The final list of principles was comprehensive and even helpful on many points. Many of its elements were already in practice, and most had appeared at one point or another in ministerial projects during 1959, not to speak of proposals from outside organizations. Delicate political problems, such as the creation of a land office under a choice of names and functions, the consolidation of ministerial authority, or the establishment of a clear new land ownership law that would overcome the inherited conflicts of Muslim and protectorate law, were all avoided.[32] Absent, too, was the comprehensive Five Year Plan *dahir*-program that the new government promised. By the end of 1962, there was still no decision to transfer the principles of land reform into law. Although the divergences of opinion within the government had been resolved to the point of agreement on the guidelines of reform, problems of politics and of detail made the government no more capable of decision than were earlier ministries or broader bodies of public opinion.

CONCLUSIONS

A clear definition of goals is crucial to the success of an agrarian reform program. It has been seen that 'Ammar's ideas were highly, even if not primarily, political. Did they further look to increased productivity of existing farmland or to the extension of land under cultivation? To the extent that they simply sought to increase the

[32] Zemmouri himself was to fall victim of political maneuvering about a variation of his own land office. A move to consolidate all irrigated lands under a single office and make them into the showcase of Moroccan agriculture was approved by the National Consultative Assembly, the CSP, and—in principle—the Council of Ministers in July, 1958. A child of Bou'abid, it was adopted in 1960 by Douiri and the prince and reaccepted in Council of Ministers in early August. In effect, the National Irrigation Office (ONI) took all the valuable lands from the Agriculture Ministry and would absorb even more of Moroccan agriculture as it became more successful. Zemmouri, whose admiration of the prince was already not great, resigned. Persuaded by the king to remain in office, he stayed on, but his political position was weakened, and he resigned again in January, 1961, to be replaced by the prince himself. To round out the cast of characters, Tahiri was appointed director of the ONI. Soon after, another portion of modernizing agriculture was given to a new agency, the office of Rural Development.

exploitation of hitherto fallow land, they might have succeeded in principle, but, unless there were close control over the use of redistributed land, the reforms might only have increased the traditional sector of the agrarian economy. Morocco is full of examples of reforms which have made no impact on the economy, from the Gharb lands distributed by the king to the irrigated lands of Imfout, where the farmers simply cultivated less land better (and left the rest fallow) to achieve the same standard of living at considerable expense to the state. To the extent that the reforms sought to increase yield per acre, they depended on continuing measures of modernization rather than on land distribution alone. Questions of mechanization, irrigation, and educated use of fertilizer, of counseling, of farmers' confidence in technicians, and, above all, of stubborn, silent resistance from that bulwark of traditionalism, the *fellah*, all made follow-up a task whose immensity dwarfed the problems of drawing up a reform *dahir*. The initial success and subsequent weaknesses of Operation Plow provide examples of both the positive and negative aspects of this problem. These problems, in turn, go back to a basic need for leadership that is both dynamic and stable, something which has never existed in Morocco, and to the much proclaimed revolution of rising expectations, which has not reached the Moroccan farmer.

Any of the reform programs would have involved a strong element of *dirigisme* that was lacking in Morocco. The conservatism of the king, absence of a strong central government to carry out coherent centralized projects, and, above all, lack of ministerial stability and continuity worked against any radical planning and reform. Most important was the lack of *élan* which characterized the Moroccan political scene. Political infighting, particularly between the warring factions of the Istiqlal, sapped the energy of the nation and destroyed the party's working unity. The time for reform was 1956, if there was ever a time; then the enthusiasm of the people was shown in their union behind the political leadership in such events as the creation of the Unity Road across the Rif. But this enthusiasm was allowed to go to waste by the divided and bickering leaders. A commentator on the educational system stated a very valid general truth when he remarked, "Experience has proven that it is perfectly possible to associate the Moroccan nation in a movement in favor of development, but also that such a movement, based on enthusiasm, is necessarily limited in time." [33]

The agrarian reform bills would have imposed immense finan-

[33] Mohammed Machrafi at a meeting of division heads of the Ministry of Education, April 6, 1959.

cial obligations on the state. Compensation; provision for state aid
in irrigation, credit, tools and fertilizers; sudden increases in the
need for trained agricultural advisors throughout the entire country—all these required a large ministerial budget at a time when
the prevailing economic philosophy was austerity. The immediate
returns from land divisions to the state would be meager, and the
sliding rent scales, although kind to the farmer, were a small source
of state revenue when compared with the increasing needs.

An attempt to follow agricultural land reform through the maze
of hopes and politics gives an idea of the conflict and confusion inherent in the problem. No attempt has been made here to follow
all the bills or a fortiori each of their drafts, but rather to show the
changes and divisions of varying attitudes. Nor has there been any
attempt to judge the merits of the competing ideas or to evaluate
the possibilities of any sort of agrarian reform in Moroccan land
and society. The basic point of departure is that some Moroccans
wanted agrarian reform, and others did not.

1. If many of the important moments in the development of
agrarian reform programs sound like kitchen politics, they were,
unfortunately, crucial to the decisions made. Such items as the rivalry of the three ministries, factional tension in the Istiqlal, the
political competition between Zemmouri and 'Ammar or between
'Abdeljalil and Bou'abid, the activists' influence on the king's distributions, Bou'abid's predilection for urban matters, and the king's
and Ibrahim's apparent idea that "something must be done" were
the keys to the rash of activity of 1956 and 1959, the lack of action
in 1958, and much of the failure of 1959–1960. Both as a slogan and
as a program, agrarian reform was a matter of politics, not policy;
it was a vehicle for ministerial rivalry, party factionalism, personal ambition, and pressure between the king and the parties. It
is remarkable that any program was formulated. In this situation,
the ministerial instability that was particularly characteristic of the
agricultural department—even to the point of causing its disappear-
ance from the ministerial level in 1958—was ruinous to any program or progress. Any continuing program, whether it be Operation
Plow, *melkization* (distribution to private owners), establishment of
cooperatives, or an agrarian reform based on confiscation and distribution, would have been more beneficial to Moroccan agriculture
than the yearly attempts at new policies brought in by new ministers
and blocked by old rivalries.

2. Besides Operation Plow, the only other change in Moroccan
farming has been accomplished by members of the UMA who have

bought land from both Moroccans and *colons,* increasing their own farms and maintaining colonial plantations intact. Until the *dahir* of November 19, 1959, land ownership in Morocco was relatively mobile, and even after the *dahir* was passed there were political ways of getting around its stringent application. There was, therefore, a process of *melkization,* although it did not involve the mass of small *fellahin.*

The UMA was also unique in that it was one of the few fully developed pressure groups in Morocco; it had more influence than its business counterpart, the Moroccan Union of Commerce, Industry, and Artisans (UMCIA), and it was no less influential—although less diffused and less loud—than its labor counterpart, the UMT. Unlike the UMT, the UMA was relatively uninterested in matters outside its own area. Its members cannot strike (except against themselves), and it has no direct control over a single responsible official. Its close contacts with the king (himself a large landowner) and its insistent visits in large delegation to the Agricultural Minister (refusing to see anyone lower) were, however, typical of the operations of a modern lobby. It should also be noted that the UMA's use of traditional religious arguments against confiscation of private property was also in sympathy with the king's ideas. The UMA supported candidates in the communal elections of May, 1960, and at least claimed successful results.

Above all, the importance of the UMA was that it bridged the dilemma of traditional groups operating in a modern atmosphere: can traditional interests effectively defend themselves against modern attacks except by adopting modern tactics that then destroy their traditionalism? Armed with persistence, repetition, religious slogans, and vague populist claims of having the farmers behind it, the UMA was able to block any sudden, drastic changes in property rights and in traditional farming, although many of its positive demands have been unfulfilled since its inception.[34] The alternative of *melkization* with state and private assistance through cooperatives could have led to improvement and gradual modernization without disruption or great speed. By including modern as well as traditional farmers in its membership, the UMA covered a sector that was so necessary to Morocco's economy and external trade that it was sacred to the country's economic planners; nothing was done in five years to disrupt its operations, despite left-wing hopes of

---

[34] Elimination of the *tertib* (agricultural production tax) had been demanded since the founding of the UMA and promised at that time by Mohammed V, but it took place only in June, 1961, under Hassan II.

egalitarian land distribution. By including small traditional farms,
the UMA could compete in the language of populism that is com-
monly spoken in developing countries. It was a marriage of great
convenience. Because of its dual membership, the UMA stood between its traditionalist members and Rabat, was able to use modern
pressure-group methods to represent its traditionalist following,
and at the same time protect the traditionalist sector from forced
or rapid modernization.

3. The UMA bore within it the seeds of a counterpressure that
—by the mid-1960's—threaten to break its influence and become a
dominant force in Moroccan agriculture and general politics. In
March, 1961, right after the death of Mohammed V, the Agricultural Trade Union (USA) was formed as a branch of the UMT.
Its members came from the more than 70,000 agricultural workers,
most of whom were employed by UMA members. The more the
private landholders increase and expand their holdings above the
single-family size, the more numerous the agricultural workers will
become. This group has the possibility of striking and of causing
violence and has powerful backing in the UMT. Its very existence
within the UMT makes it a natural vehicle for the slogan, "the
land to them that work it."

The problem of agrarian reform is a case of negative decision-
making—the blocking of decisions—and therefore the least finished
of the five cases studied. If the relation of forces were to remain the
same, there would be no reason that the results should be expected
to change in the future. But the interplay of forces that constituted
the decision-making process on agrarian reform, gave rise to a new
force, the agricultural union. The first five years are simply an in-
troduction to a more bitter battle for agrarian reform in the future,
with much higher chances for the passage of a radical and highly
disruptive land reform program.

FIVE

That which cannot be achieved in its entirety
should not be abandoned in its entirety.

—Arab proverb

SOCIAL PROBLEM
Arabization of Primary and Secondary Education

ATTITUDES

The king defined his role in government by the great problems of the moment and left other agencies to handle the rest of governing according to general guidelines which he handed down. In education there were no great momentary obstacles but rather long, slow difficulties; thus the king's guidelines were very general. His vigilant attention had fostered the establishment of the "free" schools as part of the nationalist movement before his exile, and his outstretched arms welcomed the Moroccan masses to "the struggle against illiteracy and ignorance" in posters glued to every wall after independence. His first major mention of the Arabization of education, however, did not come until his 1956 Speech from the Throne, when he reviewed the progress made and laid guidlines for the future.

> In the educational domain, our effort will consist of intensifying the schooling of children and increasing the number of students, of founding a University, of pursuing the effort of Arabizing and generalizing education, and of sending cultural missions into different countries.

This was the most explicit summary of his stand that the king ever gave. The Speech from the Throne two years later contained the apt phrase, "an education that is Moroccan in its thinking, Arabic in its language, and Muslim in its spirit," but the guidelines left all the deciding to other agencies. The same was true in the Council of Ministers, where education was infrequently discussed. In public statement and official act, the king left the academicians their freedom.

In such a situation the field was open to the development of diverse ideas, as well as conflicting attempts to implement them. Attitudes on Arabization did not represent simply a conscious decision or policy position on the isolated problem, but formed part of a complex of socioeconomic backgrounds, ideas, and cultures. One of the major elements of this complex was the future image of the country. The differing approaches to Arabization were remarkably constant in content even through the changing conditions of the first five years of independence, and the change in their effectiveness reflected the power of their proponents rather than the increased persuasiveness or appeal of the arguments themselves.[1]

Traditionalism

The most elusive of all tendencies was the traditionalist, the group that favored maximum Arabization. It was only rarely that "maximum" was taken to mean "complete." More frequently it referred to a separate *baccalauréat marocain* in Arab preparatory to a classic higher education in an enlarged Qarawiyin University, as suggested by Istiqlal leader 'Allal al-Fassi, or major emphasis on the private schools and on the *msids* and *medersas,* as advocated by 'Abdul'aziz ben 'Abdullah, head of the ministry's Division of Higher Muslim Education.[2] To the traditionalists, Arabization was simply an aspect of the desire to develop a specifically Arab culture based on Muslim tradition and the rediscovery of the Islamic vocation of Morocco. The idea was best expressed by the director of the third minister's cabinet, 'Abdelkader Lamrani, in an interview: "Arabi-

---

[1] I am grateful to Ismail Mahroug for suggesting this approach. The best annual review of Moroccan education is found in the yearly report by the Ministry of Education to the International Education Bureau's International Conference on Public Instruction held in the first half of July each year in Geneva and entitled *Education in Morocco* (Rabat: Ministry of Education).

[2] Modern education in Morocco is based on the French system, and the *baccalauréat* is the series of examinations that completes secondary education. The Qarawiyin is Africa's oldest university, founded in Fez in 859, 121 years before Cairo's al-Azhar. For a general description of the Qarawiyin system of education, see *Fez: UNESCO 1958* (Rabat: Ministry of Education, 1958). Private or "free" education was established by political parties under the protectorate to give "national" education in Arabic. The *msid* is the elementary Quranic school, and the *medersa* is the secondary Quranic school in the city; see Paul Bourgeois, *L'Univers de l'écolier marocain* (Rabat: Ministry of Education, 1959), fasc. 1.

zation is a philosophy, a civilization, a way of thinking and of expressing oneself."

Before independence, the traditionalist point of view was firmly implanted in the mosaic walls of the Qarawiyin and was propagated by the nationalist movement, particularly by the original leaders of the Istiqlal. Notions of Arab culture, the inspiration of successful nationalist movements in the Middle East (especially Egypt), reactions to the protectorate's cultural policy of spreading modern French culture and strengthening Berber customs at the expense of Arab customs, politization of the drive against illiteracy through the "free" schools, and nurturing of the neglected glories of the ancient Qarawiyin all reinforced the traditionalist cultural content of the nationalist movement.[3] Independence brought with it the hour of cultural triumph for the traditionalist group, and it succeeded in placing a representative spokesman, Mohammed al-Fassi of the Qarawiyin and the *grande famille* of Fez, at the head of the Education Ministry. After a year of experimentation, however, the traditionalists found themselves deficient in spokesmen in influential places for many reasons: such traditional groups as the *'ulema* were suspect to their former allies for having neglected political nationalism—shown by their general support of the king's deposition in 1953—in favor of cultural nationalism; only the modernists among them had access to the press and public opinion; and the detractors of traditionalism had no trouble in selling the ideas that modernism and Arabism were incompatible.

Yet the traditionalist point of view was kept alive by an outgrowth of the original attitude that can best be described as neotraditionalist. Younger figures such as Public Works and Economic Minister Mohammed Douiri gave renewed impetus to the idea of maximum Arabization by defending its place in a modern world.[4] In the process, original traditionalists were pushed into the back seat, to ride as members of large committees, rather than to steer. Those "old beards" who remained on educational councils were taken aside and subjected to the voice of reason as programs were being discussed. Traditionalist or neotraditionalist, the attitude stemmed from a cultural image of Morocco.

Modernism

The thinking at the other end of the spectrum can be called modernism, although it involved more than simple recognition of

[3] For more detail on these influences and for an excellent review of Moroccan education to 1958, see Lacouture, *op. cit.*, p. 235 *et passim*.

[4] See his speech to Istiqlal party sections at Azrou (*al-Istiqlal*, June 27, 1959).

the contemporary world, just as traditionalism was more complex than a mere outgrowth of the archaic past. The modernist attitude admitted that there was a place for Arabization, but this place was secondary to the immediate effectiveness of education. Since the Moroccan educational system had to prepare its students for a role in a world of modern skills, it was more important to teach the pupils the skills in French, a language in which there were adequate texts and words, than it was to entrust schooling to the undeveloped scientific and technical vocabularies of the Arabic language.[5] The development of the nation's culture to fit its vocation could follow the primary task of training the youth. The modernists derived their view of a proper educational system from their image of a Morocco that would be industrialized, proletarian, and universally benefiting from a basic education. To them, the traditionalists' emotional attachment to a cultural image of Morocco was putting the heart before the courses.

The most eloquent spokesmen for modernism has been Mehdi ben Barka, president of the National Consultative Assembly, exiled leader of the activist National Union of Popular Forces (UNFP), and a mathematics teacher by profession.

> We intend to conserve the use of French, not so much through love for France but by the necessity of having an opening into the West. . . . We are firmly decided to go ahead with Arabization . . . and to affirm our Islamic culture but we also propose to open windows onto Western culture by using French as a complementary language . . . so as not to remain in asphyxiating isolation.[6]

It was possibly ben Barka who wrote the *al-Istiqlal* editorial reporting,

> unanimous approval [of Arabization]. But alas, the same unanimity exists in adding, "If we are happy to see our language finally given the importance it deserves, we are no less eager that our children go to school. . . . If the number of teachers

[5] On the insufficiencies of Arabic in the modern world, see A. Faure, "Considérations générales sur la diglossie chez les Arabes et quelques autres peuples," *Confluent* (Rabat), VII (May 1960), 298–310; Gerard Lecompte, "Reflexions sur un vocabulaire technique en formation," *Orient* (Paris), V (1961), 13–25; *Education Nationale*, VII (May 1960), 23. Two rough and very selective polls in 1957 both indicated that 60 per cent of the sample did not understand classical Arabic perfectly on the radio but all understood Moroccan dialect or one of the three Berber dialects (*al-Istiqlal*, November 2, 1957, March 6, 1958).

[6] *Al-'Alam*, May 15, 1957; *Monde*, May 16, 1957; Mehdi ben Barka, *Problèmes d'édification du Maroc et du Maghreb* (Paris: Plon, 1959), pp. 34–35.

> capable of teaching in Arabic is insufficient, we would prefer
> to see our children learn French, rather than leaving them in
> the streets." [7]

Another current of modernist thought was found in a group of young leaders who stayed with the old-guard Istiqlal. Mohammed Tahiri, a forceful spokesman on economics and a former under-secretary of state in the Education Ministry, had been a leading proponent of this group. Arabization was to be a by-product of economic production, lest, in reverse order, it impede economic progress.

> The hasty Arabization which caused the resignation of several
> hundred qualified French instructors is deplorable. . . . Tech-
> nical Arabic is made in the crucible of the shop; it does not
> enter the shop by way of translation.[8]

Behind the political separation between the old guard and activists, however, lay some other basic differences. Tahiri's economic image of Morocco was essentially agriculture, requiring the teaching of basic technical skills as early as the primary grades, whereas the economic image of ben Barka was industrial. At the same time, the old guard's modernism still aimed at maintaining the religious content of Moroccan culture, whereas the activists generally cared little about Islam; this was a serious political difference, although little publicized, and since the Quran can be read only in Arabic, it was highly relevant to the problem of Arabization. All the modernist attitudes, however, were based on an economic image of Morocco.

Nationalism

A third attitude can be called nationalist, not because the traditionalists or the modernists were any less patriotic than the other groups, but because nationalist recommendations for the Arabization of education were based primarily on the view that the problem was political or post-colonial rather than as cultural or economic. The maintenance of French meant the maintenance of cultural colonialism, a less-than-perfect independence, in fact, a direct dependence on the former colonial power; Arabization meant joining the Arab brothers and other people in love with liberty, as the phrase went, and liberation from the yoke of colonialism. The

[7] October 6, 1956.
[8] February 21, 1959. For Tahiri's plan for education, see *ibid.*, September 3, 1958.

fact that proponents of this attitude usually had little technical interest in or understanding of the educational issue made no difference in their effectiveness. By moving the discussion to the level of the most popular abstractions, they could cause the educators more trouble than the more pertinent debates between the traditionalists and the modernists. Furthermore, the nationalists did not congregate in closed groups, but were found throughout the parties and labor groups or, in fact, wherever the factual argument was weak and emotions were high. Thus, the Moroccan Communist party (PCM) newspaper, *La Nation,* wrote, "There was talk of stopping Arabization completely, which would have perpetuated the colonial type of schooling"; *ar-Rai al-'Amm* once wrote of the ministries' use of French in correspondence, with the implication that the use of the colonial language was subversive; [9] and a member of the Education Ministry once said, "The UMT plays the Arabization card. I do not know what it [really] thinks." The nationalist picture was, therefore, a political image of Morocco.

Professionalism

The opposite of the nationalist way of thinking was the professional, an attitude which many employees of the ministry held no matter what their background. The professional man was a natural and frequently vulnerable target for the nationalists, since he was drowned in problems of technical detail but was frequently in enough contact with his party to feel nationalist criticism as more than wind outside the window. Employees of the ministry, particularly at the decision-making level of the divisions, were generally conscientious, and many of them simply let their party friendships and affiliations lapse under the conflicting demands and loyalties imposed by their jobs and party propaganda. The professional attitude toward Arabization recognized the cultural goal as desirable and quickly passed on to the practical obstacles, such as the inadequacy of teachers, books, and words. Since the attitude was academically, not culturally, economically, or politically based, the professional point of view stressed full heads instead of heads well filled. Under attack from the other three schools, which he considered largely irrelevant, the professional was often overcome by his own difficulties; with so many details in the way, he was un-

[9] *La Nation,* September 12, 1958; *ar-Rai,* February 12, 1960; see also *al-Istiqlal,* June 20 and October 5, 1959; National Consultative Assembly Social Affairs Committee, *PM,* April 6, 1959; Civil Service Minister Rashid Mouline, *PM,* July 2, 1957.

able to picture a doctrine of new Moroccan teaching. Nacer al-Fassi, in the Division of Muslim Education in 1956, wrote:

> It is incontestable that Arabic should be the basic language of our education. . . . But we are also aware of our present impossibility to make this desire effective. It is not a question of making great and spectacular changes which would take us back to a clean slate. . . . To the contrary, it is a matter of carrying out methodical reforms.

This is a rare and courageous statement for 1956 and one that was presented in *al-Istiqlal* with the note that al-Fassi was speaking only for himself and that comments were invited.[10] In 1959, Ahmed Salmi, head of the Secondary Education Service, wrote a memo to his minister:

> It would perhaps be more reasonable to envisage less rapid Arabization by not fixing a precise date and by Arabizing each year the number of pupils one can by following the proposed methods for the formation of teachers. . . . It is presently impossible to foresee a complete and precise plan.

Since the professionals were dealing with facts whereas the traditionalists, nationalists, and modernists were dealing with feelings, it is easy to say that the professionals were right. But right has little meaning in this context, for right is secondary to possible, and one of the facts that the professionals did their best to ignore was the existence of the other three attitudes, which continued to pressure, push, and block technical plans.[11] Since the professionals, by their position and by the willingness of the king to maintain them in that position, had a built-in advantage, the contest turned from substance to procedure, with proponents of opposing attitudes trying to unseat the deciding group.

EXPERIMENT

Mohammed al-Fassi, the tutor of the prince, an original member of the Istiqlal,[12] and a former rector of the ancient Qarawiyin

[10] *Al-Istiqlal*, April 20, 1956. No comments were forthcoming.

[11] A pathetic example of the nationalist approach to professional problems is found in some of the demands of the Istiqlal party's national meeting, "c) Installation of Arabic as the basic language of the civil service. . . . e) Make education obligatory. . . . g) Find work for all the unemployed masses . . . ," and then "f) Be economical in the expenditures of the state" (*al-Istiqlal*, July 20, 1956).

[12] He was co-founder, with Balafrej, of the Association of North African Muslim Students (AEMAN) in Paris in the 1930's.

University at Fez, was appointed minister of public instruction and
fine arts in December, 1955. His ministry bore the name given it
by the protectorate, had Frenchmen as 99 per cent of its 300 civil
servants, and carried out the program of the protectorate for the
school year 1955–1956. Teaching in Moroccan primary schools was
conducted in French for twenty hours of the week and in Arabic for
ten hours, and secondary education, including the teaching of Arabic, was all in French. Not until the beginning of the next school
year was the name of the ministry changed to Ministry of National
Education, and Youth and Sports and was serious reorganization
undertaken. The unity of public schooling was then broken by the
separation of primary and secondary Muslim education into two
independent divisions. A ministerial cabinet and three new divisions—Free (private), Basic (adult) and Higher Islamic Education
—were created and headed by Moroccans. An attempt at Arabizing
the ministry itself was begun, resulting in more inefficiency than
success.

Much of the weakness lay in the leadership of al-Fassi, who
simply did not realize the complexity of many of the problems but
was sympathetically aware of the general enthusiasm for universal
education and rapid Arabization. Upon taking office, he set himself
the goal of making education universal and obligatory, "with Arabic as the basic vehicular language," and he announced the preparation of a technical plan to overcome the lack of schools, texts,
and teachers. The extent of this enthusiasm was shown in the announcement of the "Mohammed al-Fassi Plan for the Schooling of
Moroccan Youth" for 1956–1957. With his goal already fixed at
universal education for the first three grades within half a decade
and maximum "yield (rendement)" from the current educational
system, al-Fassi had to point out that it was not possible to uni-
versalize education in the six primary grades within the initial
five years because of a shortage of teachers and funds (i.e., that it
was not immediately possible to triple the number of school children). Only a public which felt that limited education was a colonialist plot with no practical reasons would need that fact explained.

The al-Fassi plan, however, was bold and ambitious. It foresaw
a five-grade primary educational cycle with universal participation
in the first three grades by the end of five years and selective participation for better students in the latter two grades. It, therefore,
combined both universal and elite features of an educational system. The first grade was to be immediately and entirely Arabized.

The remaining four grades were each to be divided into fifteen hours of French instruction and fifteen hours of Arabic instruction a week, two grades at a time beginning in 1956; [13] on completion of this phase, the time was to be divided into twenty hours of Arabic and ten hours of French instruction, two grades at a time beginning in 1958.[14] The major initial change was teaching arithmetic and elementary natural science in Arabic instead of French. The plan thus provided for gradual and partial Arabization beginning with the primary cycle. In the six grades of the secondary cycle, no immediate change was foreseen until such matters as the lack of teachers and books and the possibility of a *baccalauréat marocain* in Arabic could be examined. The general plan stemmed from the inspiration of the minister and was discussed and approved by the division heads of the ministry.

Increased Arabization in the primary grades called at least one group into existence and rapid action. For all first-grade subjects and for second- and third-grade arithmetic, Arabic texts were needed. Mohammed al-Machrafi, head of the Primary Division, Hussein Bekkari, then head of the Free Education Division, and Mohammed Ghiati and Henri Maufrais, general inspectors of Muslim Education, formed a committee to prepare the books. By the beginning of the 1956–1957 school year, a second- and third-grade *Arithmetic Larousse* and accompanying teacher's guide were ready for use. By the following school year, a colorful first-grade arithmetic exercise book, a two-volume teaching manual, and a conversation manual were produced by different authors in the ministry, and in 1958 an Arabic reader and a Moroccan history were available. Although there were pedagogical weaknesses in the books, they were the first available Arabized texts for the program.

Despite the traditionalist views of al-Fassi, his professional position and the pressure of his colleagues made him more moderate about Arabization than is generally recognized. His careful, sometimes conflicting, attempts to define the position of Arabic and French in the school system testify to his attempt to grapple realistically with the problem.

> Education will be unified, based on Arabic with a knowledge of a foreign language that will permit students to attain the secondary cycle and to prepare to gain the greatest benefit from higher modern studies, either in the Orient or in the west. . . . With the Arabization of education in mind, we

[13] To be referred to hereafter as the "30-15-15 schedule."
[14] To be referred to hereafter as the "30-20-10 schedule."

have established a program making Arabic the basic language of education. . . . French will be obligatory as a second language. For me, Arabic is the national language, and, of course, in my mind, what I called "second language" for the *baccalauréat marocain* would be another language than French or Arabic. . . .

In the future, Arabic will be called upon to play the leading role both in the administration and in industry and commerce. It is in the interest of the Moroccans to learn French just as it is in the interest of the French [in Morocco] to learn Arabic. In the Northern Zone, we will naturally keep an important role for Spanish, as we do for French in the rest of Morocco. . . .

French will really be the second national language. . . .

For the Moroccans, [we must] make French a language coming immediately after the national language as a language of culture and expression.[15]

Arabization caused special problems with the teaching staff. Among the 6,851 Frenchmen who made up half of the teaching corps in 1956, the plans and rumors of Arabization led to a wave of doubts, shared also by the French-speaking Moroccans; both saw themselves jobless because of the cultural reorganization. Before rumors of total and immediate Arabization, the minister solemnly pledged that "not a single French teacher in the Muslim Education [Division] will be deprived of his post in Morocco," but in supporting the argument, instead of citing the overwhelming need for teachers, the minister was less convincing: "The teacher might, for example, give French lessons, even though he be replaced in the teaching of arithmetic by a Moroccan colleague or even by a Frenchman who speaks Arabic. . . . No changes will be made." [16]

Since these early doubts arose during lagging negotiations on a cultural convention with France, they were natural, even if exaggerated. Negotiations began in May, 1956, but were broken off, along with all other relations with France, following the kidnaping of Algerian leaders in October. Even in the absence of this incident, negotiations in 1956 were not near agreement. When negotiations reopened eleven months later, there was an air of greater urgency. The French fears of Arabization were not calmed by the educational disorder of the past school year, and France insisted on

[15] Quotes from press conference, June 25, 1956; *al-Istiqlal*, April 13 and 20, 1956; *Monde*, May 22, 1956; speech before Economic Commission of the Group for Economic and Social Studies and Realizations (*ibid.*, March 15, 1956).

[16] Press conference, June 25, 1956.

a dual system for French and Moroccan students. At the same time the members of the French teachers' union threatened to strike by mid-May if a convention was not drawn up guaranteeing proper schooling for their children and a fixed statute for themselves; even before the negotiations broke off at the beginning of the school year, nearly 150 teachers had left Morocco. Under this pressure, the Moroccan delegation consented to separate schooling for French children, and the convention, initiated on May 30, 1957, established a French Cultural and University Mission (MUCF) which was to be granted the use of seven *lycées* and *collèges* and 1,024 primary classes for seven years at the most.[17] The presence of the French teachers was ensured, but one-third of them taught in the MUCF schools, which were attended primarily by the French. In the general relief over the agreement, it was often forgotten that the large number of French teachers was only temporary and that many of the same problems would be posed again in 1961. In 1959, the ministry was obliged to state very clearly that "the recruitment of French teachers, indispensable as long as Morocco does not have sufficient personnel [of its own], should be considered only a complementary support, relatively limited."

Attempts were made to balance this cultural engagement by increasing ties with the Middle East, a direction more compatible with Arabization. Pressure for this action was far less than the enthusiasm behind Arabization or the interest in the Cultural Convention. Only isolated groups, such as the students of Tetuan or the Moroccan students in Damascus, publicly asked for increased cultural ties with the Middle East, although, on a very abstract level, the king and his ministers proclaimed Morocco's membership in the culture of the Arab world. The agreements with Middle East professors and teachers in Morocco were largely the personal work of Mohammed al-Fassi. As the Moroccan member of the Egyptian Academy at Cairo, as the Arab representative at the 1956 UNESCO Conference at New Delhi who proposed that Arabic be adopted as a working language of the organization, and as rector of the Qarawiyin, al-Fassi had contacts and respect in the Arab academic world. It is interesting to note that there appears to have been no drive from Cairo to recover culturally the newly liberated Arab far west. No technical assistance program could be negotiated and imple-

[17] For the text of the agreements, see *Maroc-Documents*, I (August 1957), 43–68. For a critique and comparison with the United Arab Republic cultural agreement, see *al-Istiqlal*, December 26, 1959. In 1959–1960, 11,000 of the 33,000 primary school children and 3,300 of the 11,000 secondary school children in MUCF schools were Moroccans; MUCF report, *PM*, June 30, 1960.

mented in time for the 1956–1957 school year, and the final total
of teachers supplied during the following school year from all
Middle Eastern countries totaled only 225, two-thirds of whom
came from Egypt. Egypt and Iraq also opened their own schools in
the same year, the one in Rabat and the other in Fez.

The experiment in cultural assistance was a significant failure.
The Moroccans found the Egyptians better orators than teachers,
more eloquent in praising their native land than in teaching their
subject matter. No more than the Moroccans had they solved the
problem of modern communication in an ancient language. Their
Arabic was a mixture of Egyptian dialect and words borrowed from
English and French without any standardization, their basic vocabulary was still only half that taught in European schools at
corresponding grades, and their own technical training was inadequate. Moroccans on all sides of the Arabization question agreed in
blaming Middle Eastern exchange professors for the drop in the
quality of teaching. The Egyptians, on the other hand, were un-
impressed by a system which did not pay them on time, and, with
much less stamina or cultural attachment than the French teachers
in the same situation, they went home at the end of the first year.
In concept, also, the teachers from the Middle East were criticized

TABLE 6

TEACHERS

(primary Muslim, Jewish, European, technical;
secondary Muslim, European, technical systems)

System	Nationality	1945–1946	1955–1956	1956–1957	1957–1958	1958–1959	1959–1960	Trained in Arabic
1	Moroccan	1,064	4,426	6,179	9,476	9,489	13,062	1959–1960—10,428; 1958–1959— 7,500
1	French	2,702	6,272	5,117	4,214 §	3,432 §	5,140	
2	Moroccan	63	75	216	285	350	455	1959–1960— 292
2	French	884	1,549	1,734	1,298 §	1,500 §	1,284	
1 & 2	Egyptian *	0	0	21 ‡	154	0	21	
1 & 2	Lebanese	0	0	0	34	0	36	
1 & 2	Syrian	0	0	0	31	0	4	
1 & 2	Iraqi †	0	0	0	3	0	3	
1 & 2	Iranian	0	0	0	1	0	1	
1 & 2	Jordanian	0	0	0	2	0	1	
1 & 2	Tunisian	0	0	0	2	0	8	

Source: Ministry of Education
* Not including mission in Rabat.
† Not including school in Fez.
‡ May include superior system.
§ Not including MUCF.

by Morocco. To Moroccans their teaching was no more national than was the French. Arabism was an important symbol at an abstract level, but neither the ministry nor the other political groups were interested in learning Egyptian history, Nasser's triumphs, or Middle East Arabic dialects. Other Arab countries did aid Morocco, but they had only a limited number of teachers available to send abroad.

With neither a French nor an Arab way out of the teacher training problems, the ministry was obliged to devise training programs as accelerated as the education programs for the pupils the trainees were to teach. Various systems of rapid preparation were attempted, including summer sessions, student teaching, and the creation of new regional teachers' schools (which themselves demanded new teachers). Above all, the ministry had to combat a poor opinion of the teaching profession, which involved harder work, poorer pay, and less authority than such high-status jobs as those in the civil service, police, or army—and which lacked the uniform and prestige of the latter two. Yet the ministry had neither the money nor the program to popularize the profession. Between 1955 and 1957, the increase in Moroccan teachers kept up with the percentage increase of pupils in primary and secondary education; the number rose from 4,501 to 9,761 while student enrollment also doubled. But the total number of teachers rose from 12,000 to only 15,000, since more than 2,000 Frenchmen withdrew from the Moroccan system, and the Moroccan increase could not make up the loss.

Arabization was carried out on an *ad hoc* basis, taught where there were teachers and other necessary supports, and ignored where the programs could not be changed. The language used was a hodgepodge of dialectical Moroccan and classical Arabic, depending on the teacher. The informal implementation of the program of Arabization makes it impossible to give any figures on its effectiveness, but it was widespread enough to affect the general quality of teaching without being well enough prepared to raise or even maintain that quality.[18] Had there been a systematic conversion of existing programs in accord with plans for increased Arabization, some kind of order might have been maintained, but concomitant

[18] Enrollment figures are just as deceptive; in some primary grades they refer to schooling given in double half-time classes, with a full year's program crammed into double half-day sessions. According to the plan, the first three grades in rural schools and all first-grade classes were to be half time. On the other hand, *al-Istiqlal* reported that only 460 of 6,377 rooms were used for half-time classes, indicating only partial implementation of the plan (May 18, 1957).

plans for massive increases in enrollment further contributed to
making orderly Arabization impossible. In this situation, outside
critics did not hesitate from the beginning of the 1956–1957 school
year to attack the ministry for slowness in attaining universal education and at the same time for the inadequacy of its Arabization
program.

By the end of his second year in charge of independent Morocco's educational system, al-Fassi was faced with four vigorous
and thoroughly conflicting indictments. Critics attacked the school
system for insufficient capacity and for letting "the kids hang
around in the streets, just as in the past." [19] Despite the tremendous,
if deceptive, increase in enrollment, the minister was condemned
for lack of a dynamic, radical, even explosive approach, particularly
by the modernists; his program was a drop of water in the sea. The
same ministry was also criticized for lowering the quality of primary
and secondary education, although it was the much demanded leap
into quantity that inevitably lowered the standards; this criticism
came from all groups, including those who continued to demand
increased enrollment. In a major shift of strength among the different attitudes, however, al-Fassi was also decried for his attempts to
Arabize, since they compounded the lowering of quality. Before the
end of the 1956–1957 school year, the Secondary School Teachers'
Union passed a resolution demanding

> . . . the suspension of the current experiment in Arabization
> until truly qualified cadres can be formed. If the Minister per-
> sists in wanting to continue this harmful experiment in the
> present conditions, he alone must bear all the consequences
> of this action.[20]

The first general attacks on al-Fassi's policy by his own party
began with the opening of school in 1956, but there were no
candidates for al-Fassi's post when the government was reorganized
during October, so al-Fassi remained in office. There was, however,
a convenient opportunity to broaden the lines of decision-making.

---

[19] *Ibid.*, October 6, 1956.

[20] *Ibid.*, April 6, 1957, followed by a supporting letter to the editor, *ibid.*,
May 4, 1957. For a sample of other criticism and its sources, see Driss Medkouri
(FNE-UMT) interpellation of al-Fassi in the National Consultative Assembly,
March 19, 1957; al-Fassi before the National Consultative Assembly Social Com-
mittee (*ibid.*, June 8, 1957); Association of the Teachers of Salé (*ibid.*, November
9, 1956); National Union of Moroccan Students (UNEM) Council of Administra-
tion meeting April 19–22 (*ibid.*, April 27, 1957); *ibid.*, October 5, 1956 and
January 4, 1957; resolution of UMT (*ibid.*, May 4, 1957).

Borrowing from the French institutions, the party subcommision on education had reported to the Istiqlal National Congress in December, 1955:

> A consultative council should function alongside the Ministry of National Education . . . to elaborate the programs of the different cycles of education to which it would give a national Moroccan orientation, re-establishing Arabic as the language of culture.

The following year, the Superior Commission of Educational Reform (CSRE) was created, and its members were appointed by the king after nomination by the minister. The commission had a free field in the discussion of general educational policy and little idea of precisely what was expected of it. It met for the first time in December, 1956, and the king chose a subcommission to establish its working program.

The old Istiqlal professor, Mohammed Ghazi, correctly characterized the contradictory atmosphere that prevailed when he called the members at the second meeting "idealists in the principles, realists in practice." The commission's optimistic goal for the educational system was the maintenance of

> . . . a level of culture and education equal to that in the most modern countries, permitting us to train various cadres in complete harmony with traditional Muslim and modern Western culture but always within the framework of a Muslim spirit.[21]

In the field of Arabization the commission decreed:

> Unification of the country by the greatest possible extension of the Arabic language to the teaching of subject matter, every time that this can be done without harming the quality of the acquired knowledge.[22]

It looked toward complete teaching and use of Arabic at all levels, although the formula concerned with French and Spanish was identical except for the word "complete"; the relation between the languages was made more practical and explicit in the list of imperatives, which made the choice of language dependent on the availability of competent teachers. Arabization was to be "prudent"

[21] *Ibid.*, July 6, 1957.
[22] *Ibid.*, February 9, 1957.

to the point of "harming in no way the level of studies." In principle the commission thereby recognized current practice.

Two major figures stood out in the commission debates.[23] One was ben Barka, whose participation in the discussions was lucid, organized, and to the point. He showed a comprehension far above that of most other participants, who spent their time arguing in twos and threes or wandering lamely about the subject. Ben Barka sought a pragmatic synthesis of two conflicting approaches to doctrine: the modernist, which advocated a new beginning in Moroccan education with a single system that would replace the confusion of the many existing branches, and the professional, which proposed keeping the old systems patched together for modern use. On the specific question of language, he advocated the preservation of French "wherever the shift to Arabic would bring a drop in quality even in the primary grades, and the assurance of rapid training in French for the technical branches." The minister made known his agreement.

As ben Barka moderated the modernists, so al-Fassi worked to win over the more reluctant traditionalists to an evolution in doctrine. By insisting that practical possibilities must determine—not be determined by—the doctrine and by continually showing the limitations of these practicalities, the minister gave persuasive support to bilingualism. He was particularly interested in formulating new scholastic programs, followed by a development of the necessary texts; this approach itself contributed to the support of more gradual Arabization.

The commission divided itself into subcommissions in February, 1957, to implement its principles; the division embodied a greater reform than was to be found in any of the formal proposals by uniting Muslim, private, and Jewish education in the Primary and Secondary Subcommissions. The Subcommission on Primary Education emphasized progressive Arabization and Islamic learning and supported continuation of the 30-20-10 schedule set up in the Mohammed al-Fassi plan. The Subcommission for Secondary Education adhered even more firmly to the professional line. Although it sought to "grant the Arabic language its national and vehicular role," it recognized that, pending the training of competent teachers, all specialized disciplines—history, geography, science, and mathematics—would remain in French or Spanish.

[23] The following material is taken from the transcript of the commission debates, courtesy of the ministry library, and *Enseignement Secondaire Musulman* (Rabat: Ministry of Education, 1957).

Two subcommissions, however, did germinate some ideas that were later used as initial steps in a new approach to the problem. The problem of teacher-training was finally faced, with a proposal for the Pedagogical Institute of Secondary Education (IPES) "to limit the recruitment of teachers from abroad." The IPES was opened to high school graduates for a one-year course in October, 1957, and later expanded to a full two-year course. In its first two years, 110 student teachers were graduated. The IPES was attacked by the Division of Higher Education and disparaged by primary-education leaders, but it showed growing professional awareness of the fact that quality had to be prepared, not decreed. As a corollary, discussion of the IPES brought out secondary education directors' determination to resist the inroads of hasty Arabization, which had entered and, they felt, weakened the primary program. The IPES was conceived not as an instrument of Arabization but as an institute for training in all disciplines—with training, therefore, largely in French.

The Subcommission on Technical Education, which advocated bilingualism for its branch of instruction, proposed a more important innovation as the work of the commission moved into the summer. It "wished to see a Dictionary Commission unite men of science and letters with specialists in interpretation, to establish a lexicon of Arabic technical literature." The idea would have put the nationalist and traditionalist demands in their proper perspective by first creating a complete language which could be used in texts, programs, teacher-training, and finally in progressive Arabization. But its realization was too distant, and it died.

The commission was institutionally incapable of matching its ideas to programs. The minister was too firmly committed to satisfying public enthusiasm for quantity and Arabization to turn any creative effort into implementing the commission's ideas. It was, in fact, his sincere belief that he was correctly interpreting popular will that made al-Fassi so deeply hurt, even shocked, when, in the third government, his party came into almost complete control but he was replaced. Al-Fassi felt with bitterness that he was ousted by ben Barka, who was wary of both massive enrollment and Arabization.

RETRENCHMENT

The political maneuvering that accompanied the formation of Balafrej's government brought Hajj 'Omar ben 'Abdeljalil out of the Agricultural Ministry to succeed Mohammed al-Fassi. 'Abdeljalil was an older Istiqlali than al-Fassi; his family, too, was from the intellectual aristocracy of Fez, but he himself was a prosperous agricultural engineer. He knew little of the technical problems of education, was unaided and unhampered by a past in the Qarawiyin, and was in the hospital when his appointment came up. His strong points—in addition to his amiable manner and authoritative competence in management—were his old and influential position in the party and his particular fitness for handling the problems of technical education, which so much interested the king. For the latter problem he also brought with him Mohammed Tahiri, who, as undersecretary of state for professional, administrative and technical training, helped 'Abdeljalil with matters of technical education in the minister's ailing moments.

'Abdeljalil was little conversant with pedagogical doctrine, but he was interested in a competent ministry. He, therefore, leaned heavily on his ministerial hierarchy in his decisions, and he left his cabinet to run the ministry (outside the technical education branch) when he returned to the hospital. He moved Nacer al-Fassi from his position at the head of the Secondary Muslim Education Division to the vacant post of secretary general (administrative officer). In his former office, Nacer al-Fassi had tempered public approval of Arabization with a professional consideration for possibilities. He regarded quality the primary problem and teacher-training its answer; when gradual Arabization would be possible, he felt it should be started in the primary grades on a pragmatic, *ad hoc* basis whenever the competent teachers were available. He was a respected, nonpartisan figure, effective in conciliation and articulate as a spokesman for the professional point of view. Ahmed Salmi, who was more interested in quality than Arabization, was appointed to succeed al-Fassi as head of the Secondary Muslim Education Division.

The new minister entered his job with orders for change from the highest authority. When the new government was formed, the king had specifically spoken of the problems of education. "The objectives, orientation, programs and methods of teaching must be reconsidered, in order that they answer to the demands of the modern epoch. . . ." The approach of the school year and the need to put the two-year plan for 1958–1959 into final form provided the setting for a serious debate, and the dependence of the minister on the professional competence of his ministry gave the discussion greater depth. But it did not give it publicity. The discussion over one of the most drastic policy changes in Morocco took place with a total absence of public debate on real possibilities. This was a welcome change, occasioned by the technical nature of the subject and the ministry's desire to keep its debates behind its own doors.

TABLE 7

MOROCCANS IN SCHOOL

$$\left(\frac{male}{female} = \text{total in ooo} \right)$$

School systems	1955– 1956	1956– 1957	1957– 1958	1958– 1959	1959– 1960	1960– 1961
Primary						
Muslim	$\frac{165}{50} = 215$	310 ‡	$\frac{345}{131} = 476$	527	$\frac{447}{153} = 600$	710
European	415	7	$\frac{4.3}{4.3} = 8.5$	12	$\frac{8.9}{8.5} = 17.5$	25
Secondary						
Muslim	$\frac{6.5}{.8} = 7.3$	13	$\frac{20}{3} = 24$	$\frac{20}{10} = 29$	$\frac{18}{4.6} = 23$	27
European	3	5	$\frac{3.7}{1.3} = 5$	6	$\frac{4.8}{2.2} = 7$	7
Jewish	33	31	$\frac{14}{15} = 30$	31	$\frac{16}{15} = 31$	30
Traditional						
Primary *	20	38	$\frac{42}{30} = 72$	68	72	85
Secondary and higher	3.6	9.4	$\frac{11.3}{.3} = 11.6$	$\frac{15}{.3} = 15.3$	24.5	$\frac{24}{3} = 27$
MUCF						
Primary	0	0	6	9	11	10
Secondary	0	0	3	3	3.3	3
Total †	285	415	$\frac{439}{185} = 625$	685	770	910
School-age (7–14) children	1,500	1,600	1,700	1,800	1,900	2,000

Source: Ministry of Education
* Including free or private.
† Not including MUCF.
‡ Number of girl students unavailable for 1956–1957 and for most sections in 1958–1959 and 1960–1961.

The government was scarcely in office a month when the first note of the new tune was sounded by Economics Minister 'Abderrahim Bou'abid in announcing the new plan.

> The draft for the Two-Year Plan accents above all the training of teachers and the reduction of the rhythm of enrollment to a level compatible with the financial necessities and the possibilities of teacher-training.[24]

At the same time, an article appeared over Mohammed Machrafi's signature in the ministry's periodical. "The Development of Primary Muslim Education" summarized the achievements of his division; the hand of 'Abdeljalil was evident, in the four paragraphs of the conclusion:

> ─ The principle of total enrollment . . . must be abandoned, at least for the moment, in favor of rapid formation of a technical elite. . . . The principle of Arabization has been loudly proclaimed by the Reform Commission. . . . It may, however, appear desirable to apply it only with prudence and only to the extent that the adoption of Arabic as a vehicular language does not lower the level of teaching. . . . A serious investigation of this matter is necessary. . . .[25]

On August 25, 1958, the Reform Commission met for the last time. Instead of being allowed the leisurely deliberation on principles and practice of education that it had had the previous year, it found itself seated in the auditorium of the School of Humanities of the new Moroccan University, listening to a program for drastic reform from a determined minister. With maximum politeness and lip service to its principles, the commission was asked to ratify the interment of the al-Fassi plan on which it had united the year before. The commission reacted with impotent vigor. It unanimously insisted on its attachment to the principle of Arabization as soon as possible, but agreed to the teaching of science and arithmetic in French; in order to "consolidate" the Arabic language, it proposed a lengthening of the primary grades by one year, called for increased enrollment, and requested the creation of subcommissions to formulate concrete plans for Arabizing and generalizing education. It thanked the minister for the solicitude and comprehension of his efforts, but begged him to carry their grievances to the cabinet.

'Abdeljalil and his ministry proposed to regain lost quality

[24] Al-Istiqlal, June 22, 1958.
[25] Notes et Documents, VI (June 1958), p. 12.

through the application of a professional solution not dictated by political considerations. A six-year primary cycle of full-day classes was re-established with pupils in the former first three grades (now grades two to four) redoing a year. Because of the proven impossibility of teaching arithmetic and elementary science in Arabic at the time, these courses were to be given in French, and French language instruction was increased, although additional instruction in ethics and religion were to be given in Arabic. The division of grades two through six was thus changed from 20-10 to fifteen hours in Arabic and fifteen in French. Half-time classes for the first three years were ended, full-time instruction was given, class enrollment was lowered from an average of seventy to a top limit of fifty pupils a class, and added emphasis was placed on teacher-training. In September, 1958, the cabinet met to discuss the plan and the commission's grievances. It affirmed the principle of Arabization, recognized the practical limitations imposed by the lack of competent teachers, and ratified 'Abdeljalil's proposals as the commission had done before.

In relation to other Arab countries, an additional setback in Arabization was registered under the 'Abdeljalil ministry. Although a cultural treaty with the United Arab Republic was under discussion and a similar agreement with Tunisia was signed in July, 1958, the first year's experiment had proven unsatisfactory to both sides. Egyptian professors were maintained in institutions of higher education in Morocco, but, in the school year 1958–1959, no contracts for Middle Eastern teachers were renewed for the primary and secondary cycles.[26]

Three years and two ministries were necessary to put the problem of Arabization into its proper perspective. In fact, given the state of public enthusiasm for cultural nationalism, the first stage was necessary to provoke the reaction which made the proposals of 'Abdeljalil possible. When his short ministry ended with the fall of the government in the middle of the school year 1958–1959, several new premises characterized the educational scene. From the first ministry and the Royal Commission was instilled the principle of Arabization, as incontrovertible as independence, even if granted only lip service when detailed plans were to be made. From the commission also came the practical idea of flexibility in implementing the principle. From the ministry of 'Abdeljalil came the attitude

[26] I am grateful to M. Tazi of the Office of Cultural Exchanges of the ministry for this information. See also *Monde,* October 28, 1958; *PM,* July 21 and 25, 1958, September 18, 1958.

and actions which pulled decision-making in education out of the market place and newspapers and put it into the hands of professionals in the ministry.

But the 'Abdeljalil plan was no final solution or even a long-term project. It was a stopgap measure designed to bring quality back into the educational system, and its implementation posed new problems. Given the acceptance of Arabization, which could not be totally or externally ignored, what should be the next step in effecting—rather than temporarily limiting—the principle? What would be the reaction of external forces temporarily excluded from decision-making? What would be the reaction of those in the ministry who opposed the temporary policy? What would be the attitudes of all the schools of thought on the establishment of a coherent doctrine which had been postponed for three years by *ad hoc* solutions?

EXPANSION

Benjelloun's Ministry

The answers to these questions were to be met over the next three years by a man who was as much of a newcomer to education as 'Abdeljalil. On the formation of the fourth government on Christmas Day, 1958, the king placed 'Abdelkrim Benjelloun Touimi, also a founder of the Istiqlal party, in the Education Ministry. During his three years as minister of justice, Benjelloun had won respect by revamping and unifying a system as confusing and as diverse as the school system; the king chose him to do the same in his new job. Benjelloun's training as a lawyer and a legal reform minister led him to look for the solution of problems by legislation; he was critical of *ad hoc* solutions to institutional problems and set about to transform 'Abdeljalil's stopgap program into long-term reform legislation. His goals included unification of the system, the creation of a Moroccan national school, and hence even greater attention to finding scholastic doctrine than his predecessors gave.

His first action was to impose a reorganization of the ministry —characteristically, by *dahir*.[27] Nacer al-Fassi was retained as secretary general, and the post was enlarged beyond its duties of coordination to include supervision of special administration and orientation services. The division heads' meeting was made a frequent and regular event with al-Fassi presiding, thus further co-

[27] *Dahir* No. 1-59-006 of February 9, 1959, discussed in a meeting of division heads, January 6, 1959, and in the Council of Ministers, January 14, 1959, implemented by ministerial order. The following material is taken from transcripts of the division heads' meetings, courtesy of the ministry library.

ordinating and enhancing the role of the top civil servants of the ministry. Taking the lead from the subcommissions of the Royal Commission, the minister created a single Division of Primary Education with Machrafi at its head and thus took an important step in unifying the diverse systems at the top. A single Division of Secondary Education was also created, with Salmi continuing at its head. However, the pressure of traditionalist groups was too strong to be immediately overcome; unification took place only at the top, and the body of Islamic or original education—even in primary and secondary grades—remained under the Division of Higher Islamic Education.

During early 1959, the division heads met to formulate educational doctrine and more specifically to prepare to apply it in the coming school year. The secretary general recalled the guidelines of the royal commission, which foresaw massive enrollment and a "tendency towards Arabization." He proposed a compromise between the systems of Mohammed al-Fassi and 'Abdeljalil by returning to a five-grade primary cycle with the first two grades meeting half time in Arabic and the last three grades meeting full time, fifteen hours in French and fifteen in Arabic. Machrafi looked eventually to a completely Arabized primary cycle, with the secondary cycle open to a choice between French and Arabic in its latter grades of specialization. He also proposed calling in 600 Middle Eastern Arabs in 1960 and 800 in 1961 to help with teaching. Others emphasized the opposing concept—that it was "necessary for the pupil to possess sufficient knowledge of French as an instrumental language to pursue scientific and technical education"—as the guideline for the amount of French to be retained. The ministry's Center for Research and Pedagogical Action (CRAP), a French-speaking unit, was charged with working out the school programs. Widespread Arabization in the secondary grades was aggressively fought by Salmi, who cited the French training of teachers, the pupil's need for French in scientific education, and the lack of technical vocabulary in Arabic as supporting reasons. Of the Middle East teachers he wrote, "Whatever these *maîtres* are worth, the results do not seem brilliant." In their meeting on April 13, 1960, the division heads finally agreed on a five-grade primary cycle, the first two grades full time in Arabic and the last three bilingual (15-15), followed by an option between a three- and six-year medium and long cycle of secondary studies.

Even within the ministry, there was external politics to contend with. Machrafi had the sympathy and support of the UMT through

activist associations made in his earlier work with the Committee
for the Fight against Illiteracy and for Adult Education. His presence in the ministry had been a source of annoyance to 'Abdeljalil,
and his support came from the same quarters which raised a mounting personal attack on Benjelloun in 1959 and 1960. Salmi was in
an obverse position. Never an Istiqlali, teaching in Paris during the
resistance,[28] he was the butt of a quiet campaign of insults and
name-calling for his stand on Arabization, particularly in union
and party circles. Yet support from the minister and little competition for their jobs kept all these men at their posts, where
politics could add to the sharpness of differing opinions.[29] Benjelloun never took sides with his subordinates, never even privately
acknowledged their points of view, and always maintained his own
freedom of choice. Unlike 'Abdeljalil, he had not been put into
office to impose a temporary solution, but to find a policy; unlike al-
Fassi, he kept his distance from his past political connections and—
backed by the king's confidence—was relatively immune to the
mounting political campaign against him and his ministry.[30]

The current school problem, according to Benjelloun's speeches
of August and September, 1959, was essentially one of orientation,
with the question of enrollment being temporarily outside consideration.

> The goal of unification [of French and Muslim school systems]
> is an orientation for all Moroccans, who will have an Islamic
> formation capable of reimmersing them in Muslim civiliza-
> tion, without, however, neglecting the study and acquisition
> of a foreign language or two [which opens] the only way of
> access to technical and modern culture in our times.

This attempt to walk carefully between the modernist and traditionalist positions without touching either of them was not politically satisfying, although it did have the practical value of allowing

[28] See his letter to the editor, *Express* (Paris), October 23, 1954, expressing a
moderate nationalist point of view in favor of the deposed king.

[29] 'Abdeljalil later said in an interview, "We couldn't open war on the UMT
because it is we [the Istiqlal] who created it. We could not fight against Machrafi
as long as Mahjoub [ben Seddiq, head of the UMT] was in the Istiqlal." Even
when the UMT was read out of the Istiqlal in January, 1959, Benjelloun could
not or would not purge his ministry for the same political or sentimental reasons.
This, in a nutshell, is the key to the complex political picture as it affected
the Ministry of Education and many other ministries.

[30] He lost his immunity only on the death of the king in February, 1961, and
in June, 1961, he was replaced by Rashid Mouline (as secretary of state for
education) in the new government of King Hassan II.

leeway to face the difficulties and possibilities of application. Arabic, "language of culture," would be used to teach Arabo-Muslim subjects in the primary grades, including the history of Morocco. French was considered the "basic instrument for human exchanges and for the acquisition of knowledge" and, "from the secondary but not necessarily the primary grades, an instrument of general culture." French would be taught in primary grades and would be used to teach general history and geography, mathematics and sciences in secondary grades. The long-term results of the minister's conclusions seemed to be an Arabized primary cycle—except for the teaching *of* French—and a bilingual secondary system, but the emphasis was very much on delaying Arabization everywhere until it was practicable and qualitatively safe. In the immediate future, he continued to see a bilingual six-year primary system on the 30-15-15 schedule and a secondary schedule largely in French owing to a lack of Arabic teachers. Benjelloun also began the cautious reacceptance of a new series of teachers from the Middle East "to assure the valid teaching of science in Arabic."

Yet, in a flash of realism hitherto absent from ministerial projects, Benjelloun announced that unification and Arabization could be realized only over "many years. To say to the Moroccan people that we only need a few years to create a unified National School is demagogy." [31]

The Commission of the Plan

The school year 1959–1960, with its unchanged approach to the twin problems of Arabization and enrollment, still fell within the financial and doctrinal limits of the two-year-plan drawn up in mid-1958. In early 1959 the Superior Council of the Plan (CSP) began work on the educational part of the succeeding five-year plan with the establishment of a Commission of Education and Culture. [32] The commission's membership was provided by decree, although work was divided among seven subcommissions appointed by the minister, with the division heads acting as reporters. Some members had strong points of view, such as ben Barka, Driss Medkouri of the National Education Federation (FNE), and Driss Seghrouchni of the National Union of Moroccan Students (UNEM) among the modernists and nationalists or Division Head 'Abdul'aziz ben 'Abdullah and Inspector Azziman of Higher Muslim Education among the traditionalists. Clearly the commission was to be a

---

[31] *Monde*, August 27, 1959. This part of the statement does not appear to have been given much publicity in the Moroccan press.

[32] Decree 2-59-0130 of April 1, 1959.

battlefield between modernist-nationalists associated with Bou'abid and professionalist-traditionalists associated with Benjelloun. When it first met on May 5, 1959, it was charged by the education minister with preparing universal primary education and with "adapting our education to the economic needs and social structure of the country."[33] General goals included enrollment, school construction, teacher-training, Moroccanization of programs, and creation of texts and words, in that order; foremost among the foreseeable difficulties was Arabization, followed by problems of recruitment and teacher-training.

The real antagonist was the Division of the Plan in the Economics Ministry, representing a modernist attitude. As was its custom, the division issued an orientation note to the Education Commission, giving its analysis of difficulties and suggesting solutions.[34] Instead of a gradual increase of normal-school facilities, a sector of reabsorption was proposed, to be taught by *fqihs* (graduates of traditional Muslim schools) and student teachers with a sixth-grade education and to continue to exist until this sector could be integrated into the normal-school system. The Division of the Plan suggested setting a four-year goal of 66, 85, or 100 per-cent enrollment for both sectors, with the normal sector reserved for brighter students and the sector of reabsorption immediately Arabized through rapid reconversion courses for training the teachers.

The ministry submitted its own counterplan after discussion among the division heads.[35] It pointed out the dangers to quality inherent in the memorandum and suggested instead a return to the five-grade primary cycle, with two half-time grades taught in Arabic and the latter three grades taught bilingually; it made no clear choice between a 15-15 schedule in these three grades, as in 'Abdeljalil's program, or a year-by-year increase of Arabic to a 20-10 schedule, as in the Royal Commission's program. Also included was a hybrid reabsorption sector which would combine the *msids*, the adult education classes, and night schools in order to combat illiteracy with greater intensity. The moderation shown in tempering the Primary Division's goals of full and rapid Arabiza-

[33] *Notes et Documents*, XIII (April 1959), 7. See also speech by Benjelloun before the UNEM, August 22, 1959.

[34] Division of Economic Coordination and of the Plan, *Note d'orientation* (No. 63 [Rabat: Economics Ministry, 1959]).

[35] *Notes et Documents*, XIII (April 1959), 14. See also transcript, division heads' meeting, April 6, 1959; draft project by Larbi Ammor, "Project d'Orientation, Politique de Scolarisation" (mimeographed; Rabat: Ministry of Education, 1959); "Note" by Machrafi (mimeographed; Rabat: Ministry of Education, Annex 1, 1959).

tion were probably a result both of a professional realization of the practical problems and of the professional influence of the Center of Research and Pedagogical Action (CRAP). Even its proposals, the report pointed out, imposed heavy demands on the training of teachers in Arabic, and, when Nacer al-Fassi presented the report to the commission on June 19, 1959, he set 1965 as the date for the Arabization of sciences in primary teaching.

In early August, following its national congress of the previous month, the National Education Federation (FNE) presented its own proposal for a five-year plan.[36] The project was similar to the ideas outlined by the Division of the Plan. It called for the immediate creation of a parallel sector of reabsorption to last four years and to provide a twenty-hour week of instruction in Arabic to school-age children who could not fit into the normal sector. Subjects were to consist of reading, writing, and arithmetic plus history, Moroccan geography, and religion. The sector was also to act as a practice teaching class, and teachers who became experienced could eventually move up to teaching normal classes. The normal sector would continue to increase its enrollment at the annual rate of 50,000 new students drawn from the top of the sector of reabsorption and would absorb this sector after five years. Scientific instruction would increase, and Arabization on a 30-20-10 schedule was to be adopted only when "material conditions" and "the training of qualified Arabic [-speaking] teachers of arithmetic" would permit. The normal sector was given only passing and not too precise attention by the FNE.

The proposal was made among almost immediate attacks on the minister for not including it in his announcements for school year 1959. "Outside of the simple, practical solutions presented by our Federation, there is no alternative policy." [37] In November the full Commission for Education and Culture met, followed by the Superior Council of the Plan, to discuss the work of the subcommissions and other proposals from interested groups. The UMT plan was seconded by a similar proposal by the UNEM, and the whole was supported by the weight of the premier and particularly

[36] "Plan d'enseignement primaire" (mimeographed; Casablanca: UMT, n.d.); see also *AG*, August 9, 1959. The Communist party called for an even more radical plan of universal education in seven years; cf. Tahiri in *al-Istiqlal*, February 21, 1959, one of the rare articles that even took notice of the Communist proposals.

[37] *At-Tahrir*, August 28, 1959; *AG*, September 6, 1959. The minister answered, *PM*, September 10, 1959, and the UMT replied, *AG*, September 13, October 4, 11, 18, and November 29, 1959, and July 16, 1960.

by Bou'abid. The Division of the Plan supported the general idea of the UMT proposal, but called the details of the crash program "unrealistic and costly." The result of the sharp debates between the ministry and the activist group was a draw. The ministry accepted the principle of a sector of reabsorption,[38] alongside a five-grade normal sector of which the first grade would be half time in Arabic, second grade full time in Arabic, and the rest 15-15. Arabization was, in fact, to be attained wherever possible as teachers became available. The annual enrollment quota, however, was restored to the level of the al-Fassi years, with 228,000 new school children entering school in October, 1960.

The Division of the Plan had little to suggest for the secondary cycle. The Subcommission for Secondary Education met in June, 1959, to discuss the ministry's proposal, based on the study of programs prepared by the CRAP and the division. With greater attention to a doctrine and a goal than was shown in the Primary Subcommission, the Secondary Subcommission report foresaw a branching out of programs during a seven-year secondary cycle offering eight lines of specialization in the last three grades. Contrary to the head of the division's ideas, the majority of the subcommission members favored total Arabization of the secondary grades, although they left a decision on the place of foreign languages to the commission. When the secretary general presented his report to the commission in June, 1959, his recommendations on the language question were not clear. He reaffirmed that complete Arabization of all teaching remained the goal, but admitted that scientific teaching would remain in French until 1970 in the secondary grades. Even in 1960, except for Arabic grammars from the Middle East there were no secondary school texts available in Arabic.

The problems posed by the vague and general demand for Arabization, accompanied by a lack of precision and direction as to its detailed implementation, were pointed out by Salmi in his note presenting the subcommission's report in what amounted to a one-man campaign. His own words give the clearest picture of the problems of conscience of a dedicated professional faced with powerful public pressure.

> Since Independence we have not found a solution to the problem of education. Up till now we have lacked perspective,

[38] By the time it got to the Superior Council of the Plan, it was dropped for lack of money.

a sense of realities, indeed, of conviction. After Independence, carried away by enthusiasm, obliged to take social pressure and the psychological climate into consideration, we increased enrollment in an intensive fashion and increased Arabization in an inconsidered fashion, without worrying about the methods of enrollment and of Arabization. . . . Now we see the results: quantity has replaced quality, and the level [of teaching] has fallen in French and in Arabic. . . . The basis of the problem is not to enroll or to Arabize, these are the means. The basis of the problem is to know exactly what is going to be our doctrine in the matter of teaching. When are we going to unify our teaching? Are we going to Arabize completely, at all levels, train young Moroccans uniquely in the Arabo-Muslim tradition, or institute bilingualism and permit the young Moroccan, solidly trained by means of his valid Muslim traditions, to have a wide opening onto the modern world, by the no less solid acquisition of a foreign language; [this is] a vital question for Morocco.[39]

The UMT–FNE proposals for the secondary cycle were not so radical as their primary programs.[40] Their plans also included a long and a medium cycle, of six and four instead of three plus three years, with emphasis on scientific education and an early entry of the student into economic life at the end of the medium cycle, rather than on completion of all six grades. Although Arabic was taken for granted as the "basic language of education," any attempt at Arabization was specifically put off until the next five-year plan. History and philosophy "might be taught" in Arabic by graduates of the Moroccan University at Rabat, so that during the four years of the medium cycle, at least ten of the twenty-six to twenty-eight hours a week would be Arabized. The figure was actually closer to the ideas of the Secondary Division than were most other points of the UMT's education program.

Within the ministry Benjelloun was generally thought to have a sympathetic ear for Salmi's cares. Yet, despite a vigorous campaign

[39] Secondary Education Division, "Note de Présentation, Plan Quinquennal" (mimeographed; Rabat: Ministry of Education, n.d.). For an earlier protest by Salmi in the same vein, see Secondary Education Division, *Admission des élèves de l'Enseignement Primaire dans l'Enseignement Secondaire* (Rabat: Ministry of Education, 1958).

[40] "Plan d'enseignement secondaire" (mimeographed; Casablanca: UMT, n.d.). The UMT here gives a good example of a nationalist approach; the National Union of Secondary Education (founded July 2–3, 1959, at the Second Congress of the FNE) complained that programs for Arabization meant too much new preparation for the teachers (*AG*, November 29, 1959), but by the following year the UMT was attacking the CRAP—a vulnerable target because of its French members and director—for "a ridiculously small Arabic program" (*ibid.*, April 16, 1960).

of public appearances and general statements, there was no clear-cut guideline issued by the ministry. In the beginning of 1960 Salmi sent another impassioned protest to the minister, pointing out more clearly the pitfalls of Arabization.

> I have nothing but reservations about the statements of my colleague from the Primary Division. He thinks according to a tradition inherited from the French system, that only the Primary Division has healthy and universal views about pedagogy and that primary schooling is enough to make good teachers. There are not now any competent [teachers], even in the primary schools. At the present time we have gotten together the worst students from the primary schools into certain classes to make teachers out of them. Mediocre in their aptitude, badly trained, these children become bad teachers. In appearance, quantitatively, the system seems to work. In fact, these people will be without quality. . . . At the present, no matter what the Machrafi report says, young people do not envisage becoming teachers (a dull and poorly paid profession) unless obligated, and that does not seem to be the present tendency. Teaching is a profession that is very badly exercised by obligation. . . . It is at the level of Higher Education that the University will prepare future teachers to transpose into Arabic what they have learned in French. It is there that lies the methodological problem of Arabization from above, the only effective way in my humble opinion. The Primary Division affirms that it will have Arabized all of its classes within five or six years. It then turns to the Secondary Division and asks it to do its duty in its turn. Outside of the extreme reservations that I have about the quality of this Arabization, I must insist that the problem is badly posed. It is from above that the problem should be attacked.[41]

Salmi was, however, the only person to see sense in this approach. To the rest of the ministry and especially to outside spokesmen, the problem was one of Arabizing the students, not of Arabizing the teachers. The fact that first-grade students could be taught totally in Arabic suggested that, with the annual promotions, successive grades should follow, and the delay caused by technical inadequacies could be overcome by shock measures.

When the time came to present the final draft of the Commission of Education and Culture to the Superior Council (CSP), a number of conditions had changed. The public pressure for increased enrollment that had swayed Mohammed al-Fassi was again rising, after the downswing of 1958. The UMT and the activist

---

[41] "Secondary Education Division Memorandum" (mimeographed; Rabat: Ministry of Education, n.d.).

groups, many of whom were also proponents of modernist arguments against Arabization, were no longer in control of the government. One of their most frequent targets of attack was Benjelloun. On the other hand, partly because of modernist sympathies among the opposition, pressure for Arabization had quieted, and the ministry was freer to work out or fight out its own details of this aspect of the education problem. Thus, when Nacer al-Fassi, as reporter of the commission, addressed the CSP in August, 1960, he accented raising the educational level from 38 per cent to 69 per cent by 1964 for all primary–school-age children, with total enrollment of all first graders by 1963. There was a bitter exchange between the government and the opposition in the council, but very little was said on Arabization.

The Superior Council
The debate was carried on in a second institution created by the Benjelloun ministry. Although the Ministry of National Education was one of the more stable ministries in the shifting cabinets, changes of governments and ministers had brought a half-dozen educational plans for less than a half-dozen school years. The minister, therefore, sought to create a new and permanent commission which would give continuity to educational projects, engage external elements in the responsibility for reforms in the school system, and at the same time back the proposals which emerged from the professional bureaus of the ministry.

As early as January, 1959, Benjelloun emphasized before his division heads the immediate need for a professional council to advise the ministry. The division heads rallied behind the suggestion and pressed for its adoption in March, so that the council could be used as a sounding board for proposals on the plan. But it was not until June, 1959, after the Commission of Education and Culture had shown its worth and weaknesses, that a *dahir* was promulgated creating a Superior Council of National Education.[42] Its composition, meetings, and agenda were strictly in the hands of the minister, and its creation permitted a dialogue between the ministry and its creature, giving an illusion of democratic consultation to as broad as possible an extent considering the prevailing atmosphere of political pressure. It also afforded a modicum of ministerial unification where cultural and bureaucratic jealousies made actual reorganization impossible.

The council was opened by the king on October 21, 1959; it

[42] *Dahir* No. 1-59-121 of June 1, 1959, composition designated by ministerial order of October 10, 1959.

TABLE 8

HOURS IN ARABIC AND FRENCH IN MUSLIM BRANCHES

Grade	Moroccan equivalent	1955 protectorate	1956 al-Fassi plan changes I	1958 al-Fassi plan changes II	1957 CSRE plan	1958 'Abdeljalil	1959 Benjelloun	1965 UMT	1960 5-year plan
Primary									
1	CP1	10–20	15† Arabic eliminated	15 Arabic eliminated	30 Arabic eliminated	30 Arabic	30 Arabic	30 Arabic eliminated	15 Arabic eliminated
2	CP2	10–20				15–15	15–15		
3	CE1	10–25*	15*†–15‡	20*†–10†	15–15 (20–10*)	15–15	15–15	20–10	30 Arabic
4	CE2	10–25*	15*†–15‡	20*†–10†	15–15 (20–10†)	15–15	15–15	20–10	16–14
5	CM1	10–25*	15‡ –15‡	20‡ –10‡	15–15 (20–10‡)	15–15	15–15	20–10	16–14
6	CM2	10–25*	15‡ –15‡	20‡ –10‡	15–15 (20–10§)	15–15	15–15	20–10	16–14
	Fin d'études							20–10	
Secondary									
7	6	French	13–18	13–18	13–21	13–20	20–9	10–16	variable
8	5		French	French	French	mostly French	mostly French	10–16	
9	4							8–11	
10–12	3–1							8–18	

1955: *including study hall.

1956: *half time in rural school; †1956–1957; ‡1957–1958.

1958 al-Fassi changes II: *half time in rural school; †1958–1959; ‡1959–1960.

1957 CSRE: *1959; †1960; ‡1961; §1962.

Source: Ministry of Education.

met again in December and three times in June, 1960. It discussed the matters submitted by the minister and ratified his decisions—even if they were a vague commitment to make *ad hoc* application of broad principles. As a symbolic institution which, by its composition and by its functioning, consecrated the shift of decisions within the ministry from the political to the professional level, it was extremely effective. However, as a quasi-democratic appeal board, the council fooled no one and was a public failure. In fact, this function was incompatible with its first purpose, for it could not at the same time be a professional and a national council. The most outspoken group to point this out was the FNE of the UMT, which was put into the embarrassing—but not tongue-tying— position of having some of its members appointed to the council in a private nonunion capacity. The UMT attack, the FNE was careful to make clear, was not against the competence of the members but against the undemocratic way in which they were designated.[43]

In mid-June, 1960, the council met to ratify the general principles of reform worked out by the ministry for submittal to the agencies of the plan. Four commissions of education, schooling, teacher-training and technique, and Arabization were to make their reports, which had been ready since May 15. Unanimous agreement was registered on two rather abstract objectives: "Provide the country with the trained leadership necessary to permit it to attain the rank of modern nations" and "Give to the citizen a moral and intellectual training which will permit him to fulfill his role in society." Unanimity hid serious dissents, however, and put a final seal on the dominant role of the professionals in deciding educational doctrine. Several modernists, including Mohammed Tahiri, 'Abdeljalil's former undersecretary of state, withdrew from the council in protest against the ineffectiveness of their role in a house that was against them.

[43] See *AG*, October 11 and 25, November 1, 15, 22, 1959, April 16, 1960. Although the council was an adaptation of the French organization of the same name, the French body was a truly national group composed of parents, teachers, and representatives of the ministry. The UMT had asked for a similar national group in a letter to the ministry on November 18, 1958. In his initial presentation before the division heads on January 6, 1959, Benjelloun had proposed the creation of elected organizations of professionals, businessmen, unions, parents, and alumni on the national, provincial, and local levels. As it developed, this sweeping proposal, however, clashed not only with his view of the council's purpose, but also with Moroccan reality; in a situation where universal education of children was still an insurmountable problem, it was impossible to get together a successful and informed parent-teachers association.

The final results of the ministry's new plan, beginning with the 1960–1961 school year, left the decisions on Arabization in the hands of the ministry's professionals, although the continuing attacks from the opposition forced the ministry to retreat to Mohammed al-Fassi's position on enrollment. The principle governing the use of language was pragmatic and open to leeway: "Arabize while maintaining quality." The primary cycle was to consist of five grades, the first operating half time in two daily sections to accommodate the increased enrollment; both first and second grades were taught in Arabic in 1960–1961, but there was no fixed timetable for total Arabization. Progressive Arabization would be brought to the two secondary cycles according to a series of ten rules, most of which expressed only evident relations and general principles—"Arabize non-Arabic teaching . . . ," "Set up a proper schedule for the study of Arabic." Some of the principles did, however, express the caution of the Secondary Division over the demands for rapid Arabization. Such national subjects as civics, history, and geography were to be converted before the sciences; Arabization was to be carried out systematically by class and subject matter; and Arabization was to be regarded, by the nature of the approach, only as a long-term goal. Implementation of these principles remains with the institution that created them and is certainly subject to further problems. But, at least, in setting up agreed principles of Arabization, the professionals have been able to resist much external pressure and formulate national goals compatible with the quality of their work. Soon after, another attack was made on the old problem of Arabizing the ministry itself. In November, 1960, the prince opened a twice-a-week series of evening classes in Arabic in Rabat and in other cities throughout the kingdom. Administered by the Civil Service Ministry, long an advocate of Arabization and Moroccanization, and initiated by the king himself, as a natural outgrowth of his anti-illiteracy campaign, the series was to correct "the isolation that has been imposed on Moroccan administration by the domination of foreign languages" and was compulsory for all civil servants.[44] Although this program, like all others fostering Arabization, was potentially enormous, it had to be begun on a small scale if the goal was to be attained.

The Institute of Arabization

Many of the problems of Arabization came to a climax in an institution that resulted from Benjelloun's administrative reform.

[44] *Al-'Alam*, November 20, 1960.

The role of the Superior Council, the basic problem of the Arabic language, and the paramountcy of the professional over the politician in making decisions all find culmination in the work of a single dedicated, opinionated member of the ministry—Ahmed Lakhdar. Ironically for an Arabist, Lakhdar was an Ait Ayash Berber who had taught in the French-sponsored Berber Academy at Azrou. He was one of the first Moroccan division heads installed by al-Fassi, who appointed him to the Adult Education Service; his work in this area put him in contact with the basic problem of Arabization —the weakness of the language in regard to a working vocabulary for modern day-to-day, especially technical, use. Probably more completely than any other person in the Arabization debate, Lakhdar was inspired by a mixture of all four attitudes toward the problem —modernist, traditional, nationalist, and professional. The concurrence of these attitudes produced in him a drive to overcome obstacles to a successful Arabization without sacrificing quality before blind cultural nationalism. In late 1957, Lakhdar perfected a printing system, applicable for linotype and typewriter alike, which reduced the number of pieces of type necessary to print Arabic from 475 to sixty-seven and at the same time enabled the printing of vowelized letters.[45]

In early 1959, with the approval of the minister, Lakhdar published a series of three articles in the ministry's journal and also in *al-Istiqlal.* In them he gave a historical analysis of the educational use of the Arabic language, its technical shortcomings, and the ways of making Arabic a usable modern language.[46] Most of the future thinking and discussion of the problems of Arabization were to come from these articles. If the series was bold in its plans for action, it was also harsh in its judgments of the Arabic language and made a rather unfavorable impression on the traditionalists to whom the language itself was as sacred as the book in which its basic vocabulary was immutably recorded. "I had the courage to publish them," Lakhdar has said, with as little exaggeration as modesty. The proposed solutions involved the use of the UNESCO Center of Inter-Arab Coordination of which Lakhdar was the sec-

[45] *Al-Istiqlal,* November 2, 1957. Reforms in Arabic printing and teaching were announced as early as August, 1957 (*Maroc-Documents,* I [August 1957], 42).

[46] "Rapport sur les problèmes de l'Arabisation," *Notes et Documents,* XI–XIII (February–April 1959); Benjelloun's press conference statement, "The Problems of Arabization," *Education Nationale,* IV (February 1960), 15–22, was based largely on Lakhdar's arguments. For an excellent discussion of the problems of bilingualism, see the Symposium, "Le Bilinguisme," reported in *Confluent,* VII (May 1960, 325–383).

retary general, the establishment of a center of studies and research for Arabization, and the Arabization of the ministry's Center
of Research and Pedagogical Action (CRAP). At the same time that
the first articles appeared, Lakhdar presented his arguments at a
division heads' meeting, strongly emphasizing the potential role of
UNESCO.[47] In his arguments on the weakness of the language, he
was supported by Salmi. The result of the meeting was a decision by
Nacer al-Fassi to propose to the minister the creation of an "organization of vocabulary" under Lakhdar. The two-year–old suggestion
of the Royal Commission for the creation of a dictionary commission had found root. Formal proposal of the new commission
was made in the fall, 1959, session of the Superior Council, which
called in Lakhdar to present his case. In the Council, Lakhdar's
main support—in addition to that of the minister—came from the
two most prominent spokesmen for the traditionalist attitude, Mohammed al-Fassi, rector of the Moroccan University at Rabat since
his replacement as minister, and 'Abdul'aziz ben 'Abdullah, head
of the Division of Higher Education.

In January, 1960, the Institute of Studies and Research for
Arabization was created and placed under the direction of Lakhdar.[48] Its work was to compile a picture dictionary of 10,000 words
for first- and second-grade use, then to turn to a general expansion
of Arabic in the fields of science, and finally to develop the linguistic
base for the Arabization of the three cycles of education over fifteen
to twenty years.[49] During the first year of its work, the institute also
was to prepare a French-Arabic dictionary of administrative termi-
nology. Another aspect of the institute's work lay in its attempts to
join similar efforts in other Middle Eastern countries, particularly
the Academy of Arabic Language and Literature at Cairo, where
scholars had been at work on an Arabic dictionary since 1932. Between 1927, when the Arabic Academy at Damascus was founded,
and 1958, the institutions at Cairo and Damascus had succeeded in
establishing only 16,000 words; the task of the Moroccan Institute
was to take the lead in this endeavor, without—if possible—conflict-

---

[47] He outlined ten goals: creation of "working Arabic," creation of a basic
vocabulary, unification of technical terms in the Arab world, standardization of
Arabic vocabulary, creation of new words (this goal was left out of the final
dahir, possibly because of traditionalist opposition), expansion of knowledge
in the Arab world, propagation of technical terms, adaptation of audiovisual
techniques for Arabic teaching, creation of machinery to produce national educational material, guidance for Arabization (transcript, division heads' meeting, October 15, 1959).

[48] Decree No. 2-59-1965 of January 14, 1960.

[49] The dictionary had not appeared by the end of 1962.

ing with the work already done in Egypt. It aroused a certain feeling of pleasure in Morocco to envisage an effort that would contest and perhaps even take the laurels from Egypt in the intellectual leadership of the Arab world.

The institute was staffed with civil servants, mostly from the ministry, and was divided into four sections: sorting, sampling, and publications; graphic arts and educational material; audiovisual techniques; and translation of foreign languages into Arabic. It began by examining existing Arabic words for conflicts in meanings and then by standardizing or creating, if necessary, the Arabic equivalents of French and English terms; work was organized on the basis of natural and functional groups—farming, the human body, and so on—rather than alphabetically. The institute was supervised by a council of interested specialists appointed by the minister, plus representatives of the ministry, including the division heads. The latter members constituted an administrative council of review; the former exercised technical surveillance over the work of the institute. It was to the technical group that the latest list of newly approved was submitted each month for approval before being sent to Cairo for coordination with the academy. In the last analysis, however, approval by Cairo was not required, and the administrative segment of the council served more as resistance than as a circuit breaker for Lakhdar's energy. There was also a printing plant in the ministry in the form of a book school set up by the protectorate; with the aid of the printing systems invented by Lakhdar, this plant was to produce low-cost editions of texts in Arabic, incorporating the words approved by the institute and the translations of new editions approved by the division heads.

CONCLUSIONS

The problems of decision-making on the social and cultural question of Arabizing primary and secondary education throws much light on one important way of meeting problems in Moroccan government. Effective decisions on Arabization were limited almost entirely to the ministry; the direct effect of specific outside incidents, of individual party or pressure group decisions, of collegial bodies, or of such higher decision-making institutions as the king, the prince, or the Council of Ministers was minimal. Of the latter three, only the king played any role, and this was a simple, if important, one of giving solid support to his education ministers while they were in office—and, in two cases, keeping them in office for a second term.

Public opinion was more important in many cases than it was generally recognized to be. In Morocco Mohammed al-Fassi has the reputation of having followed the crowd with abandon, 'Abdeljalil has the reputation of having ordered an about-face amid popular pressure to plunge ahead, and Benjelloun was thought to be slowly pushing forward. None of these caricatures is completely accurate. In the matter of enrollment, al-Fassi did share popular enthusiasm, but 'Abdeljalil cut back enrollment in harmony with a distinct swing in public attitudes as they realized quality and quantity were linked, and Benjelloun has had to give way before the same type of pressure that al-Fassi had to face. On the question of Arabization, however, al-Fassi conscientiously tried to define and maintain an important place for French while encouraging as widespread Arabization as possible; 'Abdeljalil's slowdown was approved by the professionals who were close enough to the schools to see the damage that was being done, whereas Benjelloun's ministry was searching for doctrine but acting with bland eclecticism at a time when Arabization was no longer a slogan that aroused much of the public.

1. The ministry's attempt to avoid interference from public groups is a significant characteristic of its way of making decisions. When, as a professional educator, al-Fassi tried to temper popular enthusiasm with a realization of what was possible, he was laying the groundwork for future decision-making in his department. Benjelloun entered the ministry with the specific goal of pulling decisions back into the ministry and removing them from the hands of popular pressure and political manipulators; since ministers were political people, he consciously aimed at removing himself as well from the field of substantive decisions and at setting up machinery designed to give the ministry stability and continuity. In a substantive sense, Benjelloun was a clearing house and a spokesman for ideas in his ministry. He allowed his division heads to fight out problems among themselves, he kept them in political anonymity, and he placed outside political forces into a position where they were obliged to fight for a role in the decision-making process, rather than being able to fight directly for a particular program. The political groups battered at the doors of decision, but they were effective only in producing delays, not decrees. Yet despite the fact that his role was largely institutional, Benjelloun was necessary to the system he had created, for the experience of 'Abdeljalil and the Royal Commission had shown that man-made institutions can be bypassed and that one minister's channels might be another's detour. The bitterest comment on this system was

found in the UMT's newspaper after the minister's refusal to give some teachers leave to attend the FNE national congress. "His supreme goal is to carry out his policies hidden from the world in the secret of his cabinets, in that official clandestinity which has become his trademark, and to hide the decisions he makes from examination in the public arena." [50] This was most certainly true; Benjelloun believed that the implementation of educational principles was a professional job and should be kept so.

2. It is natural that it should be in this ministry that some of the patterns of French action should be felt, although it is perhaps ironic that on a matter such as Arabization these should develop by themselves. The development of a ministry of permanent civil servants who ensure that the real functioning of their department flows on with only a minimum of outside influence from a succession of ministers who spent their first few months in office getting acquainted with their subject matter is a development that is only too typical of the Fourth Republic. Institutions such as the coordinating secretary general—who, in the words of Lamrani, would ensure administrative permanence as the Superior Council of National Education assured doctrinal permanence—the division heads' meeting, and the Superior Council, were borrowed from the metropole (not even from the protectorate). At the same time, unfortunately, another aspect of the French system appeared, in the *cloisonnement* or walling-off of each of the divisions into separate units. There could be no doctrinal unity as long as the ministry was so well divided, and there could be no effective modernization and unification of the system as long as the "original" system remained under the control of the Division of Higher Muslim Education instead of united with other systems under the competence of the Primary Division or the Secondary Division. Another aspect of this great weakness lay in the fact that many of the strongest opinions on Arabization were shaped by the position as much as by the person who occupied it. Thus, as head of the Secondary Division, which could least afford it, Salmi was opposed to rapid Arabization, and Machrafi looked for rapid Arabization throughout the ministry because the primary grades were the easiest to Arabize. The wisdom of Arabizing from the top instead of from the bottom was lost in a bureaucratic rivalry. A unification of the ministry was necessary to provide an over-all view, for there was no professional educator above the division heads in a deciding (not a coordinating) position.

3. At many times the problem of Arabization, in the whole

[50] *AG*, April 12, 1959.

educational context, appeared as a dilemma: it was simply too big
to handle. The principle was quickly established and was incontrovertible. In reporting to the CSP, Nacer al-Fassi stated, "Complete Arabization is the goal of any educational reform. It is incon-
ceivable that citizens of a country speak, write and think in one or
more foreign languages." One could not write about education
without mentioning Arabization, and writers simply repeated it
without any precise notion of what the concept expressed or demanded, until finally it became part of the language. As a word, it
was more powerful than any person; Lakhdar's criticism of the
Arabic language and Benjelloun's subsequent speech in which he
adopted many of Lakhdar's ideas were called courageous, and
Salmi was called a traitor for his opposition to immediate Arabization. Outside of the throne, no single value commanded such allegiance.

There was another side to this lofty patriotic principle which
made it a sham and kept Arabization on a safely abstract level, high
and out of reach of practical compromise. Although it was patriotic
to be in favor of Arabization, there was at the same time a snobbish
disdain for Arabic; French was better, more cultured, more modern.
Farmers in the *bled,* who spoke Berber in daily life and Arabic
only badly, wanted their children to learn French. Members of the
young, modern, urban middle class often regarded Arabic as an
intimate language for private remarks and French as the language
of public business and conversation. For this reason, Lakhdar's work
and Tahiri's propaganda were important in countering the inadequacy of the language—which was the factual basis for this disdain
—with concrete efforts to build up its effectiveness in the modern
world. More deadly to Arabization than rural aspirations and urban
aspersions was the attitude of the elite; Mohammed al-Fassi, Machrafi, ben 'Abdullah, and many others, including high government
officials and even *'ulema,* all sent their children to French schools,
for they knew that the education was better there, and they claimed
that their children could be Arabized at home. Salmi once wrote,
"We do not cease to repeat 'Arabization, Arabization,' all the while
sending our children to the schools of the [French] MUCF." [51]
There was almost a mathematical relationship (as Mohammed al-
Fassi once warned in an interview): to talk Arabization means to

[51] "Secondary Education Division Memorandum" (mimeographed; Rabat: Ministry of Education, n.d. [1960]). See also *al-Istiqlal,* May 30, 1959, for a trenchant
political comment and *AG,* November 26, 1960, for a bitter, outspoken letter
from Charles-André Julien, professor at the Sorbonne and just-retired dean of
the Faculty of Letters at the University of Rabat.

practice bilingualism; the more the educators spoke of bilingualism, the more they effected Arabization. For this reason public speeches are such poor (or, if properly read, such good) indexes of Arabization, and for these reasons principles received so much attention and were so unimportant.

If the public was wholeheartedly devoted to the slogan, its interest stopped at details, and the application of Arabization was a detail. It was quite impossible to make those—whether individuals or mass opinion—who believed in Arabization understand that everything could not be done at once. Arabization, unification, universal enrollment, preservation of quality, and redirection of education to fit the new economic vocation of the country were compatible as long-range goals but totally impossible to effect simultaneously. A decision for reforms in the other fields inevitably meant that quality and universality would be damaged in the short run—and, a fortiori, these latter two goals were in complete short-range conflict with each other. Rapid Arabization, inevitably if indirectly, meant leaving children in the street. It was a hard decision for a young country to make.

4. Between the extremes of slogan and reality, the civil servants of the ministry often discussed their problems with an air of figure-juggling unreality. Although the Ministry of Education has had one of the most incompetent statistical services in the government, it was in terms of figures that plans were made, and the discussions of the division heads often had the appearance of a solemn debate on whether six and six or four and two made ten. Sums of children to be enrolled, classes to be Arabized, teachers to be trained, were often made up backward, by setting the total and then assigning the components, without much reference to the possibilities. It is not surprising, then, that the plans were not successful. There was, of course, the corollary advantage that such drastic revisions as those of 'Abdeljalil were less upsetting in their effects than they would have been if the previous plans or the reforms had been totally applied. Obviously, too, what was finally done in any instance was what was possible, planning or pressure notwithstanding, and the search for slogans and doctrine played the important but limited role of suggesting where to look for possibilities only in the most general sense. Pedagogical doctrine was an obsession, but *ad hoc* solutions were a habit.

SIX

Do not go far in the path of Democracy.
—The count of Paris to
the king of Morocco

Do not worry, we only take from you that
which is reconcilable with our own
character and our own traditions.
—The king of Morocco in
reply to the count of
Paris

POLITICAL PROBLEM
Organization of Elections

BACKGROUND

Morocco's dream was to govern itself.[1] Never in history had the Moroccan people taken their national affairs in their own hands except by revolt, and then it was to put into power still another leader who would govern them. The forty years of the protectorate aroused and sharpened the desire for self-government because the governor was a foreign power. The protectorate set up elections creating partially representative but only consultative organs. The latest and most important reform embodied in a *dahir* in 1953 provided for elections by Moroccans and Europeans of city councils with real powers, but the king refused the measure, along with other reforms, because it would compromise Moroccan sovereignty with direct colonial participation in government.[2] The king was

---

[1] There is the alternative of Morocco's wishing to be governed by a single strong leader (provided, of course, that he is Moroccan). This is a debatable point and not totally incompatible with the desire for elections. Strong leadership by the king probably would have had widespread acceptance in the rural areas, but Mohammed V himself refused the role of an autocratic leader and Hassan II has had strong opposition in trying to fill this role. Party leaders, particularly among the activist opposition, may also have aspired to such a role, but they were both part and prisoner of the current of opinion that called for elections.

[2] *Dahir* of September 18, 1953; vizirial order of September 23, 1953. On the protectorate measures, see Emmanuel Durand, *Traité de droit public marocain* (Paris: Librairie Générale de Droit et de Jurisprudence, 1955), pp. 161–181.

197

deposed, but the outbreak of the resistance the same year made
the *dahir* impossible to implement. When Mohammed V returned
in 1955 to bring independence to Morocco, he declared nonexistent
all measures, including the election law, passed during the two-year
interim.

The Political Goal

In 1934 came the first demand for reforms, calling for rural,
municipal, and national elections with indirect suffrage, a literacy
test, and two rounds of voting. The 1944 declaration announcing
the demands of the newly founded Istiqlal party called for a democratic regime, and the last congress of the party before independence, in December, 1955, asked for the creation of local tribal and
municipal assemblies, followed by an elected national parliament.[3]
However, during the resistance years of 1953 to 1955, the independence movement had as its primary goal the return of the king, and
it deferred insistence on democratic government.[4] The king early
made himself the champion of democratic government. In his
Speech from the Throne in 1950 he said that ". . . the best regime
under which a sovereign country . . . should live is the democratic
system, whose principles are in conformity with the spirit of Islam
and guarantee to the individual a peaceful and undisturbed life." [5]
Two years later, in the last Speech from the Throne before his
deposition, he spoke of constitutional monarchy, and the phrase
became ensconced in the political vocabulary. In his next Speech
from the Throne, in 1955, he outlined the tasks of the first Moroccan government, which was soon to be appointed; they included
administration of public affairs and negotiations for independence,
but also ". . . the creation of democratic institutions based on free
elections . . . within the framework of a constitutional monarchy,
recognizing the rights of citizenship and the exercise of civil and
labor union rights for all Moroccans." On December 7, when the
new government was installed, the king announced that it ". . . will
remain responsible before Us until the election of a National As-

[3] For the 1944 declaration, see *al-Istiqlal,* January 11, 1958; for the 1955 resolution, given in the report by Bou'abid, see *al-Istiqlal,* March 30, 1956.
[4] Balafrej told the Istiqlal National Council on July 24, 1956, "If [since 1944]
we have not insisted that general elections take place, it is only because of the
difficult circumstances through which Morocco was passing. This provisional
position is dictated by national interest, and should not be considered a principle of our movement" (*al-Istiqlal,* July 27, 1956).
[5] For a discussion of the conditions of this pronouncement, see Jean Lacouture,
Cinq Hommes et la France (Paris: Seuil, 1961), p. 210; Rom Landau, *Mohammed
V, King of Morocco* (Rabat: Ministry of Information, 1957), pp. 48–49.

sembly; it will be up to the Government to lay the foundations of a new regime which will enable the people to administer their own affairs by means of local assemblies and a Parliament." The elections were thus given as a direct charge into the hands of the government.

No work was done on the elections during the first government. Attention was simply elsewhere. Not until two months after independence was the traditionalist sheikh Lahcen Lyoussi replaced by Driss Mhammedi, a minister of the interior capable of attacking the problem of elections. Yet, as the summer passed, a bitter political battle arose between the ministers of the majority Istiqlal party and those of the Democratic Istiqlal party (PDI), with independent Premier Mbarek Bekkai caught in the middle. On August 10, 1956, the premier spoke openly of resigning; on August 20 the Istiqlal Executive Committee demanded a homogeneous or all-Istiqlal government, and only the king's insistence on Bekkai's remaining in office until his task of setting up elections had been accomplished kept the government from splitting. Even the royal charge was not enough in October, when the diplomatic crisis with France demanded a government capable of action. The ministers resigned and reassembled on October 27, 1956 in a new government without the PDI. Bekkai again stated his charge of preparing elections, and work was begun for the first time.

The preparation of elections as a problem in decision-making can be divided into two stages which may be called, ironically, perhaps, the "easy" phase and the "hard" phase. A *dahir* was drawn up in 1957 in the general belief that elections were a simple matter needing little detailed preparation. After the failure of this attempt, a long and complicated process began to set up not only the elections, but also the preliminary components—particularly civil liberties and administrative communes—so that the operation could be a success.

The Royal Purpose

The role of the king was more important in the preparation of elections than in any other problem. His position as head of state and holder of governing powers obviously put him in a crucial position to decide an event so basic to the future of the country. The king's role in this case was threefold however, and covers all the types of action he took in the governmental process. As already seen, he was the prime mover behind the principle of elections. He was also the one who established the policy guidelines by which his

advisors acted; this was his most common role in governmental matters. In addition, he personally participated in the detailed work
of preparing the elections. This third role will be examined below
in the context of the actual preparation. It is important, however,
to look at the guidelines which the king gave, particularly in the
early stages. Two aspects of these general policy lines had to be
made clear: What elections were being prepared? Why were elections being held?

All early announcements on the subject of elections, particularly the provisions for the first two governments' tenure of
office, indicated that a national parliament was being prepared. In
the inauguration of the National Consultative Assembly in August,
1956, the king spoke both of national and local elections; there was
no indication of any order of events, except an affirmation in connection with local assemblies that "our desire is to construct democracy from the base." In his Algerian speech in Oujda at the end
of September, he also spoke clearly of general elections for a future
assembly. The king had at his disposal, however, a timetable for
elections in the resolutions of the Istiqlal Extraordinary Congress
of 1955. There the party asked for rural municipal elections with
guarantees of freedom and without administrative interference;
"the sociological structure of the Moroccan countryside lends itself
admirably to this." At the same time a consultative assembly would
be created, followed by a "fully sovereign, elected national assembly" as soon as independence had been won. These ideas were
discussed by the king and the party during 1956, but it was not until
the Speech from the Throne at the end of the year that local elections and a timetable were officially mentioned.

> Morocco's accession to parliamentary life based on general
> elections occupies Our entire attention. To attain this goal, We
> will follow the natural process by ordering first of all munici-
> pal and rural elections, then the creation of regional assem-
> blies, and finally the establishment of a Constituent Assembly
> to draw up a Constitution in the framework of a constitu-
> tional, Arab, Muslim, democratic monarchy.

This specific ordering of events coincided with the first work of the
government in preparing the election law; the prior absence of
guidelines gives another reason for the delay. It is evident that, in
electoral matters as in many other subjects of government—such as
foreign affairs, education, and agriculture—Morocco in its early

days was searching for a policy, and the earliest pronounceme
were expressions only of vague hopes.

There was one point in the timetable that remained uncle__
and which can be best understood by the examination of the purpose of the elections. Obviously the first answer was dual: the education of the population in democratic ways and the establishment
of institutions for self-government. On these points there was no
doubt, and they can be found reiterated in any spokesman's pronouncements on the subject. However, when the king again presented his timetable in 1958 in the Royal Charter he indicated that
the local assemblymen would have an additional job; from their
midst they were to elect the members of a new deliberative parliament. The indirectly elected parliament was to handle the same
matters—primarily the budget—as the Consultative Assembly and
was to be succeeded by a directly elected national assembly. In the
charter it was not clear who would write the new constitution. It
was, however, implied that each of these bodies, and hence the local
assemblies in the first place, would be political bodies, elected and
functioning with party participation. Elections were frequently
spoken of as an attempt to "distinguish the different political tendencies of the country" and "bring out a governing majority" as more
parties arose to claim to represent the entire nation. In September,
1959, Interior Minister Driss Mhammedi announced the electoral
law, which had the same aim.

> Unfortunately, at the present time all the parties and all the
> political attitudes tend to believe that they represent the ma-
> jority of public opinion. . . . Elections are the only way to
> allow competing political groups validly to test their authority
> and their representative character.[6]

In this goal, as in his early apportionment of government and Consultative Assembly seats to opposition parties, the king consistently
attempted to counterbalance the Istiqlal with other groups, such
as the PDI or the Liberal Independents. From this point of view,
too, the elections were to be partisan.

On the other hand, later mentions of the elections from the
palace emphasized their "nonpolitical"—that is, nonpartisan—na-

---

[6] *PM,* September 12, 1959; see also Mhammedi's press declaration, March 25,
1959. Bekkai had said earlier, "In Morocco, where there has not yet been real
consultation of the people, no political formation can claim hegemony" (*Monde,*
September 2, 1956).

ture, and during 1959 this aspect was almost exclusively insisted on.
When Mhammedi announced the final law, he spoke of creating
nonpartisan elites while putting the political parties to the test. The
two goals were incompatible with each other and with reality. Since,
unlike the first question, this problem was never solved, it cast a
shadow of ambiguity over the entire process of preparing the elections and was particularly important in understanding the difficulties which arose over the electoral preparations. When, in 1960,
the elections were held, their relation to the evolution of democratic
institutions was still unclear; a Constituent Assembly was promised
and soon appointed by the king without reference to the local elections or, directly, to the parties. The day after the elections, the
prince spoke of the new assemblymen as forming an "electoral col-
lege to train our representatives" in democratic ways. The bon mot
did little to tie him to a course of future action.

THE "EASY" STAGE

The beginning of government work on local elections was accompanied by important discussion within the parties. In early 1957
the Istiqlal weekly journal published a number of studies which reflected thinking in party and government circles.[7] The framework
for city elections would be the urban center or the municipality,
already created by the protectorate, with the *quartier* as the election
district. In rural areas, the human framework—the tribe, which has
been the base of all traditional political thinking in Morocco—
would be replaced by a geographical framework or *mesheikha*
(shiekhdom, since the council president might be called a shiekh).
The idea was apparently one of stabilizing rather than destroying
the tribal structure. The smallest social unit, a cluster of tents or
huts called a *douar* or *qsar* (or *tirghemt* in Berber areas) with an
average population of 250 adults, would elect two delegates to the
jema' (council) of the *mesheikha,* and the *jema'* would in turn elect

[7] *Al-Istiqlal,* January 26, 1957 (by ben Barka), February 2 and March 2, 1957
(summer civil service course based on January article). See also *Bulletin des
anciens élèves du lycée d'Azrou* (January 1957 and February 1958), cited in
Paul Chambregeat, "Les Elections communales marocaines du 29 Mai 1960,"
Revue francaise de science politique, XI (March 1961), 92, note 5, and 94, note 6;
the party's *Internal Bulletin* (June and August 1957), cited in Douglas E. Ashford, "Elections in Morocco: Progress or Confusion?" *Middle East Journal,* XV
(March 1961), 3, note 9; and also the results of the Toumliline Conference and
the United Nations Conference in Rabat, both in July, 1958, in *Les cahiers de
Toumliline* (1959) and *Confluent* (January and February 1959), cited in Chambregeat, *op. cit.,* p. 97, note 11. See *PM,* August 4, 1957, for details of the ministry's
project.

its president. Direct election of the sheikh was foreseen later. Voting age would be eighteen or twenty. Women would exercise only limited franchise. The sheikh would take over the functions of the appointed agent of authority, rather than having elected representatives and appointed administrators occupying functions at the same level. The studies also stressed the need for maturity and political education.

In the Interior Ministry, the Direction of Administrative Affairs used the nonexistent 1953 *dahir* as a starting point and drew up projects closely resembling it. A bill on rural administrative organization adopted the *mesheikha,* based on the old tribal subdivisions, without any precise notion of geographic limits; an electoral bill provided a list system of voting for the choice of representatives from sections or electoral districts in the tribal framework. Legal infractions and complaints would be judged by local commissions of the Interior Ministry. Candidates were to be twenty-five years old and members of the district in which they ran. There would be obligatory registration of voters.

A sense of urgency was imparted by the crown prince's declaration in early 1957 and by the king's May Day speech in Casablanca, both announcing that elections would be held by the end of 1957; the king was supposed to have been particularly eager to have the vote before his fall trip to the United States.[8] A rigorous schedule was imposed on the Direction of Administrative Affairs, including night sessions in which the king himself participated. House-to-house registration began on July 22; in the cities the caliph of each ward, accompanied by two potential voters, canvassed every day of the week. Three parties were recognized—the Istiqlal, the PDI, and the Liberal Independents.[9] The canvassing was to be completed by the end of the month, and elections were planned for the end of October. However, no provision was made for handling candidatures and no canvassing was begun in the *bled.*

On July 18, the day that the canvass was announced, the bill was finally ready for discussion in the Council of Ministers. The Istiqlal, bitterly engaged in a campaign to substantiate its claim that it represented the majority, if not the totality, of Morocco,

[8] *Al-Istiqlal,* May 4 and 20, 1957. There was also a desire to do better than Tunisia's one-party elections and to show that democratic elections were possible in Morocco, contrary to a "demagogic campaign of vilification put out by certain [French?] organs which are only read outside of the Moroccan community" (*al-Istiqlal,* July 29, 1957).

[9] The prince said "a fourth formation would complicate Moroccan politics" and estimated the date of the elections as December (*Monde,* June 29, 1957).

was opposed to any sort of proportional representation that might increase the chances of the smaller parties; it also wished to accomplish a revolution in the *bled* by fusing old particularisms into modern units. It therefore favored a bloc-list system and large multimember districts.[10] Mhammedi, the minister of interior, however, appears to have favored single-member districts with majority vote as the system most readily comprehensible to the voters and was supported by the non-Istiqlal members of the government. Work that had hitherto been a matter of administrative preparation suddenly became the subject of intense political debate.

The discussion was embittered by the PDI which, excluded from Bekkai's second government, was the party most threatened by the Istiqlal's gaining membership campaign. The PDI supported nonpartisan elections under a neutral government, demanded total women's franchise (because of a supposed larger female membership), and guarantees of civil liberties (because of Istiqlal pressure) and claimed that preliminary political instruction for the voters was an Istiqlal trick to delay elections and sabotage disinterested voting.[11] On the day that the Council of Ministers met, the PDI sent a telegram to the king asking for representation of all parties in the preparation of elections. On July 22, the PDI again protested to the king, and, late in the night two days later, a PDI delegation was received at the Palace to complain of falsification and sectarianism in the registration campaign. It received a rather basic assurance from the king: "To be truly profitable, an authentic democracy excludes all electoral fraud." On July 26, another PDI leader was received at the Palace, and, as the Council of Ministers then met to discuss the bill, the king insisted on a "detailed study [of the law], even if the elections are thereby retarded several weeks." The following day the council met in the presence of the king, the prince, the crown councilors, and the division heads and technical advisors of the Interior Ministry. As the council further studied the bill, the king announced that he would appoint special commissions to study detailed aspects of the law. The beginning of the end of the "easy" phase had arrived.[12]

[10] See *al-Istiqlal*, July 20 and December 12, 1957, for the party's stand and its defense of the list system to further homogeneous teams.

[11] *Démocratie*, January 7, February 18, and May 27, 1957. The PDI also called for a constitution and an elected deliberative national assembly (*ibid.*, February 25 and March 2, 1957).

[12] The argument that the disunification of the northern and southern zones or the war in Ifni retarded elections—put forward by Ahmed Hamiani in an interview and by Ashford ("Elections . . . ," *op. cit.*, p. 3), respectively—is based only on a misleading coincidence of events; the bill was simply not ready, and political opposition to its completion was too strong.

The realization that in a competitive political atmosphere elections are a complicated business led to a sudden broadening of the search for an electoral law. Information Minister Ahmed Guedira, a leader of the Liberal Independents, stated two directions of the new effort when he announced in early August that comparative studies of other countries' systems would be made, paying special attention to the protection of civil liberties. The most prominent example of the former effort was a suggestion of the prince that his former law professors, Maurice Duverger and André de Laubadère, be invited to make comments on and recommendations to the ministry's bill.[13] The two French political science professors arrived in October, 1957, and stayed until mid-November, touring the country and speaking to political leaders and administrative officials. The result of the consultation was a huge report, amounting to the first study ever made of Moroccan electoral sociology. In its four general principles, the report reflected much of the current official thinking. The elections were to be "administrative" rather than "political," and the choice of the voters should be personal rather than partisan; an electoral system should also avoid the "multiplication of parties, . . . and prevent the birth of new organizations or possible scissions within existing parties." The elections were to be educative, as the king had already made clear, and should adapt themselves to existing "tendencies, even customs," as much as possible. The elections should develop communal interest and avoid an *esprit de douar*, although only with difficulty was this goal compatible with the first two ideas. Finally, the varying conditions native to Morocco should be covered with a single, simple electoral system, applicable "for the inhabitants of Fez and those of the fortress towns of the Dra, for the workers of Casablanca and for the mountain dwellers of the Saharan regions."

Unfortunately, in its details the report did not adhere to its last recommendation. It suggested a complicated system based on three divisions of the country. The six cities with populations over 100,000 would use a majority vote to elect a city-wide list on which each *quartier* would be represented by a candidate; candidates who received the majority vote of their own *quartier*, however, would be elected even if they did not belong to the majority list. The cities with populations under 100,000 would use an unaltered majority list system. The countryside, in an attempt to reconcile the *esprit de douar* with a communal interest, would vote by election district

---

[13] The prince actually said, "I hope we can *entrust* them with the elaboration of an electoral procedure" (*Monde*, June 29, 1957; italics added). See also *al-Istiqlal*, January 11, 1958.

of one or more *douars*; each district of 300 to 10,000 members would elect one to six representatives to send to the communal council, the multimember districts using a list system. The report further proposed an education limitation on the women's vote, an age limit of twenty, no vote for security forces, voluntary registration, and a twenty-five–year age limit but no sex or education restrictions for candidates. It suggested a two-week campaign, exclusive use of radio for state political education, use of color ballots, a two-day voting period, and judicial recourse for inequities. The report was competent and detailed, and it brought to the administrators' attention the need for serious thought to particulars; but it was too complicated and too late to help the bill under discussion. When the second stage of election preparation began a year later, however, many of the points mentioned in the report received renewed attention.

The other point of attention mentioned by Guedira, that of civil liberties, had more immediate bearing on the electoral preparations and coincided with the appearance of another opposition political party. The governor of Rabat, Capt. Mahjoubi Ahardan, announced the appearance of a new rural Berber party, the Popular Movement, on November 1, 1957. The competition that it posed to the Istiqlal, compounded by the fact that it had its roots in a portion of the resistance movement that the Istiqlal was currently seeking to control, led to its immediate suppression. Despite the sympathetic attitude of the king, he was forced by Istiqlal party pressure to accept the ban. The Istiqlal reaction to the Popular Movement and its growing pressure during 1957 to crush out the other parties led the remaining independents and Liberal Independents in the government to insist on a civil liberties law as a prelude to any electoral bill. The persistence of non-Istiqlal members on this matter was heeded by the king, who shared their cause because he did not want to find himself face to face with a monolithic political organization; on November 7, 1957, in opening the second session of the National Consultative Assembly, he announced that the elections had been postponed until sufficient guarantees could be given, and in the Speech from the Throne he mentioned only the "coming elections in an atmosphere of calm." The Istiqlal nevertheless increased its attacks on the PDI for journalistic demagogy, and the language of the opposition papers—*ash-Sha'ab, ar-Rai al-'Amm,* and *Démocratie*—did nothing to remove substance from its charges.

By the turn of the year, two sides and the atmosphere in which they were arguing were evident. The air of political rivalry was so bitter that important matters could not be brought up in meetings of the Council of Ministers, and the highest council of government became useless as a decision-maker. The election bill was, above all, a touchy political matter. On one side, most of the ministers of the Istiqlal showed a marked reluctance to have any elections; or, if a vote was to be held, it would have to be under the conditions which would make good Istiqlal claims, such as a bloc-list system for large districts, a weak or absent civil liberties law, and strict party control of the government. As the months of 1958 passed, it became evident that the fall of Bekkai's second government of National Unity needed only an incident, and the Istiqlal members had, therefore, all the more reason to block the election bill until they had full control of all governmental machinery.[14]

On the other side, the Liberal Independents made the demand for civil liberties one of their major political planks and favored single-member districts. Outside the government, the PDI proposed proportional representation, and the Popular Movement favored single member districts based on tribal units. Bekkai favored elections, but only as soon as the proper guarantees of free participation for all parties were available; on October 1 he had told a political meeting in al-Huceima about the imminent and necessary appearance of laws protecting the rights of press and assembly.

Above all, the king maintained his desire for an early vote and in the first months of 1958 repeatedly called for a discussion of the Interior Ministry's work in the Council of Ministers. Under his pressure the attack on elections was led by the ministry on all fronts. In early February the governors were instructed to hasten the establishment of election districts. A single bill in April covered both the regulations for the vote and the powers of the local assemblies. The ministry had already made a number of compromises with both sides. The law was based on direct universal adult suffrage including women, a year's residence requirements or three years' taxes in the election district, majority list system in one round with bloc lists and no split votes, and registration and disputes of all kinds under the jurisdiction of the Justice Ministry. There was no date set. The supporters of elections, however, refused to accept the bill in council until the electoral system was changed and the civil lib-

[14] A letter from a Moroccan student in Toulouse, prominently printed in *ibid.*, March 1, 1958, said that the people were not ready to vote, that they needed civic education rather than elections, and that political parties were to be preferred to voting. Much of the reasoning has the ironic ring of protectorate declarations.

erties guaranteed. The minister, therefore, in rare disobedience to the king's orders, refused to report the bill.

The incident that the Istiqlalis needed to end the government came over the same issue. In the end of April, 1958, Bekkai supported a minority party declaration favoring the freedom of political association and protesting the ban his own government had imposed on the Popular Movement.[15] The immediate resignation of the Istiqlal ministers felled the government, ended the chances of an early election law, and terminated the "easy" stage of electoral preparation.

The preparation of the abortive 1957 *dahir* is rich in lessons both about and for Moroccan government. It showed, as Bou'abid was later to do in manipulating the army budget, that on rare occasions it was possible to defy the king, although only by negative actions. It also illustrated the surprising possibility of action open to parties outside the government, again most effective when negative. Finally, it showed that, despite the goals pronounced from the beginning of the electoral preparation, it was too late by 1957 to hold either nonpartisan or single-party elections; the vote would be important in training the population in democracy and would create institutions for basic self-government, but it also would be prepared during the very battle for political dominance that it was supposed to replace. It could not help having political significance, and politics would inevitably determine the shape and time of the elections, not wait to be determined by them.

RURAL COMMUNES

The first precondition to the final preparation of the elections was the creation of an electoral district. Although the task may on the surface appear to be only an administrative detail, the superficiality of the early bill showed that a profound sociological study of the entire country was needed. The choice was aptly posed by *al-Istiqlal* on October 12, 1957, after the weakness of the initial bill had been realized:

> . . . either wait until a geographic, economic and social study can be made scientifically, which would postpone the first election until a far distant date, or else accept the present administrative division inherited from the Protectorate, [which]

[15] The declaration was written by Mouline and Guedira of the Liberal Independents, Hassan Ouezzani and 'Abdelhadi Boutaleb of the PDI, Khatib and Ahardan of the Popular Movement, and Mekki Naciri of the Moroccan Unity Party.

is the result of a hasty improvisation and cannot be used as such.

The sudden concentration on electoral matters occasioned by the PDI protest in July, 1957, resulted in the creation of commissions for detailed study of electoral problems, including the Itinerant Commission appointed by the Interior Minister to set up the rural communes.

The instructions agreed to by the king and the Interior Ministry for the establishment of the rural communes illustrate how it differs from the *mesheikha* and tribal *jema'*.[16] The commission was to take account of geography, economics, politics,[17] communications, and size before ethnic considerations and create a unit of social life compact enough in area and population to act as a framework for day-to-day activity as well as for democratic government.[18] The focal element of each commune was to be the market, the center of communications and economic life and the major source of community revenue, the market tax. The market, which was often ambulatory and frequently made only a weekly appearance on a previously designated spot, was to be fixed and become an embryo town, with permanent market installations and shops, schools, mosques, and administrative buildings. It was necessary to the commission that a firm—even if not formal—hierarchy of criteria be established in its mind, for many times the elements were contradictory; thus, the high priority given to the market as the center of the commune meant that in many cases a new market would have to be created if criteria of size, geography, and communications were to be respected. Other problems complicated the need for a single focal point. Large towns acted as the market for a surrounding area too extensive to pass the tests of size and communications; populous or heavily trafficked areas had more than one market in an otherwise unified economic and social region; areas with unusual terrain or communications routes often had the

[16] There were about 1,300 *masheikhat*, each with a tribal *jema'*, in the protectorate's plan.

[17] These were not to be partisan politics but traditional animosities and legal squabbles. Two communes in Tiznit circle of Agadir province were kept separate because of traditional hostility, although their population was only 4,500 and 5,800. However, the commune of Dkhissa in Meknes was united about the possibility of an Agricultural Work Center, despite a feuding population.

[18] For broader aspects of communal planning, see *al-Istiqlal*, March 9, 1957; *Notes et Documents*, I (November 1958), 5-22; *Contribution du Ministère de l'Agriculture à l'équipement des communes rurales* (Rabat: Ministry of Agriculture, 1960). See also I. Chiva, *Rural Communities: Problems, Methods and Types of Research* (Social Science Clearing House Document No. 10 [Paris: UNESCO, 1958]).

market located in a corner of the region a long distance from many
of the people; areas having no market or a poor market were in
danger of forming a homogeneously poor commune with a homogeneously rich commune next door if the criteria of economic unity
and agricultural similarity were to be followed.

From the start the commune was conceived as an evolution of
past patterns, an institutionalization of present life, and a framework for future development. Conflicting characteristics appear
from a review of these early concepts. On one hand, all that was
being attempted was an acceleration of the natural social processes
that have generally been responsible for the creation of urban ag-
glomerations out of rural societies. In a country where many of the
previous units—the tribes—were still nomadic, primitive, rural,
and isolated, with a highly autarkic economic life and an autonomous political structure, this acceleration was necessary both to the
effective exercise of national and local government and also to the
rapid development of the country's economy and its adjustment to
an effective role in the modern world. Although the process was
natural, its speed gave it the potentiality of a profound social revolution.

On the other hand, if the revolution was to accelerate rather
than disarticulate the evolutionary process, it might be expected to
respect past social structures in transforming them into new units.
In fact, the criteria given to the commission for forming rural communes refer in many instances to a maintenance rather than a disruption of tribal patterns. Often the tribe did provide a viable economic and social unit of life. It might be centered about a permanent market which had already developed into a village—as the
names of many Moroccan towns indicate.[19] It might occupy a compact area of farming and grazing, with easy communication among
douars and with social relations, culminating in the rudimentary
election of a tribal *jema'*. In these cases, there was no purpose in
deliberately destroying the existing unit or preventing its natural
evolution.[20] Yet the most frequently heard slogan of the commission
was, "Destroy the tribal framework." So much has been made in

[19] Former Agriculture Minister Nejjai's home town, for example, is Souq
al-Arba' al-Gharb, literally "the market on Wednesday of the Gharb tribe."
[20] On the other hand, in many cases the tribe had outgrown its original socio-
geographic unity. New bridges and roads, colonial towns, and abandoned lands
often changed the tribal situation; other tribes had grown too large, had developed enclaves for transhumant grazing, or had become too compact, all of
which prevented them from being retained as a viable unit.

Morocco of the David-like prowess of the Itinerant Commission in doing away with the giant tribes that the real purpose of the rural commune is often forgotten. The criterion of success was not the number of tribes destroyed, but the number of viable communes created.

The working procedure of the commission was established in its first meeting in Casablanca, seat of Chawia province, on August 28, 1957, and followed in other provincial meetings until the last one in al-Huceima on March 10, 1958.[21] Each governor had been instructed to prepare a redistricting proposal. Usually work was entrusted to the French technical advisors attached to the governor's office; these advisors had had experience in the administration of local tribes from protectorate times and were often more conversant with the local situation than the newly appointed governors or other members of their staff. The local caids, many of them also newly appointed, worked closely on the preparation of the initial draft. Tribal *jema's* also were often consulted, and their negative opinion in several cases meant that a particular proposal was not retained; sometimes the *jema'* actually petitioned to be fused with other groups into a particular commune or voted on the proposed redistricting.

The session between the commission and the provincial office generally began with a commission member's statement of the goals and criteria, followed by an examination of the governor's draft and a discussion and rectification of problem areas. The commission decided by majority vote—although a formal ballot was rarely taken—and could overrule the governor, as it frequently did. The rectified project was then carried to the Interior Ministry, where maps were drafted, a final study made, and the redistricting reviewed through the normal hierarchy. The commission could call provincial members to Rabat for consultation and could request further study and justification of problem communes. These special studies usually took inordinately long to be submitted, the administrators apparently feeling that delay was a better defense for their projects than debate. The entire process, except for final touches within the ministry, was finished by the end of the second government, in the spring of 1958.

The best way to appreciate the problems, obstacles, and results of the establishment of communes is to review the redistricting by

[21] The following material is taken from the transcripts of the commission's meetings with the provincial officers and the redistricting plans appended thereto.

province and then compare the general results with the original instructions. In Chawia province, the 130 old *jema's* were consolidated into ninety-two communes by the governor and rearranged into a final figure of 104 by the commission. In the north-central part of the province, the Chawia agricultural plain around Casablanca, the development of embryo urban centers had already begun the process of creating communities for the governor's project; however, several communes shared an urban center. The commission located a market for each commune, questioning whether the governor's draft "has been able to remove certain ethnic particularisms and constitute real communities of interest." In the more mountainous region about Khouribga and Oued Zem, where the tribal system is stronger, the provincial project had frequently used the tribe as the natural social unit; the commission doubled the number of communes in Oued Zem to arrive at a manageable non-ethnic unit. The coastal farming plain of the Doukkala about al-Jadida is densely populated, homogeneous in its land, and strongly centralized about existing markets; the resulting redistricting made large communes averaging slightly more than 15,000 inhabitants, double the size of the old *jema's*, but constituting well-to-do units which broke up the tribes.

The province of Marrakesh includes an area to the south in the Atlas, three tribal confederations on the northern plains next to the Chawia, and the former province of Safi along the coast. In the mountains, the communes are based on geography tempered by considerations of size; a valley or communicating valleys were used as the unit unless the resulting communes would be too large or too poor. The result was a commune averaging less than 10,000 population, with tribal groups split or mixed. Among the northern confederations slightly larger than average communes were traced, and tribal unity gave way to economic and geographic regrouping. In reapportioning the former Safi province, the commission and the province clashed on concepts; the province felt that "the tribe is that framework which best permitted a sufficiency of resources and which best suited the educative action of the public spirit that is essential in the rural commune." Unlike Marrakesh, the commission tripled the number of communes and split the tribes in order to arrive at a manageable economic unit. Even so, the coastal communes have a population of over 15,000 each.

Tadla province is small but lies half in the heart of the High Atlas and half in the rich irrigated Tadla plain to the north. In the irrigated plain, the small tribal fractions were regrouped into units of about 10,000 inhabitants, corresponding to already established sectors of irrigation; in the mountains, the communes had about 5,000 people, in accordance with the governor's desire to provide geographic and economic unity.

Rabat province is composed of the rich farmlands of the Gharb in the north and the hilly farmlands of the Zemmour and Zaer tribes in the south bordering on the Chawia plain. The commission made few changes on the governor's report. The communes vary from about 10,000 members in the south to 15,000–20,000 in the north; the number of former *jema's* was cut in half by the fusion of small, market-less tribal fractions into viable communes. Since the tribe was often the unit of cultivation and ownership in Rabat province, it was frequently maintained or used in conjunction with others as a base for the new communes.[22]

When the commission met at Meknes on August 30, 1957, the instructions of the committee were not forcefully put across, and the province succeeded in maintaining the old divisions. The commission asked for the dissolution of communes of under 5,000 inhabitants "except when natural ethnic or geographic conditions prohibit their regrouping." Lack of cooperation from the governor made it necessary for the commission to return nine weeks later. The northern quarter of the province was a rich but highly colonialized farm plan—the Sais—mixed with mountains; here the commission found a solution with little difficulty, fusing of tribal groups—often with their permission—to form arbitrary but homogeneous communes of about 10,000 members, "whenever the former *jema's* showed evidence of a common economy when united."

One of the major problems of the mountainous south of Meknes province shows the depth of ethnic particularism that the commission had to face. Tribal lands were often noncontiguous and even widely scattered over mountain and plain for use in seasonal migration, but the tribe wanted to be with its land. The governor's draft faithfully reflected the ethnic division with a mosaic of enclaves—three to five a commune. On its second visit the commission could insist only on a regrouping, so that each commune was a territorial unit, obviously no longer with any ethnic basis. Elsewhere in the south the governor resubmitted the protectorate's plan for a multitude of *jema's* too small to be viable. They were as individually distinct as beads in a necklace, held together by a basic line of communications and tribal unity that ran through them;

[22] One such was the tribe of Beni Hakim about Tedders, in one electoral district of which Zemmouri successfully ran for communal councilor in 1960.

yet a tribal grouping would result in elongated communes as much as forty miles long with populations ranging from 4,000 to 23,000. Faced with a problem of units too big or too small, the commission chose the former. "The basic idea here is to determine a geographic area with common interests. It happens, in this case, that that area is that of the tribe."

Parallel and to the east of Meknes lies the province of Fez, which stretches from the pre-Rif in the north, across the Sais plain into the Atlas and the desert valley of the Moulouya in the south. The commission accepted most of the governor's rectifications of past structures. In the north the communes averaged about 10,000 inhabitants, but in the mountainous south, even an average size of 5,000 meant communes of large area and poor communications. In a high percentage of cases the tribe was used as the basis for the commune (30 per cent) or was split into several communes without disrupting ethnic homogeneity (30 per cent).

Parallel to Meknes and Fez provinces, continuing east, are Taza and Oujda provinces. Taza is a highly mountainous region where the Rif and the Atlas meet; half of the province also falls in the Moulouya valley desert in the southeast. Communes in the Rif and Middle Atlas were based on purely tribal considerations, varying between 5,000 and 25,000 inhabitants but averaging about 10,000, and were maintained even after the Rif dissidence which shook the region the following year. Although the population of the larger communes was high, the territory was small (six by ten miles), and there was no natural basis for redistricting. In the valley of the Moulouya and in the southern desert of the neighboring province of Oujda, huge communes were formed, containing only 10,000 people on an average; here pairs of the protectorate units were fused because of the native poverty and the availability of adequate communications, for many of the inhabitants were nomads. Although an effort was made in northern Oujda to keep the units between 10,000 and 15,000 inhabitants, the problem of juggling resources, population, and area led to communes as small as 2,000 people about Oujda city, the other two factors being dominant. The important mines in the region were distributed among the communes to provide a basic source of revenue.

In the three largely desert provinces to the south [23]—Tafilalt, Ouarzazat, and Agadir—the same problem of balancing resources, population, and area is evident although the tribal lines are relaxed

[23] Tarfaya province had not yet been returned to Morocco, was only later divided into three communes, and voted for 107 councilors in October, 1961.

enough—partly by nomadism—to constitute a lesser problem than they do in the north. Here, too, the tribes are canal-, well-, or spring-centered, rather than having defined territorial boundaries as they do on the other side of the Atlas; around these populations are vast areas of largely uninhabited desert, crisscrossed by nomad's trails. In the Tafilalt and Ouarzazat, a number of former tribal units were consolidated, but two-thirds of the communes still have fewer than 5,000 inhabitants. Even in the south-slope valleys of the Atlas, tribal groups were fused into larger economic and geographic units; here and about the more populous centers of the large Tafilalt oasis, the communes attained 10,000 or more inhabitants. The units in Ouarzazat, largely accepted by the commission, varied in size; half had 10,000 or more inhabitants, including the geographically rich and large commune of Agdz with an unexplained population of 21,000, whereas a quarter of the communes had 5,000 or fewer people. Foum Zguid, in the extreme south, illustrates another part of the complex problem; the local tribe, cut in two by the Dra River and by the protectorate's administrative division but now united in one commune, spoke Arabic on one side of the river and Berber on the other.

In Agadir, the governor, who presided over the meeting with the commission, reduced the number of units from 180 *jema's* to ninety communes, fusing tribal units for economic and administrative reasons, which the commission accepted. The basis of the commune remained ethnic only in about 15 per cent of the cases. Agadir presents such a heterogeneity of economic and physical conditions that no general rules seem applicable to the redistricting. The result varied from 2,000 to 20,000 but most communes had populations of about 9,000.[24]

In the former Spanish zone in the northern part of the country, an easy relation has been established between the tribes and the communes. Here, except in the agricultural Loukkos plain that formed the old province of al-'Airash, the mountainous terrain of the Rif divides the inhabitants both vertically, by altitude, and horizontally, by valleys. It was, therefore, a matter of regrouping the tribal fractions to create communes with a high degree of uniformity and with 5,000 to 12,000 inhabitants. This system does nothing to mix tribal fractions; they are either split, retained, or grouped by the communes. Several trips by the commission were necessary to overcome local obstacles in part of the north.

[24] Contrary to the experience in Meknes, three communes in Agadir included enclaves in the territory of other communes—and, in one case, in another circle.

An over-all view of results permits comparison between the
final redistricting and the original instructions to the commission.
Between half and three-quarters of the 726 new rural communes
differ in shape from the corresponding *jema's* of the protectorate,
although a large number were made by merely fusing two or more
protectorate units. A few more than 15 per cent of the communes
are coterminous with tribes; this is especially characteristic of the
northern half of the country—Rabat, Meknes, Fez, Taza, Oujda,
and the Rif provinces. Four per cent of the communes are composed exclusively of two or three fractions grouped together; this
occurs in Agadir as well as the other provinces cited. Thus less than
one-fifth of the communes are coincident with one or more tribal
units. On the other hand, in more than 20 per cent of the cases,
tribes were split into two or more communes; here ethnic unity is
preserved, although tribal unity is broken. This solution is extremely common in Oujda and the Rif and little used south of the
Atlas. One other consideration helps emphasize tribal orientation.
Except in Ouarzazat and Tafilalt, practically all provincial boundaries are tribal, and over 75 per cent of those boundaries coincide
with large tribal federations. Furthermore, in the provinces of the
great tribal confederations—Chawia, Marrakesh, Rabat, Meknes,
and northern Oujda—the district, comprising several caidats, is frequently coincident with the confederation, thus reinforcing the
tribal influence at a higher level.

The communes were finished, except for some small subsequent
changes, in August, 1958. The four months following the last provincial meeting had been spent in drafting and eliciting special
studies from unresponsive provincial offices. Along with the communal reorganization, the Interior Ministry prepared a new and
totally revised map of provincial boundaries in keeping with the
commission's suggestions. In August, the Council of Ministers accepted the proposal, which consecrated the integration of the former Spanish zone in the north by dividing Nador province between
Taza and Oujda, enlarging Tetuan province to include the northern part of Rabat, and rectifying a number of other geographical
and economic anomalies. Before the provinces could be reshaped,
the tribes of the Rif broke out in armed revolt against the government, and the project was delayed until January, 1959, and then
only partially implemented.

Thereafter, the communal redistricting awaited the progress
of other election details until it could be made public. The first
map was presented to the king by Hassan Zemmouri, president of

the commission, in April, 1959, but the decree creating the communes did not appear until December. Even at election time, over two years after the commission's work, there was still evidence of the old tribal system; newspapers referred to the communes as *mesheikha* and gave the results in terms of the tribes, and the *chef de cercle* at Khemisset accurately reflected the ethnic composition of his communes by telegraphing to the ministry: "Honor to report you following lists of candidates elected in rural elections of following tribes." Zemmouri claims that the tribal framework was broken in two-thirds of the communes. Considering the centuries of entrenchment supporting the tribal structure and its frequent coincidence with economic and geographical patterns, this result was both realistic and impressive, if not remarkable.

CIVIL RIGHTS

The nationalists had emphasized civil liberties since the protectorate's restrictions in the mid-1930's and the declaration of a state of siege in 1939. Some of the most stringent measures were put into effect in connection with World War II, but they remained on the law books to be used against the Istiqlal Movement. The arrival of independence posed a real dilemma for the successful nationalists. On one hand, they expected their long-standing demand to be honored, the restrictive legislation to be rescinded, and a bill of rights to be proclaimed; in its pre-independence congress of December, 1955, the Istiqlal made special mention of the measures it wanted abolished in the name of human rights. On the other hand, since the protectorate legislation of 1914 and the "emergency" limitations of 1939, the Moroccans knew only a legal system by which certain liberties were *authorized,* not *guaranteed.* They therefore found it natural to envisage a restricted list of civil liberties for which the state would grant permission on individual application, rather than a broad protection of civil rights. Furthermore, there was still enough opposition—even within the Independence Movement—against leaders other than the king to make such restrictions not only natural but also useful. The Istiqlal was facing the embarrassing problem of successful revolutionary movements which find in all good conscience that what they wanted was freedom for themselves but not for others.

A year after independence the feeling sharpened. The Istiqlal saw division in opposition when the nation needed unity, colonialism in criticism when the nation needed patriotism, and hence treason in all that was non-Istiqlal. This chain-reaction reasoning, which could be persuasive to the sincere nationalist, threw a heavy onus on the opposition, and it was a convincing argument for postponing or at least carefully wording any protection of civil rights. Thus by 1958, when the Political Commission of the party met to formulate its position before the choice of the third government, it was ". . . unanimous in emphasizing that . . . civil liberties, particularly of association and expression, should find permanent guarantees while respecting the interests of the nation"; but the new government would

> . . . nevertheless have the duty to take measures necessary to incapacitate the seditious and the traitors who have plotted against their country and who take advantage of the freedom regained through the blood of the martyrs of the Resistance, to create a climate of excitation and of anarchy.[25]

Work on civil liberties began with the preparation of the 1957 election bill by the second government, with various interested ministries preparing drafts. A preliminary experience indicated the sort of problems to be faced. 'Abdullah Ibrahim, Istiqlal labor minister, and Guedira, Liberal Independent information minister, both prepared a *dahir* on labor rights; a compromise law appeared, granting freedom of trade union association, one of the most insistent demands of the urban resistance.[26] On the same day, however, an "exceptional and transitory" decree was promulgated by the labor minister, giving the secretary general of the government the right to oppose the creation of any new labor union. In November a young electrician named Mohammed Jorio was expelled from the Istiqlal-affiliated Moroccan Trade Union (UMT) in Rabat for refusing not to strike on the anniversary of the Algerian uprising; he was charged, rather curiously, with "intelligence with colonialism and anarchist intrigues," but he went ahead to form the Free Confederation of Moroccan Workers. The secretary general was opposed and was upheld by the king in the name of trade union unity. A precedent was established, both for civil rights laws and for handling opposition to the Istiqlal.

Guedira nevertheless continued to prepare a law on freedom of the press, and Mhammedi had a law on freedom of association drawn up in connection with the electoral law. After the PDI pro-

[25] *Al-Istiqlal*, April 27, 1958.
[26] *Dahir* No. 1-57-119 of July 16, 1957 and decree No. 2-57-0571 of July 17, 1957. The powers of the secretary general followed the precedent of a protectorate law of 1914.

test in July, work on the rights bills took precedence, and in the
Council of Ministers meeting of August 30, 1957, an interministerial
council was formed of the Justice, Interior and Information Ministries and the premier's office. Three drafts of a press bill were
drawn up before the end of the year; the third draft was presented
by Guedira to the Council of Ministers on January 18, 1958, and was
sent to the council, where it was picked to death in the partisan
arena. At the same time the PDI press was banned for excesses, and
a bill was prepared giving the interior minister the power to forbid
the formation of political parties.

When the second government fell in April, 1958, two conflicting attitudes were evident. On one hand, the *dahirs* on civil
liberties clearly stood out as a preliminary to any election law. On
the other hand, the Istiqlal had declared the transition phase ended,
prepared to take control of the government, and made known its
highly circumscribed stand on full exercise of civil rights. National
Assembly President Mehdi ben Barka, the first person the king consulted on the new government, called the new *dahir* the corner-
stone of a true democracy, but insisted that the law could be passed
only if it were constructive and if it protected against "demagogy,
outbidding (*surenchère*), [and] . . . imperialism." [27] "Some say that
the Government wants to snuff out liberty. You know the truth.
Morocco is going through a delicate period," he told party leaders
in Casablanca.[28] The Royal Charter that defined the duties of the
new Istiqlal government, however, stated clearly:

> Desirous of permitting Our subjects to exercise the basic lib-
> erties and to enjoy the rights of man, We will guarantee free-
> dom of opinion, of expression, of reunion and of association.
> This guarantee will be limited only by the respect due to the
> monarchial regime, the safety of the State, and the impera-
> tives of the general interest.[29]

The government was charged with creating "an electoral law and
a law on public liberties."

The government, however, did not move, although more than
one text was already prepared. On June 24, the king called in a
commission headed by Ahmed Bahnini, secretary general of the
government, and asked for the *dahirs* by July 20. It was not until
the last day of July, however, that the secretary general had made

[27] *Al-Istiqlal*, April 20, 1958.
[28] *Ibid.*, April 27, 1958.
[29] *Ibid.*, May 11, 1958.

his observations on the bills prepared by his offices and nearly a
week later that Bahnini presented to the king bills on freedom of
assembly, association, and the press. During the months of September and October, the Council of Ministers met and discussed the
bills, but no action was forthcoming, and it began to appear as if
the government of Balafrej would try to sit on the measure as the
preceding government had done with the electoral law. It took a
polite note from the king recalling the charges of the Royal Charter and implicitly threatening the government with dissolution if
no action were forthcoming to bring the *dahirs* to publication on
November 15. A week later, the growing tension between the two
wings of the party was shown by the resignation of the economics
minister, and a month later the Istiqlal government fell. The way to
elections was finally cleared of two of its major obstacles.

Nearly all the legislation was drawn directly from previous
French laws or from legislation of the protectorate. The General
Secretariat once commented, "The new legislation is rather extensively inspired by French legislation, to the point of sometimes
arriving at nonsense. The differences [arise] particularly on the
amount of the fines." [30]

Of the press code's eighty articles, fifty-nine were found intact
in all five drafts except for small changes in wording, fines, and
sequence.[31] Of the remaining twenty-one articles, five were new to
the 1958 drafts; these comprised a definition of the foreign press
and the rather useful Article 77, which gave the minister of interior
the power to order "administrative seizure of any issue of a newspaper or periodical whose publication will be of a nature to trouble
the public order." The General Secretariat of the Government
(SGG) received the first draft from the Information Ministry on
August 12, 1957, after the PDI protest. In addition to the above-
mentioned five articles, it lacked provisions to protect the public
morals and penalties for criminal action against guilty editors. The
second version took care of these loopholes; the third version
omitted some earlier provisions on ownership of the press. The difference between the substance of the 1957 and 1958 drafts, with the
exception of Article 77, was thus remarkably slight.

[30] General Secretariat of the Government note, SL/SGG of September 13, 1957.
[31] *Dahir* No. 1-58-378 of November 15, 1958. Preceding legislation includes
dahirs of July 13, 1951; February 19, 1945; December 5, August 24 and 30, and
July 26, 1939; October 7, 1932; and April 27, 1914; Order of the Superior Com-
mandant (OCS) of April 26, 1944; French decree law of July 29, 1938; and French
law of June 11, 1887. The three 1957 drafts are numbered 1-57-254, and the two
1958 drafts are numbered 1-58-378.

Similar characteristics are evident in the *dahir* on freedom of association.[32] Only titles III and IV, covering authorization of federations and conditions governing political parties, were new to Moroccan law; the latter were open only to Moroccans, closed to members of the security forces, and liable to fifteen days maximum suspension followed by court trial if they contravened the limitations imposed on the exercise of civil liberties in the Royal Charter, already cited. Any political party could be constituted after a formal legal declaration of purpose. The publication of the *dahir* was immediately followed by the legal appearance of the Popular Movement, which had been banned thirteen months before. It is ironic that, when the Istiqlal finally split in January, 1959, and the seceding activist Confederated Istiqlal and then the National Union of Popular Forces (UNFP) were formed, both of these parties benefited from the *dahir*, although they were the bane of the old-guard Istiqlal and the most outspoken critics of the king. The third *dahir*, that on public assembly, was also taken, with no exceptions, from the protectorate regulations.[33]

> This draft does little more than unite in a single bill the provisions of [protectorate] laws of 1914, 1936, and 1945, themselves tightly based on the French laws of 1881 and 1848. . . . The editors of this bill have thus not done much new work.[34]

THE "HARD" STAGE

The new Istiqlal government took office on May 12, 1958, amid general expectations of elections in mid-summer. Just before the fall of the previous government, Mhammedi had called on the king and promised elections by July on the basis of the 1957 bill. The Royal Charter, which incorporated the general political objectives accepted by the Istiqlal Political Commission, specifically imposed on the government the task of preparing the electoral law as well as the civil liberties *dahirs*. The charge was no longer a promise to the government—such as had been given twice to Bekkai, who was supposed to hold office until elections took place; it was an obligation. But from the very formation of the government, conditions

[32] *Dahir* No. 1-58-376 of November 15, 1958. Preceding legislation includes the *dahir* of May 24, 1914; OCS of December 20, 1944; French decree law of April 12, 1939; and French laws of January 10, 1936, and July 1, 1901.

[33] *Dahir* No. 1-58-377 of November 14, 1958. Preceding legislation includes *dahirs* of July 20, 1936; March 6, 21, and 26, 1914; OCS of March 14, 1945; and French laws of June 20, 1881, and July 7, 1848.

[34] Observations of General Secretariat of the Government, July 17, 1958.

which hindered its fulfillment arose or were imposed. Mhammedi, who is said to have considered the preparation of elections as his personal contribution to independent Moroccan government, was no longer in office. In the list of ministers submitted by the new premier, the left-wing Economic Minister Bou'abid was transferred to the head of the Interior Ministry. The king, however, was anxious to keep the Interior Ministry, with its control of the police, in more decidedly loyal hands, and he replaced Bou'abid with his own former head of the Royal Cabinet, Messa'oud Chiguer. The ministry remained attached to its former head, and work slowed down to a camel's pace. The government itself was beset by political troubles among its ministers, foreshadowing the party split that was to cause its demise seven months after its formation, and the Rif dissidence in October only added to its political difficulties. In early December, the king accepted its resignation, because of Balafrej's incapability to hold his government and country together and because the obligations imposed by the Royal Charter—the preparation of elections—were not fulfilled.

The disappointments of the 1957 bill and the problems of administrative delay were frankly recognized by the king in speeches of November, 1958. In the beginning of the month he addressed the opening session of the Consultative Assembly: "We have been confronted with difficulties of all sorts and of a complexity and number that we did not foresee. Much clairvoyance and wisdom was necessary to surmount them." In prolonging the terms of the assembly members to May, 1959, he indicated that he expected the elections to take place by that time. In his Speech from the Throne in the middle of November, 1958, the king again recognized that, "If the election of communal and municipal assemblies has been put off, it is because we are dealing with a new experiment that we sincerely wish to see succeed." He spoke of particularist difficulties in creating the communes and of the necessity of guaranteeing civil rights, and he announced that the elections would be held as soon as possible. *Al-'Alam* and *al-Istiqlal* both echoed urgency.[35]

Conditions were more favorable for the success of the election bill in the new government, which took office on Christmas Eve, 1958. The impending split of the Istiqlal, which took place a month later, actually favored elections by injecting a spirit of partisan competition into the proceedings. The new government was specifically designated as an interim, nonpolitical group chosen according to individual competence for the preparation of the elections.

[35] *Al-Istiqlal,* December 13, 1958; *al-'Alam,* December 12, 1958.

It will be expected to govern in the present while preparing the municipal and communal elections, which will give the Sovereign an indication of the currents of opinion and political orientation of the Moroccan people.[36]

Although no time limit was set for elections, the official announcement estimated June, 1959. Mhammedi was recalled to head the Interior Ministry. To assist him as undersecretary of state for rural and communal affairs, Ibrahim named his former cabinet head, Hassan Zemmouri. In his new position, Zemmouri asked to be put explicitly in charge of election preparation, and the king indicated that he wished to see him often. As a protégé and sympathizer of Ibrahim's, Zemmouri was at home in the new government as he had not been under Chiguer and Balafrej. He had good relations with Mhammedi, but since the minister was seriously ill during 1959 and finally went to the United States for treatment, Zemmouri was largely his own master. He saw the king as instructed, sometimes as often as two or three times a week, usually alone to explain the progress of his work, but occasionally accompanied by Ibrahim. Zemmouri was aided by a small staff made up of an Algerian to handle the Arabic aspect of the work, one or two French technical advisors for legal advice and acquaintance with the groundwork laid by the protectorate, and four Moroccans of diverse political views.

With the elections finally so close to reality, preparations entered a precautionary stage. The bill that was ready by the end of 1958 was now scrutinized and restudied. Mhammedi told the press on March 25, 1959, "We have no right to throw five million Moroccans into an adventure." An additional occasion for final verification came in early March, when communal elections were being held in France; a special delegation of Zemmouri, a member of his office, and four lieutenant governors was sent to observe the event and bring back conclusions for Morocco. In a sharp contrast to the administrative delays which characterized earlier work, the observers prepared their reports within five days of their return to Morocco and presented them to the prince and the king.[37] The sug-

[36] *PM*, December 17, 1958. Special symposia during 1959 discussed problems of local administration in preparation for the *dahir* on the councils' powers; the discussions were printed in *L'Administration locale et ses problèmes* (Rabat: Ministry of the Interior, 1960).

[37] *Rapport de Mission des Secrétaires généraux des provinces* (Rabat: Ministry of the Interior, 1959); quotations are from pp. 10 and 22. The first suggestion was implemented in April, 1959, indicating that someone was looking to early elections. See *PM*, April 2 and 16, 1959; party criticism is in *al-Istiqlal*, April 18, 1959.

gestions included a complete review of the local administrators and replacement where vacancies or incompetence appeared, use of the courts for review of election irregularities in the absence of an administrative court system, and use of electoral cards and colors to distinguish candidates. On the other hand, the observers were nearly unanimous in favoring a simple majority list system with one round of voting, so that the councils would be "homogeneous in their decisions and united in their responsibilities"; they also supported a permanent obligatory system of registration, although they admitted that the burdens this operation would place on the civil service would be heavy and that "the under-administration in the *bled* threatens to eliminate administrative activity during the entire period of the elections." These two features—list system and obligatory registration—were still part of the bill as it stood at the beginning of 1959.

Soon after the observers' report had been filed, Mhammedi announced that the long-awaited elections would take place in September. There were to be 800 rural and about fifty urban communes, with councils ranging from nine members to the fifty-three members for Casablanca. The 1957 age provision of twenty-one for voters and twenty-five for candidates was maintained, as was unrestricted women's suffrage. The electoral system provided for the subdivision of the communes into a number of multimember sections or election districts, so that each section would vote for a small bloc list of candidates—a system close to de Laubadère and Duverger's suggestions for urban communes. But there was no final agreement on the number of sections for each commune or on their boundaries, and it was details such as these which, in an unfavorable political atmosphere, had delayed the elections to this point. In March the sections were to be three a commune; in April, when Zemmouri gave the king the first provisional map of the communes, there were to be two to ten sections, as yet unmapped. On April 23, the Council of Ministers settled another detail by fixing the legal delay between the promulgation of the *dahir* and the elections themselves at six months; elections were thereby put off until October.[38]

The bill was finally submitted to the Council of Ministers in early May. After a heated discussion, the king made the rare move of calling a vote. The council approved the provision for obligatory registration but split in half on the electoral system; the members

[38] Note of Mhammedi to Ibrahim, June 4, 1959, for breakdown. Part of the following delay was the result of the intervening fast month of Ramadan.

from both factions of the Istiqlal supported the list system provided, whereas the independent ministers and the king's men supported single-member districts. The government threatened to resign. The bitter conflict between the two sides, so clearly expressed, led to action in a number of directions. Outside authority was again appealed to; three governors were sent on an information trip to England to study communal administration and elections, and the president of the Indian Electoral Commission arrived the following month.

Mhammedi and Zemmouri's response to the delay was to send a letter to Ibrahim on June 4, 1959, with the object "of Remedying the Delay in the Publication of *dahir* 1-59-161." The bill, "still being studied," would be corrected and ready for publication on June 30. With the legal six months' delay, elections would take place at Christmas, but by immediately promulgating a *dahir,* the delay could be reduced, permitting elections by the end of November. The principle of obligatory registration, which had hitherto been the policy of the ministry, was therefore abandoned. Voluntary registration at the office of the local urban or rural authorities would begin a week after the publication of the *dahir.* The *dahir* was drafted on June 16, sent to the General Secretariat of the Government for editing on June 20, and then it, too, fell into administrative and political delays. Meanwhile Ibrahim departed for the Middle East and in Cairo, on June 17, announced that the 180-day legal delay for elections would begin within a week, thus anticipating the publication of the electoral law. The elections were therefore put off until Christmas.

The king's response to the governmental split was to follow his usual custom of turning, paradoxically in this case, to the political parties. Representatives were called to the Palace on June 8 and given a list of questions on the electoral system; party dossiers on the elections were to be returned by June 22, when a synthesis was to be made by the Royal Cabinet and passed on to the king.[39] The two most important reports were given by the old-guard Istiqlal

[39] The Istiqlal, in *al-Istiqlal,* June 13, 20, and 27, 1959, September 12, 1959; Confederated Istiqlal, in *al-Istishara al-malakiya haul al-intikhabat al-biladiya wa al-qarawiya* (mimeographed; June 21, 1959); the UMT, in *AG,* June 28, 1959. The UMA and UMCIA were not consulted until the Istiqlal protested; the UMA was partially negative in its report, saying "someone has simply forgotten to integrate the rural masses in order to make them capable of carrying out their national duties" (*al-Fellah,* December 15, 1959). The Communist party was unhappy at not being consulted and published its own report anyhow (*al-Jamahir* [Casablanca], June 25, 1959).

and by the National Confederation of the Istiqlal Party, the seceding group; the latter report was endorsed by one of the resistance organizations and repeated, except for changes in language, by the UMT and by the Communist party; the former report was later supported by the Moroccan Agricultural Union and the Moroccan Union of Commerce, Industry and Artisans. The important characteristics of the two dossiers were their disagreement with the ideas of the ministry and their frequent resemblance to each other despite the bitter partisan rivalry.

There were seven compound questions. On voter's qualifications, both parties required a year's residence or three years' taxes in the commune and excluded criminals, bankrupts, and legally declared traitors, although the old-guard Istiqlal's definition of a traitor appeared to include some members of the government. The Istiqlal asked for a voting age of twenty; the Confederated Istiqlal, for eighteen. On registration, both supported the use of voters' lists, publicly displayed, in the absence of a definitive census; the Confederated Istiqlal was specific in requesting voluntary registration whereas the old-guard Istiqlal appeared to insist on permanent voters' lists. On candidatures, both parties agreed to exclude civil servants, local authorities, security forces, and members of the judiciary, in addition to unregistered or ineligible voters; the Istiqlal asked for an age limit of twenty-five; the Confederated Istiqlal, twenty-three. On women's franchise, both parties supported complete equality with men. On the electoral system, both parties agreed on a multimember list system without split votes; they expected the elections to be political and supported the list system as a means of acquainting the voters with capable candidates and electing homogeneous councils. In the dossier it submitted, the Confederated Istiqlal's additional proposals went even further and are particularly interesting.

> Of course, the lists of candidates must reflect the population of the villages and must take into account *the social position of the candidates*. The villages are divided into sections and the number of candidates from every section is proportional to the population of the section. Election will depend on the number of votes in the first round and on the proportion of votes in the second round. Proportional representation is not necessary because this would cause differences in opinion and *eventually new parties would arise*. One party list would be elected, on the condition that its members represent all sections of the village and all social levels of the community. [*Italics added.*]

On the election rules, there was a wide variation of details but basic agreement on secrecy. On the electoral irregularities, the old-guard Istiqlal favored the normal judicial hierarchy for all legal complaints, but the Confederated Istiqlal wished only questions of voting fraud to be submitted to judicial authorities; registration and candidacy disputes were to be judged by the local election board, and, if there was no response within ten days, the matter would be submitted to a punishment committee composed of local administrators and voters.

The Istiqlal enclosed a second document with five annexes, complaining of partisanship and repression on the part of the Ibrahim government and demanding a change of government before the elections. The activist report also began, curiously enough, with a demand for a revision of the government to weed out members of the government and local administration "suspected of disloyalty, . . . carelessness, and partisanship." The king, however, was not yet ready to press for a change in government. Instead, scarcely had the dossiers been submitted when he prepared to depart on a medical and diplomatic trip to Switzerland and France. Just before leaving, he held a formal consultation with his governors, many of whom were said to have spoken against holding the elections at all.

On August 3, the king returned suddenly after a two months' absence and was operated for tonsillitis two days later; it was another month before he made a public appearance. However, on September 1, 1959, accompanied by a decree on registration and a *dahir* on legal details, the election law was promulgated.[40] As the culmination of a history strewn with ironies, it was closer to the nonexistent law of 1953 than to the recommendations of the French political scientists or the dossiers of the rival political parties.

The elections were to be held under a single-member–district system, with universal and direct suffrage, secret ballot, one round of voting, and a relative majority necessary for election. The voter had to be twenty-one and could vote either in the commune where he was born or where he had his residence during the past year or where he had paid three years' taxes; criminals, bankrupts, legally declared traitors, recently naturalized citizens, and members of the security forces could not vote. Communes would return between nine and fifty-one council members for a three-year term, each commune to be divided into the corresponding number of election districts. A voluntary system of registration, to be revised annually,

[40] *Dahir* No. 1-59-161 of September 1, 1959; legal provisions given in *dahir* No. 1-59-162 of September 1, 1959.

was established, and voters would be identified by a voters' card; the
registration *dahir* which had been prepared in June was printed as
an accompanying decree and thus could be modified without going
through the Palace.[41] Candidates would be identified by colored ballots; their campaign would last two weeks.

On election day the voter would identify himself by his voters'
card, receive an official envelope and a ballot for each candidate,
and then retire to the election booth where he would put one ballot
in the envelope and throw the rest of the ballots into a waste basket;
he would then come out and publicly deposit his sealed envelope
in the ballot box as his name was again verified. Electoral operations were controlled by an electoral board appointed by the governor, but each candidate could name a poll-watcher to inspect the
proceedings; the president of the electoral board had the police at
his disposition. Counting was done by the poll-watchers and the
board after the polls closed; following the French system, uncon-
tested ballots were burned after the counting was done. All challenges of registration, candidature, and voting were to be handled
by the court system; an accompanying *dahir* provided rules for the
campaign and penalties for all types of fraud and infractions. The
date of elections was to be set by decree forty-five days beforehand;
no date was set at the publication of the *dahir,* but the legal period
of six months put off elections until February.

The *dahir* was an admirable piece of legislation. It provided
an electoral system that fully filled the criteria of simplicity, secrecy,
and honesty, and it provided, as much as any law can, for what
has been variously called "administrative," "nonpolitical" or, more
accurately, "nonpartisan" elections. Each district would have its
own representative; the party entered the voting by way of the
candidate and not vice versa. On the other hand, the provision for
poll-watchers ensured the presence of party representatives over the
entire proceedings. The exclusive use of judicial machinery was
sufficient guard against administrative abuse; any citizen could ini-
tiate judicial proceedings. A uniform and easily comprehensible
system of voting with sufficient guarantees of equity and justice
made the *dahir* a model regulation, well adapted to the Moroccan
situation. The satisfaction of the Palace was indicated in the
Speech from the Throne, when the king announced that the elections would take place in mid-May.

[41] Decree No. 2-59-1287 of September 1, 1959, originally prepared as *dahir*
No. 1-59-229.

OPERATIONS

One phase was completed; another was about to begin. In announcing the *dahir,* Mhammedi wisely looked to future problems. "Everything is not completed," he announced. "We have erected a structure, we must now furnish it." Registration had to be begun, candidatures had to be declared, the election districts had to be drawn up, and the exacerbated party bitterness had to be handled. Each of these operations threatened to upset the structure already so long in the building.

The decree provided for a registration period of thirty days, which the Ministry announced would begin November 25.[42] The potential voter was to appear before the local sheikh, caid, or caliph with papers of identity and age, and with proof of birth, residence, or taxes in the commune in question; however, since there was no reliable record of births and deaths in most of Morocco, identification could also be made by two voters who had already registered. The operation was accompanied by a press and radio campaign to educate the people in the functions of the commune and urge them to do their civic duty by registering. In rural areas, the sheikh dispatched the traditional town crier with his goatskin tambour literally to drum up interest, particularly in the weekly market. At the other extreme from this carry-over from an ancient system was the rather ingenious competition set up by the ministry; weekly and even daily quotas for an ideal registration figure were calculated for each province and city, and regular reports were published showing which local administrators had succeeded in most nearly fulfilling their quota. Administrative zeal and a system of calculation that underestimated the population growth since the 1951 census led to some provinces' registering more than 100 per cent of their quota.

For the most part, however, registration went very badly in the beginning. In the countryside there was often little awareness that a *dahir* had been passed or that elections were being held or, for that matter, what elections were. When the sheikh became overworked, the *muqaddem* had to be allowed to aid in registering. It was decided to let men register their wives, although this precedent posed problems on election day. Even in the cities, identification proved difficult, since certificates of residence required a fee and two photographs; the authorities therefore distributed residence affidavits to voters' domiciles. In the countryside there was criticism

---

[42] Decree of November 17, 1959, implementing decree No. 2-59-1287.

of the distance to the authorities' offices, although this does not seem valid in view of the traveling habits of the countryfolk. There were also a number of officials who refused to register members of various parties, so that re-education by the ministry was necessary. Nevertheless, during the first week, less than one-third of the anticipated 1,143,000 registrants appeared, and the ministry was obliged to ask the king to make a personal appeal. The prince also visited the Tafilalt, where he encouraged participation.

The royal appeal also did much to correct the second reason for nonparticipation; with the notable exception of the National Union of Popular Forces (UNFP), the political parties had been extremely dissatisfied with what amounted to the rejection of their suggestions for the electoral law and were bitterly critical of the government in power, which they called too partisan to administer democratic elections. At the national level, the Istiqlal, the Popular Movement, and the Constitutional Democratic party (the renamed PDI) boycotted the registration. At the local level, the control of the national leadership was not always sure, and, if the boycott was not always heeded, at least participation was spotty. After the king's appeal, abstention became unpatriotic, and by the second week participation had tripled. However, at the end of the thirty-day period, only 3,921,592 out of an expected 4,582,000 Moroccans had registered; the goal had been set at half the estimated 9,000,000 population, but the 1960 census later showed that the population was 11,600,000, and the goal was therefore barely 40 per cent.

The entire question of holding elections was again posed, and Zemmouri was extremely discouraged. However, he decided to extend the registration period by three weeks, and additional press bulletins, radio announcements, and other means were employed to increase participation. A telephone call from Zemmouri is said to have overcome the last doubts of the Popular Movement; in any case, after the party leader Mahjoubi Ahardan gave instructions in a meeting in the Tafilalt, the participation increased to 108 per cent of the expected goal. In Marrakesh, a letter from Hassan Ouezzani to the PDC also instructed participation. As registration continued in December and January, the parties began to campaign as actively as they would for the actual election. Particularly in Fez, Meknes, and Marrakesh provinces, both in the cities and the countryside, the Istiqlal added to the government's efforts to explain the significance of the elections, although not always in the same terms. In rural markets trucks equipped with loudspeakers harangued the gathered people. The UMT and UNFP campaigned less extensively, concentrating on the cities where their following was; the Popular Movement started late and spread its instructions through meetings and by word of mouth, as did the lesser parties—the Constitutional Democrats and the Liberal Independents.

The final total of registered voters increased by the end of the seven weeks to 4,172,080 or 91 per cent of the estimated figures and 72 per cent of the goal based on correct population figures. Provincial totals ran from 118 to 60 per cent of the assigned goals, with Tafilalt and Tangier holding the highest and lowest ranks. Registration was particularly low in Rabat city, Fez province, and much of the northern zone and was high in the trans-Atlas south, in Rabat and Tadla provinces, and in Casablanca city, showing a big turnout in both the traditionalist pre-Sahara and Morocco's largest urban center. The absence of any party correlation with these gains indicates both the decentralized nature of party organization and the regional particularism of Moroccan politics.

There is no doubt that at the end the first complementary operation to the election *dahir* was as great a success as the law itself. The period for judicial recourse which followed the close of the books brought only about 10,000 complaints or less than three per cent of the registered total. The high participation shows an unusual spirit of civic duty and political interest among an underdeveloped people, although it must be admitted that the current of rumors which held that the registration was obligatory or was for medical aid or was the vote itself probably helped raise the number to a small extent. The diligence of the local authorities was also to be commended, for any kind of operation which deals with Moroccan names—with no fixed last name, an optional article, no agreed spelling, and an infinitely variable number of first names, ancestors' names, and nicknames—is in itself a challenge in any language. The relatively free participation of women, who made up 39 per cent of the registered voters and attained a percentage as high as 48 in Nador, is also noteworthy.

The second operation, that of creating the election districts, also nearly destroyed the elections. The communes were finally fixed by a decree on December 2, 1959, in most cases in the shape originally decided in early 1958.[43] The same decree also apportioned the number of seats due to each of the 799 communes on a

[43] Decree No. 2-59-1834 of December 2, 1959, based on *dahir* No. 1-59-351 of December 2, 1959, establishing provinces. For the latest figures on communes, population, and composition, see *Population légale du Maroc* (2 vols.; Rabat: Service Central des Statistiques, 1961), appended to decree No. 2-61-213 of May 29, 1961.

population basis. Zemmouri had already sent instructions to the governors' offices to divide each commune into election districts corresponding to the number of communal seats.[44] In a sense, the entire problem of the communes was again presented. The instructions established the criteria as *"principally* economic, or geographic or, if need be, ethnic," thus perpetuating the socioeconomic nature of the commune. However, since each district was to be centered on a point of social life such as the Agricultural Work Center, the market, a well, or a village or make up a geographic or economic region such as a valley or a *douar* and since internal communications were important to smooth operations on election day, the 10,349 election districts were most often ethnic units or at least ethnically homogeneous. Each district was to contain about 900 people or some 400 voters, although the final results varied between rarer extremes of 100 and 2,000. In most cases the local authorities were successful in incorporating a point of social life in each district, and this was verified toward the end of the preparations when it became necessary to set up polling places. There were 11,652 polling places, indicating that a few districts were oddly enough shaped or populous enough to need two or more voting facilities. Casablanca, notably, had ten polling places for each district, and Rabat had four. In the *bled,* tents and private huts were used for voting, and the problem of distance was countered by setting up another tent across the road, building a fire, and making hot mint tea to refresh the voter before his trip home and to mull over the possible outcome.

The election districts were created over several months, much to the credit of the provincial office, who worked with truly unusual speed under pressure from Rabat. It is at this level that gerrymandering might be expected, and yet there is almost no report of it.[45] Apparently the local authorities who had the knowledge of the commune's political composition did not have the sophistication to consider dishonest districting, and the Rabat office did not have the necessary information. Zemmouri had a report drawn up defending the practice of establishing strangely shaped districts for the defense of local and minority interests in Europe and America, but there is no evidence that he ever needed it for a specific district. No map of election districts was published, making verification difficult, but

[44] Memorandum No. 538 of November 5, 1959.
[45] The only criticism in the usually alert party press concerned one district in Rabat (*ar-Rai,* May 20, 1960). See also *al-Istiqlal,* May 14, 1960, on fears of gerrymandering aroused by the absence of an electoral map.

the absence of neatly defined areas of political sympathy, plus the parties' uncertainty over their own followers and even their candidates, makes gerrymandering a minor likelihood.

Scarcely had the election districts been established when a new disagreement arose. By using the word "uninominal" in the election law, Zemmouri meant a single-member district; further articles of the law made the method of voting clear. The head of the Royal Cabinet, Ahmed Hamiani, interpreted the word to mean only one vote for one person and opted for a list system in which each voter would vote for one name on a large communal list of candidates. Zemmouri had suspected Hamiani of wishing to discredit the Ibrahim government by imposing a system open to criticism for partisanship; certainly the Royal Cabinet was not in sympathy with the activist government, although such reasoning is somewhat devious. It is also possible that Hamiani was attempting to synthesize the party proposals, which the cabinet had gone over before handing to the king, in order to make the elections more acceptable to all factions. Zemmouri threatened to resign and is also said to have threatened to take all the ministry's Berbers with him. The prince, who favored a single-member district, suggested calling again on Duverger, who was then vacationing in Zagora. The French professor supported Zemmouri, pointing out that in the multi-member system advocated by the Royal Cabinet, a new *dahir* would be necessary, and a small but organized minority could elect its followers while the rest of the voters concentrated on a few well-known personalities.[46] The king was convinced and ruled in favor of the planned system; a brief communiqué affirming the *status quo* was all that was made public of this near crisis and the possibility of a further delay in the elections.

The problem of finding a candidate for presidency of the old tribal *jema'* was frequently difficult, and the Ministry of Interior once complained with evident disgust at the ignorance and lack of civil spirit shown by the rural population in this matter.[47] The election law provided few restrictions on voters who wished to be candidates; only certain civil servants and local administrators down to the level of caid, pasha, and caliph were excluded. The local tribal officials—the sheikhs and the *muqaddem*—were allowed to run, according to Zemmouri's wishes, thus giving a chance for

[46] Duverger and the king specifically mentioned the Communist party.

[47] *Revue des communes rurales et des municipalités* (September–October 1958), unpaged. Rudimentary councils set up in connection with Operation Plow failed for lack of interest among the farmers, and one rural member of the National Consultative Assembly had to be replaced because he did not appear.

the integration of traditional and active elites into the new system. Declarations of candidature were to be filed in the two-week period following the announcement of the election date, to be made forty-five days in advance. If the elections were, therefore, to be held in May, as the king had announced, and not put off again, the necessary decree would have to be published by mid-April, "that is, practically, in the *Official Bulletin* of 8 April 1960," the General Secretariat warned. At the end of March, a brief bill was drawn up by Zemmouri setting the date for elections as May 2–, 1960. A number was handwritten into the blank, and the bill was sent to the General Secretariat of the Government on March 26, to Ibrahim on March 31, back to the General Secretariat two days later for publication. It actually appeared on April 14 in the *Official Bulletin* dated April 8, announcing the elections for Sunday, May 29, 1960. The date was set.

Candidatures came even more slowly than had prospective voters. Although the same official means of propaganda were used to create interest, there appeared to be very little response. As in registration, a delegation of officials from the ministry was sent into the *bled* on April 18 to inspect the operations and, if possible, accelerate them. Instead of apathy, they found that political and ethnic groups had in many cases set up an additional step to the electoral process by staging primary elections among party cells or tribal fractions while prospective candidates attempted to enlist the support of a *douar* or *jema'* or the backing of the local party unit before filing. By the end of the legal period, candidatures had risen to an average of almost five for each election district.

At the same time, the Istiqlal began a persistent campaign to prevent the candidature of sheikhs and *muqaddem,* on the grounds that their official position gave them unfair advantages. Toward the end of April, the party presented a formal protest to the king, charging that the presentation of these local officials was against existing legislation, even if not specifically stated as such in the election law. If the sheikhs and *muqaddem* were declared ineligible, the number of candidates would be reduced in many areas, particularly the northern zone, for the ministry had often put pressure on these officials to run if no other candidates appeared in their district. However, on May 5, a *dahir* excluding the local officials from participation was passed.[48] The effect was often discouraging to the individual districts, since the deadline for filing and withdrawing had already been passed on April 29; in some districts

[48] *Dahir* No. 1-60-120 of May 5, 1960.

where the sheikh or *muqaddem* was a popular figure, his withdrawal brought a drop in participation on election day.

There were 47,164 declared candidates, ten of whom were
women. In fewer than a hundred districts there was no election for
lack of a candidate or lack of competition. In the politicized urban
areas candidatures were generally party inspired and few; in the
rural areas there was frequently little control over personal ambi-
tions. In Marrakesh and Rabat provinces, the highest number of
candidates for one seat was forty-seven and thirty, whereas in Casablanca there were no more than fifteen candidates in the highest
district.[49] Party control, however, was a very uncertain thing. The
Istiqlal established two categories: official and nonofficial party
candidates. In many cases, candidates claimed to represent two or
more parties, which shows to what degree the elections were apolitical. One device, however, did favor the partisan element. Local
authorities were strictly instructed to assign colors in order of registration; by being first to declare their candidatures, Istiqlal representatives were frequently able to build up a communal slate of
whites, the first color assigned, to aid party voters.

In the legal period of four days following the close of filing,
only nine complaints were taken to court, although during the actual filing period a number of local officials had to be re-educated
by the ministry after they refused to allow more than seven candidates (the number of basic colors) or refused to register candidates
of certain parties.[50] Despite the original fears and occasional confusion, the filing phase was also a success, resulting from the alert-
ness of the ministry, the parties' activity, and the surprising interest
of the population.

The largely technical emphasis on the "hard" phase of election
preparations did not mean that the political parties were uninterested. Although the two halves of the Istiqlal had been in general
agreement in their proposals of June, 1959, their battle on purely
political grounds during the summer of 1959 was heightened by
rivalry for the Istiqlal name and by a realization of the moment of

[49] The ministry announced that it tried to limit candidatures in some areas;
see Zemmouri's press speech of May 18, 1960. This was more an overstatement
than the flagrant breach of democratic practice that it appears to be. The
boldest step was giving publicity to declarations suggesting that candidates be
sure of their qualifications before filing and pointing out the disadvantages of
too many candidates. In an interview, Zemmouri admitted that any intervention
of this type was delicate and generally unsuccessful.

[50] See *al-'Alam*, April 20–22, 24, and 28, 1960. Zemmouri's instruction No. 314
of February 29, 1960, was confusing, for it suggested to local authorities that
candidates should not number more than the seven colors.

truth that the elections would pose to their conflicting and exaggerated claims. During the registration campaign at the end of
1959, the activist press educated the population in its duty to register and called the authorities' attention to irregularities and bot-
tlenecks in the system. "Think a little, O responsible officials," *at-
Tahrir* once admonished.[51]

However, the UNFP also took a critical view of operations
from the beginning. On December 6, 1959, the party's National Assembly expressed reservations on the election proceedings; in preparation for possible defeat, the party maintained its reservations in
its National Assembly in April. Once registration began, its criticisms of insufficient civic education and sloppy administrative pro-
cedures took the proportions of an organized campaign. The party
press also claimed that the current government attacks and seizures
of *at-Tahrir,* the party organ, cast doubts on the fairness of the
election. Its pressure did, however, result in a worthwhile extension
of the registration date, and criticism eased during the second period. During the later months, the activist papers simmered down
to a typical election campaign, recalling their activity and their
promises, indicating the tricks and conspiracies used against them,
but showing how "the wakefulness of the citizens foils all the ma-
neuvers of the Istiqlal reactionaries." [52]

The Istiqlal press, essentially in an opposition position, was
far more outspoken. As soon as Mhammedi announced the election
plans in March, 1959, *al-Istiqlal* launched the party's slogan: "This
Government Is Not Capable of Holding Elections." [53] The argument, to be repeated endlessly during the next year, was that some
of Ibrahim's ministers, chosen as nonpartisan technicians, had
identified themselves with the January 25 scissionist group of the
party and were thus incapable of impartial administration. The apparently unpunished repression of Istiqlal followers by a number of
local administrators was persuasive evidence of the Istiqlal's
charges. It is interesting that, although neither party showed great
enthusiasm over the elections, there was no longer an attempt to
block them but only to change the political color of their admin-

[51] *At-Tahrir,* December 10, 1959; see also *ibid.,* November 25, 1959; *al-'Ahd,*
November 24, 26, and 30, 1959. The UNEM congress in Agadir in August, 1959,
called for a postponement of elections until the people were ready, foreign troops
were evacuated, and the administration had been purged (*at-Tahrir,* August 21,
1959).

[52] *Ar-Rai,* May 17, 1960; see also *ibid.,* April 4, 27–28, May 15, 17, 19, 25–27,
1960; *AG,* April 16 and May 21, 1960.

[53] *Al-Istiqlal,* March 28, 1959; see also *ibid.,* May 14 and June 13, 22, and 27,
1959; *al-'Alam,* March 5, April 1, May 14, and June 24–25 and 29, 1959.

istrators; the pressure of the king had finally engaged the parties in the electoral process. When the *dahir* appeared in September, the Istiqlal revived a second theme to join to its attacks on the government's integrity and repeated it with equal constance—only the list advocated by the party since 1956 would lead to capable, cooperative, homogeneous communal councils. The important role of the administrative hierarchy in the election process, particularly in nominating the election boards, caused the party to renew its protest against the government in power; "the voters demand . . . the departure of the bankrupt Government AS A PRECONDITION TO ELECTIONS." [54] As a hesitant participant in registration, the Istiqlal played a lesser educative role than did the activist press; when the registration progressed badly, the party press used it as further proof of the government's ineptitude in handling the elections.

The Istiqlal's attacks on the government's competence were also joined by other newspapers, particularly *al-Maghreb al-'Arabi*, the Popular Movement's paper, which asked for a longer period of preparation supervised by all parties, and *an-Nidal*, the Liberal Independent's paper, which was close to the palace and which incisively criticized the contradictions and abuses of the government. Istiqlal newspapers which had consistantly called for a change in government even began to ask aloud whether it were not too late for such a change to be effective, thus casting doubt on the elections themselves. On April 26, a *dahir* prepared in Zemmouri's office delayed the elections until June 26 or July 3.[55] Three versions were drawn up, one freezing candidatures, another allowing additional filing, and a third canceling all candidatures and beginning all over again for elections on June 26. On May 5 the first choice was adopted by Mhammedi and Zemmouri and discussed in Council of Ministers with the king. It was felt that the shock of another delay would be too discouraging to the population and that the elections should therefore be held on schedule. The elections had narrowly escaped another postponement.

The Istiqlal nevertheless continued to demand the installation of a disinterested government; party newspapers seized on the resignation of Rashid Karami in Lebanon following riots against his government and suggested that Ibrahim might follow a good

[54] *Al-Istiqlal,* November 12, 1959; see also *ibid.,* May 14, 1960; *al-'Alam,* May 18 and 27, 1960.
[55] *Dahir* No. 1-60-120. See also Interior Ministry memo to General Secretariat, No. 288.

Arab precedent. The most important question at this time hung on the meaning of a word: when Ibrahim was chosen to "prepare" elections, did this include presiding on election day as well? There is no indication that the king himself knew the answer when the government was first appointed, nor is there any indication at what point the final decision was made. During May a number of events involving attempts of the premier to act without the authority of the king brought the fall of the government. A military advisor to the prince was refused by the government, and, more important, 350 French policemen were dismissed from Moroccan service, presumably to be replaced with Ibrahim's sympathizers.[56] On May 20, the king thanked his ministers and ended their term of office; on May 26 a new government was sworn in, with Bekkai as interior minister, Zemmouri as agriculture minister, Mhammedi as foreign minister, the prince as vice-premier in acting charge of the government, and the king himself as premier. The first Council of Ministers met on May 27, two days before election day, to make a final decision on the elections.[57] The Istiqlal ministers were in favor of respecting the date set, since their demands had been fulfilled. The Popular Movement ministers and activist sympathizers favored a six months' delay to perfect their campaign. Zemmouri literally bet his head on the elections, saying that, even if there were disorders in 1,000 of the 11,652 polling places, the risk would be worth it and the elections would be a success. Again, the king backed the man who had quietly worked to set up the elections. The elections were still to take place on May 29.

On Sunday morning, Zemmouri got up early and made a tour of the polling places in Rabat. He was at last reassured. Another last-minute crisis had threatened to destroy all success; a shortage of the colored papers needed for the ballots was discovered in the French printing shop in Rabat that was contracted to handle supplies, and a special plane had to be flown to France to pick up more paper. Of the 4,172,080 people registered, 4,008,529 were eligible to vote, the rest being disfranchised by the absence of a candidate or a contest in their district. Of the registered and eligible voters, 2,978,595 (74.3 per cent) voted, 79,335 ballots—less than 4 per cent

[56] For the UNFP side of the story, see ben Barka's article in *Tribune Socialiste* (Paris), June 4, 1960. Fuller analyses of the crisis are given in *Monde*, May 22 and 24 and June 28, 1960.

[57] The electoral procedure had already been successfully tested in the elections, arranged by Zemmouri's office, for the Chamber of Commerce and Industry on May 8, 1960.

and a low figure considering the high illiteracy rate and the novelty of the proceedings—were declared invalid. Compared to the thousand disorders on which Zemmouri bet his head, there were 360 occasions on which the local presidents called on their police forces. None of them was serious, and there was no call for the army troops standing by on alert in their barracks.[58] There is no doubt that election preparations were a total success.

CONCLUSIONS

Success is an ephemeral matter, quickly left behind in the continuum of events, but the patterns of action are more durable and their lessons have application beyond the borders of Morocco. The election was far more gratifying than the future powers and activities of the newly elected councils. These powers were not defined until a *dahir* was passed on June 23, 1960; no government had been able to agree to a text until this time, and it had finally been decided in mid-1959 to separate the powers from the election bill in order to pass at least one measure. Instead of being fully autonomous in their small spheres of activity, the councils were circumscribed by administrative mechanisms to the point at which they had little more governing power than the creations of the protectorate. The cause for this caution in releasing governing powers to the people lies largely with the prince. The government found 799 communal councils clamoring for the powers which they thought they were elected to exercise, and the transition to democratic government was made more delicate than if there had been no frustrated councils.

How ready is a people for democracy? This is a question that never can be accurately answered. The Moroccan people showed that it was mature enough to understand and participate in elections, at least on the local level. But there is a crucial question which is usually not posed: How ready are the leaders for democracy? The success of the first half-decade of any new country depends above all on the ability of its leadership to put the abilities of the country to work while utilizing the enthusiasm and support of its people. Essentially this is the basic problem of Moroccan decision-making. The success of the elections means that the early

[58] By-elections were held in the towns of Oujda, Agadir, and Marrakesh and a Rabat rural commune on November 24, 1960. The Istiqlal charged the UNFP with election frauds in Casablanca, but the election results were upheld in court (*al-'Alam,* June 29, 1960).

leadership was capable of harnessing, channeling, and giving means of expression to the population; the weakness of the councils is largely the weakness of subsequent leadership.

1. The first year was spent searching for a policy. Yet the longer the wait during this period, the harder it became to agree. Politics in the absence of elections then turned to cruder methods of showing strength. Since 1957, violence, strikes, riots, and demonstrations, even murder, have increased, not decreased. These are not manifestations of basic bestiality, but an attempt to substantiate claims of strength in the absence of formalized processes for so doing. A contrary theory might suggest that violence made such processes impossible and that only when civil liberties were fully respected could elections take place. This is true only in theory or when there are two incompatible extremes—violence and elections—in a vacuum. In fact, interparty violence did fall off after the elections were finally held (with the possible exception of labor ranks, where the same absence of formalized processes for determining the strength of the two rival unions—Istiqlal-UGTM and UNFP-UMT—left only cruder ways of showing strength).

2. The slow progress of the preparations had a technical and a political aspect. It is undeniable that the country suffered badly from a shortage of civil servants. In the failure of the "easy" phase, the lack of technicians was crucial, for, to take advantage of the early enthusiasm, there had to be civil servants who were familiar with details and who could rapidly translate the dreams into policies and the policies into action. In the "hard" phase the lack of personnel was also evident. Although the Itinerant Commission was endowed with sufficient power to decide questions, overrule governors, and call for reports, it could not hurry the provincial offices, better the liaison between Rabat and the provinces, or force studies where there was no one to write them. "We did not get the impression in France that elections stopped the administrative machinery," a provincial administrator remarked wistfully in his report on the French communal elections. "We have talked for two years of elections, but we have never thought to organize the apparatus which would assure their execution." The importance of trained personnel is shown above all in the success of the law; it was the work of one office and primarily of one man, Zemmouri, whose technical competence and political skill created the communes and the bill and had them both approved.

3. The political parties' role in the decision-making process was purely dilatory. Unable to force a measure, they were fre-

quently successful in enforcing their will only by blocking action. A Frenchman in the ministry commented, "The King did not realize the opposition that he could meet in his own country and his own party."

4. Some of the strong points of the system adopted should be recognized. Two of the wisest decisions were the king's policy of creating communes and of beginning at the grass roots, where the representation was direct and observable and where, in some Berber areas, a quasi-democratic practice already existed. Both of these points made the elections part of a natural development; they meant a step ahead at a more hurried pace than nature moves, but they built on what already existed, and this contributed to their success. Another helpful decision was the policy of reducing the role of political parties as such, one of the largest differences between the Moroccan law and the French system from which it was copied. The king's decision to keep the vote nonpartisan caused much criticism and confusion, but in a backhanded sense it enhanced the value of elections as a measure of strength. Since there were no official reports giving the party breakdown of the results, the parties were left arguing about details, and their attention was called away from the basic claims of exclusiveness. By this decision, the government also avoided making judgments in many borderline cases where the candidate claimed to represent two parties, all parties, the prince, or the king.

Party organs criticized the election staff for extemporization; the charge was valid but was actually a compliment. There was much *ad hoc* regulation of details, and it showed inventiveness and flexibility, both of which were helpful. The decision to cancel all weekend markets imposed a slight hardship, but did more to propagate the news of the elections than any other move. Unlike other Arab countries, women underwent no special economic or education test, no separate voting booths or lines, no limit on participation or candidatures—although all ten women candidates were beaten. It is likely that the integration of women in the electoral process also encouraged the male turnout, for Moroccan women are a powerful social influence and an effective—even if not always accurate—communications channel. And, of course, the decision to hold the vote on a clear, rainless day did much to guarantee success.

Debate over the electoral system itself simmers down to the usual debate between proportional, bloc-list, and single-member representation. Councilors were often elected by very small proportions of total voters; in fact, those who had the luck to be unop-

posed had no need to be voted for at all. The parties charged that
adventurers and feudals could win seats in the single-member districts, but the parties had every occasion to put up candidates of
their own to oppose such people. Presumably the feudals would
coerce the voters, although the choice here was between rare personal coercion and a greater danger of party pressure. There was no
mention of any notorious "feudals and adventurers" who actually
were elected, fairly or unfairly, although there was criticism of party
pressure in Casablanca. On the other hand, the single-member district provided the occasion for the two parties to pick off a number
of prominent opponents.

Given the desirability of nonpartisan elections based on traditions, the single-member system was most in keeping with policy
decisions. Given the necessity for a simple, comprehensible operation, the single-member system was also best. Furthermore, there
is no doubt that a bloc list presented under a symbol or party name,
without chance for direct voting for individual candidates, would
have broken the voter-representative contact that is an integral
part of democratic evolution and would have put the elections
completely in the hands of the parties, who had neither proven their
capability for such a responsibility nor their ability to provide a
slate of candidates in all the communes.

SEVEN

EVOLUTION AND DECISION-MAKING

The process of decision-making and evolution in the governments of developing countries recalls the sign frequently seen in growing American cities: "Open for Business during Alterations." The most important characteristic of government in new nations is that it is forced to govern while it undergoes transition and that decision-making therefore becomes both a governmental and an evolutionary process. Since neither process operates independently of the other, the relation between decision-making and evolution is crucial.

This conclusion will examine this relation in light of Moroccan experience and attempt to situate decision-making in the evolution of developing government. The generalizations presented here have thus been arrived at inductively, based on the conditions in newly independent Morocco; they have been verified deductively, by checking them against experiences in other Arab and African societies. Morocco's location in both of these worlds makes it an apt case from which to draw broadly applicable lessons.[1]

I

The processes referred to under the title of evolution are pluralistic and complex. The broad range of material covered in the pre-

---

[1] There is no claim that these conclusions are universally valid in the Arab-African area, but it is suggested that in this region these ideas are generally valid and universally helpful as guides to the questions to be asked in research and in a search for typical or deviant behavior.

ceding five cases and the emphasis on the relation between decision-making and evolution might suggest the necessity of examining all facets of social and economic as well as political evolution. Fortunately, from this broad span of concomitant evolutions that characterize a new nation's development, detailed attention can be meaningfully focused on seven types of evolution that are pertinent to decision-making. In each case, evolution will be described in three stages—roughly, traditional, transitional, and modern. There is no intention of suggesting that these steps are sharply defined plateaus; rather, they are phases through which a nation passes as it brings its institutions into harmony with the modern world. The aspiration to modernity is universally typical of developing societies, as much by their very nature as by the forces of change which are acting within them. First colonialism and then independence unleash evolutionary pressures and evoke the sister-value of independence—democracy.[2] A traditional society, particularly a traditional society which has just gained independence from colonial rule, cannot face the demands of modernity without creating institutions which challenge its traditionalism.

There is, therefore, a tendency to move forward and a concurrent tendency to feel uncomfortable or be unstable during the transition. Over a short time, instability may appear to be dominant even over the direction of evolution, and frequently temporary regression occurs. This is evident in the Moroccan Council of Ministers, which, hovering between a vizirial and ministerial system, slipped back into the former, from whence it came, when the pressure to move toward the latter was temporarily removed. Yet such regressions are only transient. The relation that exists among the various types of evolution means that any one area of activity is subject to modernizing pressures from evolution in other fields. Over longer periods, the progression remains valid, for the pressures of multiple evolution remain constant in direction, even if they are not predictable in time.

1. Morocco is undergoing an evolution in its legal system. From a formerly customary basis of authority, the government has moved into a statutory stage and is heading toward constitutionalism. The customary stage in the pre-colonial period depended on the ruler's will operating within broad socioreligious limits in which every member of the society knew his place. Under the protectorate and in the first five years of independence, legislation was a collegial

[2] For a development of this theme, see I. William Zartman, *Government and Politics in Northern Africa* (New York: Frederick A. Praeger, Inc., 1963).

emanation, carried out by law (*dahir*) and subject to change by law. The country was given its first constitution in December, 1962, written by politicians and jurists and accepted by a popular referendum. Not only governing institutions, but also basic legal guarantees, which formerly were given by promise of the sultan or by law, are included in the constitution. In its first two stages this evolution corresponds to the present sources of Moroccan public law—Muslim tradition and Moroccan history on one hand and French and Spanish precedent on the other. These sources, too, held together by a good dose of *ad hoc* glue, are the bases for a constitution.[3] This evolution is clearly visible as a search for stability in a new type of society. The customary stage was a static legal order, fitted to a traditional way of life; the statutory stage is highly flexible, and the constitutional stage brings new rules for rule-making in a new way of life. The constitutional stage also has the crucial characteristic of permitting amendment, thus permitting stability through orderly change in a society more complex and changing than was the traditional society.

2. Morocco is undergoing a parallel evolution in the position of the masses. Its people are changing from an inert mass, through an instrumental position, where the people are manipulated but not effectively consulted, to an integrated status, where they take part in public life. The position of the populace in the first two stages reflects the sociological phenomenon which Edward Shils so aptly terms "the gap." [4] Between the masses and the traditional elite, there is a great gulf and little social mobility across it. In the inert stage, the population is not only far from access to government and incapable of political activity, but its characteristic autarky and local autonomy leave it little touched by governmental activity from above. Popular reactions in this stage are anomic or nothing. When we read about the *bled as-siba* or the circuit of a newly selected sultan to gather allegiance, reference is to local lords, tribal sheikhs, displeased *'ulema,* or army clans, and obviously not to a popular constituency having any political relations with the sultan.

Similarly, it would be a great mistake to see the present stage as democracy. The relation between the government and their leaders is closer, but the gap is only narrowed, not abolished.

[3] For a discussion of the sources of Moroccan constitutional law, see I. William Zartman, "The King in Moroccan Constitutional Law," *Muslim World,* LII, No. 2 (1962), 129–136.

[4] "Political Development in the New States I," *Comparative Studies in Society and History,* II, No. 3 (1960), 265–292.

Neither before nor during the reign of Mohammed V had there been any national representative body, elected or appointed, in Morocco. The Consultative Assembly (1956–1959) and the Crown Council (1956–1960), which were conceived as a prototype house and senate and then abandoned, functioned merely as advisory groups to the king. But once the dynamics of evolution have been set into motion by changing the masses' inert position, the shift to the second or intermediate stage creates new pressures. Since traditional leaders and colonial oligarchies held a monopoly on all other types of power, the nationalist leaders were forced to adopt the populism which characterizes all emerging societies. The democratic slogans of World War II and the democratic ideologies of the colonial powers made this appeal even more natural. The adoption of democratic forms, particularly of universal suffrage, increases the pressure toward political integration of the population, and paradoxically this pressure is even greater when the initial elections have been limited to the local level, as in Morocco on May 29, 1960; local voting seems so easy that democracy must be, too. Finally, the growth of mass communications media and the spread of literacy increase the pressure for integration.

As long as the gap remains, however, the mass is condemned, by evolution and by definition, to remain in an instrumental position. Political leaders continue to seek to establish their claims on government in terms of their popular followings to which they are not responsible but which they use as instruments of pressure. They are not ready to submit themselves to the vagaries of public opinion which may put them out of, as well as into, power. The revolution of rising expectations is transforming the needs and demands of the population, but the initiative and political action reflecting this revolution still come only from the political elite that leads the restive masses. This relation is as clear in the actions of the Moroccan labor left—the UMT and the UNFP—as it is in the more conservative groups—the UMA, the Istiqlal, and the traditional urban masses, as well as the Popular Movement and the rural masses. Until the population is homogenized,[5] mobilized,[6] or integrated, the mass will not be able to exercise an effective role in government.

[5] The term best fits the views of Shils in this matter (*ibid.*, pp. 282, 285). Note that the developmental role of a rising middle class is to bridge the gap.

[6] The term is used by Karl W. Deutsch in "Social Mobilization and Political Development," *American Political Science Review*, LV, No. 3 (1961), 492–515. Gabriel A. Almond and James S. Coleman speak of a similar phenomenon as "political socialization" in Almond and Coleman, eds., *The Politics of Developing Areas* (Princeton: Princeton University Press, 1960).

3. Meanwhile, on the other side of the gap, the elite is also undergoing an evolution. For convenience, the terms "traditional," "mixed," and "modern" may be used to describe the stages of this evolution. On one hand, there is an elite whose power is based on land ownership, descent, respect, relationship with the monarchy, and religious authority. In the sultan and in members of the *makhzen* (governing household) these elements coincide, although in such powerful figures as Hajj Thami al-Glawi, pasha of Marrakesh, such elements as land or respect for kinship may be dominant. On the other hand, there is an elite whose power derives from monetary wealth, education, occupational skills useful in government service, and from popular support. 'Abderrahim Bou'abid or Mohammed Douiri—despite their political differences—may be the best examples of this type, although Ahmed Balafrej and Mehdi ben Barka are partial examples. Between lies a hazy area of mixed authority, typified by the enigmatic figure of 'Allal al-Fassi, who enjoys both mass and religious appeal, or by Ahmed Reda Guedira, whose power is based on wealth, skills, and royal favoritism.

The relation of these trends is visible in the undercutting of traditional elements in favor of the modern. A move away from the customary stage of the evolving legal system reduces the effect of family respect and religious authority, increased popular participation in government brings forward the importance of mass support, and the social integration of population breaks down local autarkies and increases the importance of monetary wealth. The direction as well as the slowness of these evolutionary processes is visible in the traditionalists' success in blocking agrarian reform and their failure to impose a traditional concept of Arabized education in Morocco. Traditional forces—in particular, tribal leaders, intellectuals of the Qarawiyin University, "feudal" caids,—are weakening, largely because they are losing their importance in the evolving society and they have found no place in new political institutions from which to defend their positions. A converse phenomenon is also present: traditional forces that do organize to preserve their interests find themselves forced to adopt modern methods to defend their traditional position and so join the evolution that they are fighting. Landowners in the UMA and tribal councils (*jema's*) in the rural communes are notable examples.

4. A complex evolution is noticeable in the development of political organizations. The initial reform group broadens in goals and membership into a nationalist movement and then develops

into a political party.[7] The complexity in this evolution occurs in
the later step, for the term "political party" and the development
toward it include a number of specific possibilities.[8] The awakening
of national consciousness is first reflected in the creation of pressure
groups content to press for certain reforms—generally the establishment of political equality—within the political *status quo*. Significantly, both success and failure lead them into the second stage, the
formation of a comprehensive nationalist movement. This movement seeks universal membership, and its goal sharpens to that of
changing the existing political system, be that system one of colonial
domination or traditional government. The sharpening of goals is
usually accompanied by concentration on a single goal—independence or the overthrow of the traditional ruler, whichever is applicable—to the exclusion of the previously emphasized reforms or
at least to their complete subordination. Privilege and partisanship
are also subordinate to the symbolic unity of the single goal. At this
stage the term "political party" is still inappropriate, largely because the classic *raison d'être* of a party—competition for power
through elections—is lacking. Nevertheless the movement seeks
nationwide power and is therefore a political group, often organized to the point at which it can bear the name of political organization.

[7] I have used as a starting point the typology of James S. Coleman in "The
Emergence of African Political Parties," in C. Grove Haines, ed., *Africa Today*
(Baltimore: The Johns Hopkins Press, 1955), pp. 226–227 *et seq*. However, I have
substituted the reform group for the pressure group as a more accurate first
stage. Pressure groups exist throughout the evolution; they may remain as
pressure groups, or they may follow their own evolution as either political
parties or special interest groups. This is, however, a sidelight, whereas the reform group has an initial place in the evolution of political organizations. The
typology in Almond and Coleman, *op. cit.*, especially pp. 286–287 and 397–398
and subsequent discussion, is at least adaptable to this evolutionary pattern,
although it is less concerned with evolutions than with typology itself. "One-
party dominant systems" and "dictatorial parties" equal our "single-party system," and "competitive-party systems" equal our "multiparty systems," but both
fall under the evolutionary stage of political parties. "Competitive nationalist
parties," which are rarely, if at all, political parties, equal our "nationalist movements." "Ideological parties" are omitted as being a rarer animal, differentiated
according to criteria different from the previous typologies and, therefore, not
meriting a special category in the evolutionary typologies or, for that matter, in
Dankwart A. Rustow's (Almond and Coleman, *op. cit.*, pp. 397–398). Nationalist
movements and their outgrowth as single-party systems are also called congress
parties in some areas. See also Thomas Hodgkin, *African Political Parties*
(Baltimore: Penguin, 1962), and H. B. Sharabi, *Government and Politics of the
Middle East in the Twentieth Century* (Princeton: Van Nostrand, 1962), ch. 20.
[8] For a discussion of the pre-independence political groups in Morocco as
parties, see Robert Rezette, *Les Partis politiques marocains* (Paris: Colin, 1955).

Attainment of the unique goal creates a new set of political conditions that change the nature of the movement. Independence or the change of traditional government removes the unity that was formerly imposed by the single goal. National self-government (i.e., independence or the change of traditional government) changes the nature of the movement by opening the direct competitive struggle for power, often through newly instituted elections. The attainment of power by the nationalist movement, or a part of it, brings up the need for governmental programs, thus reviving aspects of the reform-movement stage but also creating the likelihood of political differences over these programs. These differences may have been reflected in debates over tactics during the second stage, but the unity imposed by the single slogan and necessitated by the nature of the struggle is now removed.

The resulting third stage, however, offers two choices: a multiparty or a single-party system. Conditions governing each of these possibilities can also be characterized. A multiparty system is to be expected where the country, through size or through natural ethnic or geographic divisions, favors a pluralistic society,[9] where free elections are held, or where the concept of national unity or national allegiance is not developed to the point at which it overcomes residual localism. The single-party system will develop under three conditions: (1) where the unifying slogan of independence is carried over as comprehensive anticolonialism into the post-independence period to the satisfaction of the movement's followers, (2) where the movement adapts to the new situation and adopts a governmental program that attracts the adherence of all its former members,[10] or (3) where the movement has organized to the point at which it can manipulate the means of coercion to the exclusion of any competing political groups.[11]

The second condition is most difficult to attain; the third may be created not only through the more usual use of police powers, but also where the organization of the movement can control the means of political sanction (expulsion that is tantamount to excommunication, as in Tunisia) and gratification (patronage, consultation with the potential opposition) to the preclusion of effec-

[9] Thus also in a federal state or a state where tribal influence remains strong.
[10] In such a case opposition usually develops within the party, but is proscribed outside.
[11] This organization may center about a single charismatic leader, but it would be wrong to consider his existence a condition for a single-party system. Either ben Barka or 'Allal al-Fassi had stature comparable to Bourguiba or ben Bella, but their leadership was contested by each other and above all by the king.

tive external opposition. It is also important to emphasize the need for satisfaction and adherence of all followers as a part of these conditions, for in their absence the movement may be unsuccessful in its desire to develop a single-party system. Finally, it is apparent that the development of either a single- or a multiparty system depends on a number of important—even difficult—conditions, the uncertainty of which tends continually to challenge one system in the name of the other. This inherent instability is overcome only when other elements of the society mature and when other evolutions clear their unstable transitional stages.

The Moroccan experience illustrates all of these stages and possibilities. The prewar reform movement that grew up in response to the Berber *dahir* of 1930, and then splintered, united in an independence movement under the leadership of the Istiqlal. This movement contained serious internal divisions and rivalries that were subordinated to the single-minded goal of independence (*istiqlal*) and was in no way a political party, a weakness it hastened to overcome after independence was attained in 1956. For a period after independence, the Istiqlal party retained its dominance through the magic of its sloganistic name, the appeals of camaraderie from pre-independence times, the use of opprobrium in nationalistic terms against opponents and internal deviants, and a dominant claim on patronage. Largely through the influence of an outside force, the king, however, the counterclaims of smaller nationalistic groups were given weight, and the Istiqlal was never able to make good its claim to exclusiveness.

With its sloganistic unity breaking down, its carry-over program of independence in all fields unsatisfying to its activist wing, its attempt to control police powers held in check, and its demand for a homogeneous government refused, the party split under its own weight in 1959. In the process, the size of the country, its ethnic divisions (between Arab and Berber), geographical differences (mountains, desert, and plains), and social heterogeneities (modern coastal cities with their growing proletariat, traditional inland centers of population, rural agricultural and pastoral districts) all worked to the splintering of the political structure; the passage of the civil liberties bills provided the legal conditions for a multiparty system.

The result in the Moroccan case was a single party which grew out of a reform group and a nationalist movement into a multiparty system. In other countries both of the substages may not (or not yet) have appeared. But the pattern of evolution still exists, despite varying conditions and rare exceptions, and it is a valid guide for understanding the development of political organization.

5. There is also a significant evolution in ideology, the pattern of values governing political action. This evolution involves a change from a narrow goal of personal interest through a broader but exclusive goal of national power to a complex of values called national interest.[12] Government has traditionally been a business rather than a profession, political power a goal rather than a means, and government employees "fortunate participants in the central drama of life" [13] rather than civil servants in the literal sense. The profit motive is dominant not merely in terms of material gain, but also in terms of the acquisition of personal power for power's sake. The problem-solving function is a purely secondary matter. Classical Muslim theory canonizes this view of problem-solving by limiting the ruler to adjudication and administration, since God has already granted all the law that is necessary to the solution of human problems.[14] The expectation that those in power will solve problems or else get out (or be expelled) is a patent intrusion of modern political morality.

In the transitional period, corresponding to the rise of the nationalist movement, the acquisition of national power becomes a group goal. In Morocco, the goal of independence became the sole ethic of the nationalist movement, particularly after 1944. Whatever might be the idealistic hues which color a movement of national consciousness, its purpose is to attain power—that is, to replace foreign domination with self-government. Even justice and equality become subservient or equated to power; the colonial peoples have a right to power and to govern themselves, and independence becomes the rationale even of injustice and inequality. Probably the clearest illustration of this point is the independent government's retention of most of the colonial legislation, including many of the

[12] I have here tried to use words with their accepted meanings, not as concocted symbols. I am forced to deviate from this practice in the case of "national power" simply for want of a better word to describe the combination of independence and political power as a goal. Obviously there is no reference here to elements of national power in the traditional foreign-policy sense. For the concept of national interest in developing Africa, see Coleman, "The Politics of Sub-Saharan Africa," Almond and Coleman, *op. cit.*, p. 331.

[13] Lucian W. Pye, "The Non-Western Political Process" in James N. Rosenau, ed., *International Politics and Foreign Policy* (New York: The Free Press of Glencoe, 1961), p. 293; see also Max F. Millikan and Donald L. M. Blackmer, *The Emerging Nations* (Boston: Little, Brown & Co., 1961), pp. 69, 71, 138.

[14] See Zartman, "The King . . . ," *op. cit.*, p. 184.

police laws which were so highly criticized when they were in colonial hands. Thus the coin of national power has two faces: domestically it means power to the nationalist movement; in external relations it means anticolonialism.

It might seem that the attainment of independence would end this single ethic; in reality comprehensive anticolonialism—which has been called the "colonial hangover"—exists. After many years of seeing all evil in the protectorates, the Istiqlal party in Morocco was little prepared to judge issues on their merits, but was well trained to search out further evidence of colonialism in Morocco or to look for independence in wider, more subtle fields.

There is, however, another part of the continued national power ideology. The Moroccan nationalist movement that sought political power from the protectorate continued to see its enemies as traitors after independence, and it turned the same sort of attack onto those Moroccans who blocked its rise to total power. Even nationalist opposition was called a tool of colonialism and an instrument of the protectorate, which they saw seeking to re-establish itself. Here is another reason for the retention of much protectorate legislature, now turned against a new enemy. Reasons of partisan politics heavily outweighed reasons of state.

The other ideology, which *grosso modo* characterizes the actions of the modern states, may be called national interest. In general, reasons of partisan politics or emotional prejudice are subordinate to the welfare of the nation and the preservation of the state—or, if they are not, the criticism is sounded as a grievous reproach. Independent Morocco operates between these two ethical extremes, evolving slowly and unevenly away from national power toward national interest.

This evolution is of prime importance in understanding the place of ideology in political life, for it shows that ideology grows with the society. Its development is concomitant with, not anterior to, political action. The process of developing ideology is part of the process of enculturation, a problem which the enormous impact of modernization renews for developing societies. Since enculturation is defined as a process of cultural learning, it involves unlearning as well, often by trial and error. Cultural traits, especially ideology, provide the basis for automatic responses to and interpretation of stimuli and events and, as such, must provide satisfying answers and explanations to external challenges. When these ideologically determined answers and explanations prove themselves inadequate, this inadequacy and frustration pose the need for new ideology.

This is the pressure that modernization—that is, concomitant evolutions—brings to bear against traditional ideology, but it is also the pressure that is exercised against ideology in the national-power stage, encouraging its development to the stage of national interest. The hypothetical conclusion of this understanding is that national power is inadequate as a policy guideline for meeting the challenges of modernism, and this is borne out by examples of this evolution in Morocco.

Despite emotional sympathy for the Algerian rebellion, the decision to overrule the Army of Liberation's demands for active intervention in Algeria and subsequent military decisions along the same lines showed an appreciation of the danger for Morocco in following an emotionally guided policy. The Arabization of education, on the other hand, was discussed in terms of cultural nationalism, of arguments on quantity and quality, and of conflicting ideas of the future image of Morocco that an educational system was to create; the mixed criteria for decision-making resulted in uneven progress and policy reversals. The battles over the constitution and the role of the king, frequent successful attempts to block the election law, the split in the dominant Istiqlal party, and the subsidiary battle for control of the labor unions were elements of a procedural struggle for power. After heated debate between the proponents of anticolonialism and national interest had resulted in a year of no policy, Morocco devalued its money and changed its currency in 1959 in response to French devaluation in 1958. Although there are deposits of iron and hopes of oil in Mauritania, the propaganda for Morocco *irredenta*—a policy which has put Morocco in conflict with many of its potential African friends and supporters—is couched entirely in anticolonial terms.

6. A corollary evolution is that of programs. It is a frequent mistake to think that new nationalist elites come to power with a good idea of the policies they will enact following independence; this is particularly untrue where nationalist agitation has concentrated on independence as an exclusive goal. The Moroccan experience shows a clear post-independence evolution from dreams to principles to policies. The first stage is characterized by an expression of general hopes and goals in the atmosphere of a broad search for a desirable new world. In this period there is generally more accent on desired ends than on available means.[15] The second stage involves the formulation of principles which embody the goals and hopes once they have received rough consensus. Only in the

[15] For a contradictory interpretation, see Pye, *op. cit.*, p. 290.

third stage are policies to correspond with the agreed principles formulated. The evolution is a deductive, not an inductive, process. Where possible, policy-making and action on policy are simply suspended while the process is going on, for there are no programs to implement. However, in some fields, day-to-day problems demand treatment and cannot be postponed. In these cases, even a futile attempt at postponement will be an integral act in the evolution of policy itself, just as will be growing pressure of unsolved problems and the evolution of the problems themselves.[16]

This pattern is characteristic of nearly all important policies of independent Morocco. The search for a framework in foreign policy led to the rejection of the king's slogan—Morocco conceived as a hyphen between East and West—and the adoption of ben Barka's idea of non-dependence. Thereafter, a policy on American bases could be formulated. Lengthy debates in press and council led to the slogans of Arabization, enrollment, and unification for the school system and only then, after 1958, were specific policies and doctrine possible. The agrarian question bogged down between the first and second stages of policy evolution on disagreement over the meaning of agrarian versus agricultural reform, and even attempts at policy, such as the encouragement of cooperatives, came to nought. Nearly a year was spent in airing dreams of democracy before the king formally decided the type and form of elections. Such new principles as the creation of a new election unit— the rural commune—and the guarantee of civil liberties as a precondition to elections further held up the final enactment of an election law until the end of 1959. Understanding this evolution is important because it gives content to the sometimes confusing battle of emotional slogans that characterizes the early years of new nations' government.

7. Finally, Morocco is undergoing an evolution in decision-making. From personal decisions, the government is moving

---

[16] This also explains why it is so hard to make policy decisions immediately after independence, when it would be so helpful to be able to capitalize on the concurrent outburst of enthusiasm, or why policies made during this time are often soon subject to important changes. In Morocco, the hastily enacted policy of Arabization was soon reversed and then subjected to lengthy—if not too fruitful—deliberation. Similarly, although it has been suggested that a base agreement could have been signed between Morocco and the United States soon after independence if the United States had acted "correctly," it is highly unlikely that this agreement would have lasted or that the picture by 1961— evacuation in process, policy of active non-dependence—would have been any different. On the element of *élan* and its clash with the dream phase of policy evolution, see ben Barka, *op. cit.*, pp. 15, 22.

through an *ad hoc* phase toward institutionalization.[17] The difference between the first two phases should be emphasized. The *ad hoc* phase does not mean an absence of patterns of decision-making as does the personal phase; it means a search for patterns, a fluid use of many patterns, in sum, an evolution—sometimes unconscious—toward institutionalization. It is particularly characteristic that in this phase, as in contemporary Morocco, there is a great concern for legality, respect of forms, and a public embarrassment over the institutional nudity.[18] In this stage, the institutional structure is still incomplete and the institutions' functions are not formalized, but prototypes and essays at institutions proliferate. The transitional stage is therefore no less complex because it is still underdeveloped, and there is still little relation between formal or theoretical and informal or actual systems of government. Far from being absent, patterns of decision-making are present in abundance; like a wadi in torrent, they are searching for a permanent channel as they flow, and the result eludes the neatness of usual political organization charts.

Evolution in decision-making, in conjunction with the other evolutions, explains why it is so futile to impose classical institutional analyses on new nations' government as an attempt to understand the decision-making process. It also explains why there is no constant pattern visible in the histories of concurrent government problems. There is no one pattern because there are so many, not because such patterns of action are totally absent. In the *ad hoc* stage, variable roles and changing functions are arrogated by existing actors, forces, and institutions, and yet there is a tendency to seek stable institutional patterns in order to exert influence. Today anomic manifestations lead to formal groups and unrepresented groups organize or lose their influence. Thus, the 1958–1959 Berber dissidence preceded the appearance of the Popular Movement. Agricultural labor, long without a voice, formed the Agricultural Trade Union (USA) in 1961 and sought membership in government

[17] Of course, in the narrow sense personal decisions can be institutionalized, but the forms are rudimentary, the functions concentrated, and the institutions generally comprise one person (king, vizier, and so on) rather than collegial bodies.

[18] Examples of this embarrassment are the insistence on prototype democratic institutions in the absence of the real thing (cf. emphasis on symbols and plans in the absence of policies and achievements, below) and the defensive reaction to Tunisian elections and constitution. Concern for legality and respect for forms is an important characteristic of the creation of the election *dahirs* and decrees and of the choice of decrees over *dahirs* to change dates, to bypass the king, or to tone down the seriousness of the matter.

economic councils. In governmental procedure, even the formulation of a constitution is an attempt at institutionalization, an attempt to attain stability in a transitional, *ad hoc* stage of decision-making.

These seven aspects of political evolution are concomitant, yet nothing could be more misleading than to suggest that they are marching in step with one another. Morocco is not advancing from a customary society with a traditional inert mass, dreams for policies, and personal interest in ideology; through a statutory stage with an instrumental mass and mixed elite making *ad hoc* decisions on principles according to a power ethic. The former picture may never have existed at all at a single moment in all its details, and, if the second stage somewhat approximates the present situation, it is only a caricature. At some future time, Morocco and other developing countries may become constitutional societies that have modern elites and integrated masses and that decide policies according to national interest in an institutionalized process. But they will have arrived at this stage only by the interacting pressure of each of the seven political evolutions—and others in other fields—creating conditions which set other evolutions into motion. These evolutionary processes are therefore going on at rates which differ from one another and which even differ from one problem to another. This may complicate the picture, but it clarifies the analytical tool. The whole emphasis on the analysis is on the transitional instability of the current situation and on the relation of its various components.

II

The relation of concomitant evolutions goes far to explain the context of decision-making in a developing society such as Morocco. In guise of a conclusion, an attempt will be made to delineate, if not fully answer, the question of how decisions are made. The answer stems largely from previous considerations and is given in four propositions.

First, problems are chosen for decision by reaction to pressure; the solution, therefore, will go no further than necessary to assuage the pressing force. Decisions are made under two circumstances: (1) when the pressure of external events makes a decision imperative or (2) when the pressure of external forces such as the opposition requires a token measure to be enacted to undercut the substance of the opposition's claim to power. Bad harvests, the breakdown of a military column in the desert, tribal dissidence, or the inadequacy of the Arabic language for advanced teaching are examples of the first. Pressures for agrarian reform, the demand for Arabization of education, and popular attachment to the symbol of elections or the evacuation of foreign troops are examples of the second. The pressure more frequently arises from the needs of day-to-day operation than from the direct demands of a political force. But the narrowness of pressure that can be brought to bear on any issue in an evolving and unintegrated society means that the opponents to change outweigh the proponents and that the decision-makers will seek to alleviate the problem just to the point of reducing the pressures and no further.

Second, inertia and conflicting pressures foster inaction rather than action; decisions are, therefore, left to external events, which eliminate alternatives and strengthen unconscious commitments. Although both inaction and the limiting action of circumstances occur anywhere in the world, they become characteristic of decision-making in a developing society such as Morocco. The decision-maker stands by and watches his hands being tied, either to a particular action—the narrowing of choices on American and French base evacuation, the necessity of devaluation—or to no action at all—army organization, the evolution of Operation Plow, the first election bill. In either case, the only decision by a responsible official is the decision to accept the *fait accompli*—or *inaccompli*. This choice can be refused, but the refusal tends to have little effect on the course of events. It takes rare single-mindedness to impose a program and almost-unheard-of perseverance to follow it through over a long time.

Third, problems are handled seriatim; short-term pressure, therefore, determines priority in the absence of a clear structure of goals. The simple numerical deficiency in the evolving elite means that problems can be dealt with only one at a time. Since the elite also lacks intermediaries—political brokers and bodies where special interest spokesmen are tied to general policy tasks—the horse-trading, logrolling, and haggling typical of representative government are absent. Each issue is decided on its own strength, and there is no compelling long-term majority. In such a political picture, perspective is lost, depth and vision are absent, and all problems are treated as short-range concerns.

Fourth, decisions are based on symbols; they are, therefore, not discussable, public participation is reduced, and problems are exorcised instead of solved. There is frequently more power in slogans than in people. In Morocco, even the king would not allow himself to be outflanked on issues couched in terms of the protection of in-

dependence. However, since evoking symbols is a better way to
silence debate than to solve problems, there is a real gap between
plans and implementation, and there is a tendency to substitute the
former for the latter and to substitute manipulation of slogans for
real discussion. Yet the repetition of Arabization or agrarian reform
or Moroccan Mauritania as slogans has not brought these issues to
consummation. The alternative is to take the problems under consideration in the offices of the ministries or other specialized
agencies, as in the case of Arabization, the setting up of elections,
and, in a sense, the base negotiations. Shielded from the clangor of
symbols, some work can be accomplished.

MAP 1

Agriculture and Geography

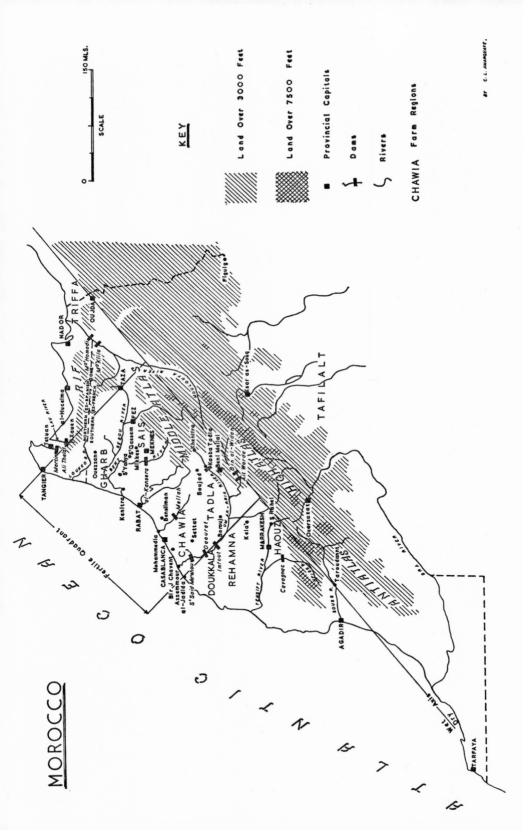

MOROCCO

KEY

Land Over 3000 Feet

Land Over 7500 Feet

■ Provincial Capitals

⊥ Dams

∫ Rivers

CHAWIA Farm Regions

SCALE

0 ——————— 150 MLS.

BY C. L. HARMSWORTH.

MAP 2

Politics and Military Bases

MOROCCO

ATLANTIC OCEAN

SCALE

125 MILES

BY K.F. BAUGHMAN

Legend:

ZAER - TRIBAL REGION
RABAT - PROVINCIAL CAPITAL
RABAT - PREFECTURE
— · · — PROVINCIAL BOUNDARY
— — — INTERNATIONAL BOUNDARY

ROYAL ARMED FORCES
■ - MOBILE BATTALIONS
◆ - GARRISON BATTALIONS
▨ - CAVALRY & MEHARISTS
▨ - ARMOR & ARTILLERY
□ - ARMY SCHOOLS
▣ - ENGINEER BATTALION

ARMY OPERATIONS
▨ - TAFILALT 1956
▨ - RIF & MIDDLE ATLAS 1958-1959
▨ - SOUTHERN ARMY OF LIBERATION 1957-1960
▨ - BASHIR BEN THAMI 1960

(BOUNDARIES OF DISSIDENT AREAS ONLY APPROXIMATE)

AMERICAN BASES
▼ - U. S. NAVY
▲ - U. S. AIR FORCE
△ - U. S. AIR FORCE (STAND-BY BASE)

Place names:

TANGIER
TETUAN
OURIAGHEL
AL-HUCEIMA
NADOR
AHFIR
BERKAN
OUJDA
BERGENT
FIGUIG
BOU ARAFA
COLOMB-BECHAR
KENADSA
BOUDENIB
KERRANDO
HASSI ZERZOUR
TAL-AMAGAIT
TARGUIST
KETAMA
XAUEN
AL-'AIRASH
AL-KSAR AL-KEBIR
QUEZZAN
SOUQ AL-ARBA'
ASILA
SI' SLIMAN
TAOUNAT
TIOUZLLI
TAKNOUL
TAHALA
TAZA
FEZ
SEFROU
AHERMOUMOU
IMMOUZER
AZROU
BOULEMAN
MIDELT
RICH
ERFOUND
RISSANI
KSAR AS-SOUQ
GOULMIMA
ZAGORA
MHAMMID
FOUM ZGUID
OUARZAZAT
TATA
MEKNES
KHEMISSET
EL HAJEB
ITZER
KHENIFRA
ZEMMOUR
OULMES
ZAER
O. ZEM
BERRECHID
KHOURIBGA
KASBA TADLA
BENI MELLAL
OUAWIZAGHT
SETTAT
BENSLIMAN
KENITRA
RABAT
SALÉ
CASABLANCA
AZZEMOUR
AL-JADIDA
YOUSSOUFFIA
SAFI
AS-SAWIRA
BEN GUERIR
MARRAKESH
AMIZMIZ
AGADIR
INEZGAN
TAFRAQUT
AKKA
FOUM AL-HASSAN
TIZGUI REMZ
TIZNIT
MIGHLEFT
SIDI IFNI
GOULIMIM
HASSI TANTAN
PLAGE BLANCHE
TARFAYA

INDEX

Moroccan names are listed by the generally accepted last name. In such names as publications and the like, the article (*al-,* etc.) is ignored in the alphabetical listing; however, filial last names beginning with ben, ou, or ould are listed alphabetically under those prefixes. Army units, branches of education, international agreements, rivers, and tribes are listed under those headings.

267